for YOU the w is over....

SAM KYDD

EDITOR JONATHAN KYDD'S NOTE

This is Sam Kydd's own record, and nothing has been done to change
his phonetic spelling, personal understanding or individual
interpretation of the numerous foreign language dialogues and
discussions in which he was involved.
It was written in 1972. Please bear with any language or attitude that
was permissible at the time but which might now be considered
offensive.

Dedication by Sam Kydd

For You the War is Over is dedicated to all those POWs, who never
made it, and to those who did. To the Red Cross Society. To my
mother, Mary Tyler Kydd, and all the other Kydds, wherever they may
be – on the job, 'inside' or just released! Also, to my wife, Pinkie and
my son, Jonathan, born out of captivity.
Last, but not least to my accountant, my bookie, the Inland Revenue,
Hammersmith Labour Exchange, and the Halifax Building Society,
who hope the receipts from this book, will at last pay off the
mortgage.
Also to the bailiffs for their forbearance.

Contents

1. "Sergeant—it's all a mistake…." 5
2. "For You the War is Over" 31
3. "Alles ist Verboten" 50
4. "Streng Verboten!" 80
5. "Ist Verbauten! (But not if you're Irish)" 102
6. "Better Plead Guilty" 132
7. Un-Finnished Censor Business 161
8. "Prisoner's Pie" 180
9. The Cockney Obergefreiter 202
10. "Alles ist not Verboten" 213
11. "Tovarich! Angelski!" 241

Sketches throughout by Sam Kydd

The author in 1939.
For him the war was just beginning.

CHAPTER 1
"Sergeant-it's all a mistake…"

It was the night before war was declared – the 2nd September, 1939, a Saturday, and there was I standing on guard like a lost soul. A lonely, self-conscious, terrified twit with my pick handle ("No rifles yet– Cop 'old of this—an' sign 'ere!") clutched tightly in my moist, right hand.

I was on guard outside one of those fabulous houses, rumoured to belong to the Duchess of Windsor, in Cumberland Terrace, Regents Park.

I cogitated as I looked up at the stars; looked up the road, and listened to the chattering of the monkeys as the sounds of the zoo wafted across the Park. And when the wind was in the right direction, it wasn't the only thing that was wafted across!

I talked to myself seriously, to reassure myself, to chide myself, and to keep myself company, and finally, I stopped when the Corporal of the guard came out and said "You challengin' someone?"

"Er—No, no Corporal", I said, "Just musing out loud and cogitating."

His eyes narrowed, and he looked at me oddly, then looked around into the inky blackness—back to me, back to the inky blackness, and then back to me again—snorted, as if to say, "We've got a right one 'ere!" And turned on his heel to go in again.

He stopped at the door, did an about turn, and said "You're supposed to be on the lookout, not bleedin' cogitatin'."

I ignored the interruption and carried on with my thoughts. It was my own fault being there, I couldn't blame anyone else. For that moment, I was a raw rifleman—well, a pick-handle-man— in the Queen Victoria Rifles, and I had been "called up" about 5 or 6 days earlier to fulfil the obligations that I had so lightly and foolishly embarked upon in that crisis-ridden year of 1938.

It must've been the sight of the sandbags being filled and gunpits being dug in the London streets that first stirred my conscience. Or it could've been the fact that I was keeping company with a quivering virgin called Susie Blueall, (whom my friends referred to as Susie "Blue Hole") who would go so far and no farther, leaving me to limp home with a pain in the groin after our every meeting. And on this particular night, she was doing her usual routine of moaning and writhing and pushing me away, and during a lull in the sexual manoeuvres, I told her I was going to join the Territorial Army–well, I was thinking about it. She gasped, nearly swooned, and almost fell, as if I'd touched the forbidden zone, and was off to the War tomorrow!

"Look—I'm only going up on Thursday (To the T.A. I meant) to see about it."

"If you join up on Thursday," she said, "We'll make love before you go away."

I couldn't believe my ears. She was naive as well as a virgin. Or was she? Anyway, I had to join in order to seduce her on the Saturday.

Looking back, neither was worth it.

Whatever the reason, I joined this gallant band of civilians playing at soldiers – "The Territorials." Nicknamed by some dog lover as "the Terriers".

After about five weekly meetings (or "Parades", as they were called) the tension of imminent war receded, and so did my patriotic enthusiasm. And I never went back.

Little did I know that once you've signed for "King and Country" then *that* is it. There is no way out. Unless of course you suffer from flat feet, ride side saddle, and have only one testicle, and then you have to have a Doctors Certificate to prove it. Foolishly I kept my side saddle prowess a secret, otherwise I might have been a C3 reject!

And as I said before, I never went back, so it came as a surprise when my mother phoned me at sunny Scarborough to say that I had a telegram from the war office "Calling me to the Colours."

"Calling me to the what?" I said speaking into the indistinct phone.

"The Colours" she said, with a capital C, as if genuflecting.
"What colours?" I said.

"Your calling up Colours," she said apprehensively. "The Territorial Army."

"But I don't belong to them anymore," I said desperately, "you know that."

"Well, they want you," she said.

"Blimey" I said, and hung up.

This was about the second week in August and I was appearing with Oscar Rabin's Broadcasting Band in an arcade called "Gala Land". I was acting as Compere and doing gags and impersonations, (Syd Walker, Vic Oliver, Hitler, Charles Laughton, and my favourite Maurice Chevalier). We did two sessions a day lasting about two hours every day and I was getting £10 a week, which was great. One old lady, after sitting out front for one of the shows, came to me afterwards and said,

"Well ah've sat through your show twice and your jokes get worse each time. My late 'usband was a comic, ah'll bring you some of his jokes, ye could do wi' 'em!"

I related what she'd said to Oscar's son Bernard, who was overseeing the box office and accounts, and he said,

"Don't take any notice. Take the gags though. There might be something you can use. You *could* do with them!" (Ooh him and his cheeky badinage!)

I never saw the woman again for after about another week, Oscar Rabin's Band and I were disbanded—through lack of customers brought on by the looming 1939 crisis.

I returned from-not-so-sunny Scarborough, to apprehensive London, to find my mother very agitated–the Police had called– Twice! To see what had happened to me.

"But I don't belong to the T.A. anymore, you know that. I left ages ago."

"I know, and you know," she said, "but *they* don't seem to know. Why don't you go along to the police station and tell them?" I did. I went to the Police station at Chiswick High Road and pointed out the mistake.

"Well," said the Police Sergeant, "I don't know about that son. All I know is that we've had the War Office bumff, asking us to check up on you, and if you don't report they might treat you as a deserter."

I froze where I stood. A deserter? Me?! Where could I desert to? It was all a mistake.

I reported to the Territorial Army—Queen Victoria Rifles—Headquarters in Davies Street, hoping it would be sorted out.

I sought the advice of the Sergeant, who was receiving everyone. He was a Regular—a professional soldier, who had been with a famous regiment, the Kings Royal Rifle Corps, the K.R.R.'s, and although he was brusque, and had a voice like a ruptured corncrake, he listened to me sympathetically.

"You see, Sergeant," I said humbly, "It's all a mistake really. I left the T.A. ages ago. I don't belong anymore."

"Did you," he said, twirling his military moustache with a tobacco stained trigger finger, "Did you sign the papers? The Embodiment papers?"

"Well –er— I think I did."

"What do you mean *think* lad? You either did or you didn't!"

"Well, oh yes, I suppose I did."

"Did you accept the money? For signin' on an' that. Did you get the Bounty?"

"Well, I'm not sure. I think maybe I did."

"Well– (he gave me an old-fashioned look) that's it lad, ennit? You signed the papers and you've got the money. There is no way out, is there?"

I looked suitably crestfallen. In fact, I heard it fall.

"Look, son," he said sympathetically and well-meaningly, "If you want my advice, you'll stay where you are. You're among friends 'ere. You'll be called up sooner or later, but this way you'll 'ave a start on all the others. You might get promoted, become a Sergeant like me, and who who knows, you might even get to be a nofficer. You'd like that, wouldn't you?"

His psychology worked. I nodded—weakly. My fate was sealed....

I telephoned my mother with the news.

"How did you get on?" She queried.

"Well, I've decided to stay. I had a talk with the Sergeant and he advised me."

"Well, I'm glad it's all cleared up. You'll get some leave before you go overseas."

"Blimey, I should hope so." (They hadn't even declared War yet!) She'd been through it all before with my father who'd finished up as an officer in the Royal Berkshire Regiment.

"Is your camp bed comfortable?" she asked.

"We're sleeping on the floor"– my voice dropped as if it were unspeakable– "in the Drill Hall."

"Can't you get a mattress?" She queried.

"It's not allowed, Mother, Army regulations. Anyway, it'll be alright once I get used to it." (I never did!) "I'd better go now."

"Telephone me tomorrow and let me know what you need."

"Yes thanks, mother. Alright. Good night."

"Don't worry, Sam, you'll be alright."

"Yes–I hope so. Thanks." I said in a very low voice full of self pity and hung up.

I went straight to the pub in Oxford Street and had three large Scotches and some bloke from the Stock Exchange bought me another and tried to pick me up. I may have been a very young soldier, but I wasn't *that* young!

"Right—Fall in outside in three ranks for Breakfast Parade. Come on, let's 'ave yer!"

It was September the Third, 1939. War was declared at 11 a.m. And the air raid siren went off immediately. We scurried to our billets, put on our steel helmets and looked up at the sky, expecting the Jerries to rain down bombs on us right away.

We "stood to" and I grasped my pick handle even tighter.

"What's that knocking?" said the Corporal. It was my pick handle.

I was tapping it nervously on the floor. I didn't mention that my knees were knocking as well.

After two or three weeks we got into the swing of things. It wasn't too bad really if you accepted your lot and settled down—there were some good blokes there—and some not so good, but wherever you ended up you'd run into *them*. They were nearly all London blokes in the Q.V.R's with more than a sprinkling of cockneys very witty and sharp and good fun to be with.

"D" company, of which I was a member, were a pretty useful lot of all-rounders, which was shown when it came to games like football. We played regularly, most afternoons, in the Park. After reveille, usually blown full of wrong notes (well, he hadn't got the hang of it yet) by the Bugler. we had to get into P.T. (Physical Training) Kit and charge around the Regents Park Inner Circle twice, a distance of about 2 to 3 miles—for a pre-breakfast run. The more conscientious did the full trip; the less so set off at the same pace as the others–stopped at the nearest "Gent's convenience" or the bushes, and hung about for a while, relieved themselves, had a smoke, and then joined the others, who had run the full circle, on the way back. If they were gasping from being out of breath, it looked quite authentic, they weren't used to running anyway!

After a quick rub down or cat-lick wash, depending on how you felt, everybody paraded for breakfast, complete with tin plate, knife, fork and spoon, and a tin mug.

Breakfast always took place in different or staggered shifts, in order to accommodate all the companies at Company Headquarters (Coy. H.Q.), another largish house not far from us, also requisitioned by the Army.

Breakfast varied, but usually consisted of watery porridge or thick "swamp" porridge—your spoon stood up and slowly sank— followed by two or three rashers of burnt or raw streaky bacon, and a dollop of half-baked beans, washed down with a mug of chlorinated tea.

Then would follow a session of Bren gun training—How to fire (no real bullets used, only dummies). How to clean. How to unjam the magazine. How to pull it apart. How to put it together —

"Alright, Kydd. Your turn!"

"Blimey!"

I never fired one in my life as it turned out. Just like the Mortars. I had a course in *them*—3 inch Mortars, and we never had any shells (blanks or real) to fire, not even in action in France. We had the Mortars alright, but no shells!

I also took a course on how to decontaminate contaminated water with special tablets. I never even saw the tablets.

A bout of square bashing—marching in threes—followed, by which time it was time for lunch.

Lunch parade—same tin, plates, knife, fork and spoon, consisted of meat, lamb or beef, two veg, potatoes, and for afters, a chunk of duff, or ginger cake, covered with syrup, or a piece of jam tart, covered with coconut chippings, known affectionately as "Toenail Tart." And of course, chlorinated tea, which was kept hot in a huge bucket-like dixie. I think there was more thrown away than drunk. Mind you, it did get better as the weeks wore on, or perhaps our tastebuds had disappeared by then!

There might be a short talk or lecture about army discipline, or a session of map reading after lunch, and then came what was known as Physical Recreation, which I always enjoyed. Usually it was playing football in the Park.

After tea—bread-and-butter, meat loaf, jam, biscuits and/or cake. Unless you were on guard duty or something like that—fatigues for instance—the rest of the time was your own.

You weren't supposed to stray out of the area, but of course everybody did, there was no check on them. The nearest flea-pit (cinema) was in Camden Town and there were stacks of pubs in the vicinity.

Once a week we had a "Bathing Parade"—we marched or went by lorry to the local council slipper baths, where high jinks always occurred. You'd be lying contentedly in your bath when suddenly a bucket of cold water would be emptied over you by the bloke next door (the walls were about eight foot high, but with the aid of a chair, you could easily get up). By far my favourite, however, was the occasion when a "Fairy Black Dye" was surreptitiously dropped into a rifleman's bath (he was dozing at the time), and he came out looking grey—like an African who had been frightened! He whitened, and came clean eventually!

And so the days rolled on. Nothing much was happening on the actual war Front, but we were certainly having fun at the rear.

Gradually, we were being welded into some sort of fighting unit —not yet ready to go into the ring, perhaps—but a "team" (Or "company") spirit was being forged, which augured well for the future. We were never going to become totally dedicated as professional soldiers are meant to be, although from what I saw of *them*, then, and later, I was never very impressed. Most of the regulars that I met seemed to be bound by Kings Regulations (The Regulars' Prayer Book) when it suited them. The vast majority of them were boorish—lacked humanity and a sense of humour. They were very good at taking the mickey out of people—especially in front of others. Maybe I was too sensitive, but that was how they struck me— verbally many times! There were a lot of "I'm all right, Jacks" amongst them.

The Queen Victoria Rifles were a mixed bag of Stock Exchange types and Cockneys from in and around Paddington and even further afield. What the Cockney riflemen lacked in intellect, they made up for with their natural wit, craft, and friendly approach to everything. I'm not saying they were all angels—of course they weren't—but they wouldn't do you a bad turn deliberately. I looked on most of them as Sam Wellers!

One Sunday, after Church Parade, there was an appeal for a driver to deliver an army vehicle over to the other side of London (to some army depot in Mill Hill, I think it was) and as there seemed to be a reluctance to volunteer (most of them had planned to nip off home or have a kip afterwards) I stepped forward. I had never driven a car and I wanted to prove to myself that I could do it.

"Well done Kydd!" (He knew my name!) said the Company Commander, Captain Morgan. "Would you deliver it right away?"

I was given the necessary papers referring to the car and found the vehicle, a khaki Austin 7, parked outside Company H.Q.

I got in and switched on the ignition and pressed the starter. The engine revved but didn't start. I tried again, and after about five minutes choking and revving she started.

Clouds of black smoke belched out of the exhaust pipe and a cheer went up from a group of onlookers.

I put her in first gear, released the clutch and she stalled. I repeated the process and put her in second gear, released the clutch gently, and she tottered forward about 15 yards and stopped.

I knew next to nothing about what went on under the bonnet, but I got out, lifted the bonnet and looked at the engine as if I did. I pretended to make some adjustment, replaced the bonnet, got in and tried again.

This time I started in third gear and only half released the clutch. She juddered forward reluctantly but gradually picked up speed until I was bowling along at 20 miles per hour. At this pace and in this manner I travelled across London—downhill I touched 30. It was at Hendon at some traffic lights where she misbehaved again. The lights were red, so I had to break and stop, and to keep the engine going I kept flicking the accelerator pedal. All was well till I went to move forward, which she did like a jerking juggernaut and finally stopped in the middle of the crossroads.

A policeman who had been watching my efforts came over to my assistance.

" 'Ow long you been driving a car?" he asked.

"If you want the truth" I said, "Since 12 o'clock this morning!"

He looked at me sideways, and gave me a push!

I finally arrived, having taken about two hours when I should've done it in 30 minutes.

But as a result of that little jaunt of endeavour, I became a temporary despatch rider. One of the regulars had been injured in an accident and they asked me would I take his place till he got better.

I agreed, of course, and was henceforth known as the spare "Don R."

Being a despatch rider, even though only temporary, gave me a new interest, status and many advantages. I had owned a motorbike of my own in 1936, a 250 cc broken-down Velocette, but had never taken a driving test, having driven, off and on, for over two years on a provisional license. So when they asked me if I had a license, I naturally said "yes". Not mentioning that it was only provisional!

I was issued with the goggles and gauntlets (crash helmets came later) and I wore my ground sheet if it was raining.

After two days, I bought myself a sort of khaki waterproof "on safari" jacket from the shop—a naval and military store—at Marble Arch, and looked quite dashing, playing my new character, part delivering "Top Secret" messages to Whitehall and other self-important sanctuaries.

The great thing was you could exceed the speed limit with impunity, drive on the pavement if necessary, and if checked by authority in the shape of the police, the "magic" words "Urgent, Despatch" saved the day.

I always kept a phoney gargantuan buff envelope handy with the words "O.H.M.S. URGENT SECRET" written on it, and to make it bulky, I stuffed it with buff toilet paper—Army issue, of course.

On one occasion, I was challenged by an overzealous "special" policeman, when I was on my way home to my mother's place for a quick bacon and eggs, and just gone against the lights at Edgware Road. I haughtily and pityingly produced my "O.H.M.S. URGENT SECRET" envelope, and he retired in confusion!

Eventually, I learnt how to suck petrol out of a petrol tank without swallowing it, but that was later in the war when petrol rationing was more acute. Not that it was ever really acute in the army, it was just that some bod in the higher up echelons was making a nuisance of himself, instituting an economy drive.

After a while, the rifleman, for whom I stood-in, recovered from his injuries, and I returned to my normal duties, P.T., Rifle Drill (We'd finally got rifles, of 1914 Great War vintage "All pick 'andles must be accounted for!"), Marching, Map Reading, and the inevitable Bren Gun training. How to fire—How to clean—How to unjam the magazine —well, you know how it goes!

"Your turn to put it together, Kydd. Right? MOVE!"

"Blimey!"

Then came the day when I learnt from the landlord of the "local" pub in Albany Street, that we were moving shortly– "in about five or six weeks time" he said.

"France?" I asked him.

"Oh, no, nothing like that, you're nowhere near ready for that are you." I didn't answer —I knew I wasn't!

"You're goin' to a hop farm, in Kent."

"Oh, really. Isn't that where the beer comes from?" I queried.

"That's how I know" he smirked, sinking his pint. "That, and the fact that your N.C.O.'s are 'avin' a goin' away party the week before they leave. I'm doin' the drinks and eats."

"Oh, I see," I retorted, "Thanks for the info."

I hurried back to the billet to report the news, but I had been forestalled—they knew already.

And so it came about that we of "D" company after various meetings and get-togethers at first planned a bun fight with drinks or buffet and dance with wives and mums and dads and girlfriends or mistresses or just casual pick ups!

All to celebrate our departure from our salubrious surroundings in Cumberland Terrace, Regents Park. *Finally,* it was decided upon, or turned out to be, a "Grand Concert–cum Dance and Buffet." The recruiting of the Acts for the concert part was left to me–

"Ah well, Kydd, you know all these people" (I didn't know any of them! Well. A couple.)

And the "Getting hold of the Dance Band" was left to me!

In other words, I was detailed for the job. By our Lieutenant Field Fisher——"Fi fi" or Fee Fee—to his friends and acquaintances.

How does one start collecting people to perform at a concert for no payment? I took the bull by the horns and went straight to the top. Patriotism plus some white lies here and there can go a long way. And it did.

It was much more successful than I could have imagined.

We had hired a hall in Marylebone, with the help of Company funds, donations, and collections, and with the generous help of the aforesaid subaltern—"Fi fi."

I went to the London Palladium, where the "Crazy Gang" were in residence and breaking all records. I didn't know any of them personally. (Well actually I'm fibbing as I had worked with Bud Flanagan briefly in Scarborough), and they were all wonderful pros and would help out if they could. So the stage door keeper told me. I asked to see Bud and was taken along to his dressing room.

"Hello Sammy!" He said. "Lovely to see you again. What's happening?" I told him that our Regiment was "on the move, probably overseas" (Liar) and "we wondered if he—er they could come along, and do their stuff at a farewell concert." For free—"of course, there will be a drink and the usual hospitality etc…" He was sweetness itself. Of course they would come along—the whole Gang — just leave it all to him. And they did—Flanagan and Allen; Nervo & Knox; Naughton & Gold; Monsewer Eddie Gray. The chorus, dancers and other members of the Palladium Company. They all came.

Elated with my success, I jumped on my 350 cc BSA and shot down to the London Hippodrome and used the same dialogue on Mr Vic Oliver, saying of course that I had Bud and the Gang—and again it worked. Finally, I shot over to the Hammersmith Palais and asked Oscar Rabin if the Band would come and play for dancing. (I of course knew him already as well). Not only would they come said Oscar, but as they would be playing late at the Palais, he would arrange for a relief band to play until he and the Orchestra got there. Looking back, I should've been mentioned in despatches! The show went on for three or four hours and was a complete riot, followed by drinking and eating and dancing long into the night. Years later, I was in a film with dear old Bud Flanagan and though I looked like a Mongolian (well, I'd been through Russia) he remembered me again. Once seen…! Needless to say that bill of Artistes would have cost a fortune but "D" company got it for about £100!

The thing was, a good time was had by all, and especially by the rifleman next to my bed in the village, who took his girlfriend back with him, and had a hectic farewell session on top of his blankets. She kept saying it was "Great!" And he replied, "You can say that again"– and she did, so they obviously enjoyed the show too! On the morrow, we departed for Whitbread Hop farm, Beltring.

Leaving London in a pall of exhaust fumes, and not a few regrets, we made the journey in convoy without incident—apart from getting my wheels caught in the tram lines in the Old Kent Road—and arrived long past the estimated time of arrival (we got lost twice) at our new mild and bitter billets near Paddock Wood.

A quaint romantic name is "Paddock Wood", as of course is Beltring Hop farm. They both roll off the tongue or past the tongue, depending on which way you're facing when you drink. Our billet on this vast, hop, step and mind the cows' pancakes, was an Oast House, and it's not everybody that gets the chance to sleep in an Oast House. If you're ever offered it—refuse. Read on, and I'll tell you why….

An Oast House in case you don't know, is a Kiln where hops or malt are dried, and if you look it up in the dictionary, it says "a Kiln to dry hops." In the same dictionary, you will probably see the word "Oasis" which comes before "Oast." Now the definition of Oasis, in my dictionary, is "any place of rest or pleasure in the midst of toil and gloom" and I suppose you could say that I found my oasis in the Oast House, which is the nearest I've ever got to perversion! We, the Q.V.R's, or as some people said "Those Black Buttoned Bastards", had arrived at the hop farm at a most unfortunate time, I mean, the hops had long since been hopped and dried and squashed, and fried, or whatever the hell they do with them, and as far as we were concerned, the whole thing was very small beer—if you pardon the pun. The hoppers had long since gone, but you could see by the hop prints where they'd been. *Graffiti* abounded there. Living conditions were primitive—there was only one bog with the door half off, and the washing arrangements were suitable for one wash per week!

We, "D" company, were assigned to the number one Oast House, which was immediately on your right as you came into the camp, and unfortunately our arrival coincided with what is known as a "very cold snap" and consequently, snow and ice were everywhere and it was to remain so for several months! It was so cold, so freezingly cold, that if by chance you took your socks off, overnight, they'd be frozen solid in the morning—standing to attention! There was only one way to defeat this. Go to bed with your socks on. And your trousers. And your tunic. And your balaclava.

You see, the Oast House is so conically constructed that the wind comes up like Barney's Bull—in a mad rush—and the lattice work flooring is specially made to allow the draught to soar through unimpeded. But we were young and healthy until half the Battalion went down with pneumonia, or just wanting to get away from it all for a few days. In other words "swinging the lead"—that's Army slang for "pretending". There was a lot of it about. The Cockneys were very good at it. So were the Irishmen, Scotsmen and Welsh, in fact, any other nation too I suppose. Maybe not the German (I found out later they do. It's called "swinging the Sauerkraut!")

As time went on, we hardened to it, and as usual gradually settled down into the routine of it all.

The farm belonged to Colonel Whitbread, and whenever his name was mentioned, it was always with bated breath, standing to attention, as if we were expected to mention him in our prayers. "And God bless the Colonel for allowing us to use his facilities."

He, of course lived at the big house—not, I hasten to add, the Big Oast House. All mod. cons. And all that. Well, why not, after all, he was the Colonel and he had *lent* his place—the hop farm I mean— for the good of the troops. At a nominal fee to the nation, I suspected. I know I had barrack room damages deducted from my seven shillings every week. I never did find out what I was supposed to have damaged. Anyway, there followed a period of training and, to quote "daily orders," "intense activity" which really amounted to the usual marching, map reading, drilling, exercises, guard duty, and the inevitable Bren Gun training. How to load the magazine—How to strip it—How to put it together again.

"O.K., Kydd, your turn. You have 60 seconds to put it together again. Move!"

"Blimey."

It's even more difficult to assemble a Bren with mittens and frostbitten fingers!

We went into Tonbridge quite a lot—it was the nearest point of civilisation. To the pictures, a dance or just for drinking and "that". There was quite a bit of "that" about as well if you knew where to look.

I was out on an exercise one day driving my 500 cc Norton Motor Cycle Combination (Sidecar) known as M.C.C. and we were all to rendezvous with some particular map reference at a place called Yalding, and turning into a side street there was this sultry piece of homework I met at the dance on Saturday night. She was waiting at the bus stop—presumably for a bus. Claire her name was—I never got the surname—who had the reputation of being a "man eater" whatever that meant! I had taken a yen to her (yes, she *was* slightly Japanese looking) and I danced a lot with her. She had hinted at "things to come" when I moved in closer during a spot waltz, but had nipped off sharply at the end of the dance to catch her last bus, she now said.

Anyway, I stopped the machine and offered to give her a lift to her home where apparently she was going. I put my ground sheet round her shoulders and made her wear my steel helmet. (it was strictly forbidden to give civilians rides on the motor-cycles). Any ride after dismounting was our own affair (Think about it). I stopped outside the house in which she had a flat, and she invited me in for a cup of tea and crumpet and that was how my exercise ended that afternoon. Tea and crumpet on the floor with the gas fire full on.

I never got to the map reference point that day. I went back to camp and told them that my brake had seized up, but it was alright now.

I went back to Yalding for my belt that I inadvertently left there on purpose, two days later.

I put another notch in it before I put it on. Even with all that tea and crumpet I was getting thinner.

Of course we had several week-end passes, which entitled us to go home to London. I've forgotten exactly how many free travel warrants you were allowed, but all other times you had to pay, which was a bit of a blow if you were on seven shillings a week as I was. I'd noticed that when some of the fellows got to the main station (Charing Cross) they would not show their tickets, but just sing out "Scotland" or "Wales" or "Ireland" or wherever they were going, which necessitated going across London to another main station. Usually the ticket collector would reply "Euston" or "Paddington" or "Kings Cross" and just wave them through, so I determined to try the same idea for myself.

The following week-end, fancying a bit of home cooking, I bribed the company office clerk to give me a week-end pass, which he did (but no free railway warrant, the sod!).

So, arriving at "Beltring Halt", where you got on the train to make the connection at Tonbridge, I mingled with the rest of the riflemen, who had bought legitimate tickets to take them all the way to London, and when we got to Charing Cross Station and approached towards the barrier, taking care to keep closely behind a crowd as they surged forward, and clutching my suitcase in my hot hand, I sang out "Scotland" in my pseudo Scottish accent expecting to be waived on and through. But no, not this time.

A big towering conceited ape of a military policeman stopped me and said "Where are you going?"

"Scotland" in my now not so confident Scottish accent.

"Where's your ticket?" He said, smirking.

"Ticket?" I said forgetting my accent and producing the week-end pass.

"I want to see your ticket," he reiterated through his thick lips.

"Oh yes." I went through the routine of looking for the ticket which I never had in the first place.

Somebody else called out "Scotland" and was waved through. (Just my luck!)

"You haven't got a ticket 'ave yer?" he sneered.

"Oh, yes, I have. I've just mislaid it."

"C'mon," he said, "I'm puttin' you under arrest. Follow me!"

I shouldn't have. I should have bolted, but that might have made it worse, if he'd caught me. I followed him meekly to the R.T.O.'s office, there to await the officer.

I carried on doing the turning out the pockets routine looking for the non-existent ticket, but he wasn't fooled.

He said to the other Corporal, who joined him —"I got another one. No ticket."

"Right," said his carbon copy, " 'old him till the Captain gets back."

"Do you want to make a statement?" said sneering chops.

"About what?" I said dopily.

"About your fucking ticket that you never 'ad, that's what!"

I didn't answer. I wasn't going to commit myself.

I waited three hours in the office and the officer never did turn up. They were having me on a large piece of string. He'd probably gone on leave too without a ticket!

They made me leave a deposit for the ticket, leaving me just enough money to get home. They threatened me with all sorts of reprisals—arrest—glasshouse—and finally told me to fuck off. And if they ever caught me again, they'd throw the book at me.

They were kidding, but I didn't do it again. Well, not often.

Whilst still at Beltring Hop Farm, we had what was known as a new intake. A batch of youngsters mostly around 18 known as "The Militia"—called up or conscripted and sent to our battalion. For a long time they went around in L.G.O.C. (London General Omnibus Company) overcoats and looked very pathetic, especially in the cold weather, but like us they soon found their feet. Frozen mostly. It was all that standing around listening to lectures like— "Now you see before you, the Boyes Anti Tank Gun, which is not in case you might think it, to be fired by Boys" (Alright joke over. What joke?) "But by men—soldiers of strength and sagacity." (What's that got to do with it?) "Kydd pay attention. Wot have I just said?"

"The Boyes Anti Tank gun is not to be fired by boys, but by men of length and tenacity er capacity…?"

It was getting as bad as the Bren Gun!

The Militia perked up considerably when they were finally kitted out with battledress and the regulation overcoats. At least they looked like part of the Establishment instead of Lithuanian mercenaries. I don't think they were meant to go overseas for sometime until they had had at least six months training, but if my memory serves me right, I think a lot of them did. So much for Government ruling.

Eventually... the winter passed and Spring as always was not far behind, and a beautiful Spring it was, which gave birth to a glorious summer, but I'm getting ahead of myself... First of all. Surprise! Surprise! I was promoted to Lance Corporal—Acting. Unpaid. And as it was never confirmed in what they call Battalion Part 2 orders— don't ask me why, I never *stopped* asking, I needed the money—and although I was ordered to wear the stripe, I remained unpaid for the duration. A sort of sorcerer's apprentice Corporal, who never got his certificate.

And I still only had 6/6 a week for painting the town red.

The only thing I didn't distinguish myself at was, yes, you've guessed it—reassembling the Bren gun.

"All right, Kydd, sorry, Corporal Kydd. Your turn. Move!"

"Oh blimey–not again!"

As I said before, the blossom came out, and so did the soldiers. They became even better known in the locality for their valour, their manners, and their exploits, like helping lame ducks over stiles, and then ringing their necks on the other side and selling or flogging petrol, which was severely rationed. I myself was involved in a local fracas with the long arm of the law.

But before that, I met a very charming girl called Nora O'Neill at a "Tea Dansant" in Lyons Corner House, Coventry Street, whose Aunt was the Mother Superior at a convent near Saint James's I think. I can't remember what I was doing there exactly—apart from having tea that is—I mean it was on a Thursday, and what was I doing in London on the Thursday—perhaps I was on leave—anyway there she was, in all her sweet religious Irish glory, sitting at a table, delicately nibbling a piece of toast. She had wonderful sleek black hair pulled back to a bun in a sort of Spanish fashion, beautiful dewy grey-blue eyes, and it wasn't long before I was gazing into them. She was delightful in a naive sort of way, pure and unsullied, she danced well and was very vivacious. I was very taken with her. You can say that again! I will—I was very taken with her.

We exchanged addresses, and she wrote to me, on and off, calling me her "green eyed Apollo", all through the war years.

But I never saw her again, and when I got back from the war, she was already married and had two children and was living in Newcastle.

So you see what nibbling a piece of toast can do for a girl.

I returned to Beltring to carry on with my war efforts to outwit those in authority, and to enjoy life to the full in that mad maelstrom of exotic swinging, Tonbridge!

It was a Saturday in March, and I wanted to go to the local dance in Tonbridge. I and my clique had become well known there as sporty lads, but on this particular night I got caught up in having to issue some ammunition to an officer, and he of course, was late. (I was working in the Armoury stores at the time, and kipping there as well. Needless to say it had its advantages such as the roast duck party— local duck enticed from a nearby farm. Beer—roast duck—and "crumpet."—The "crumpet" enticed from Paddock Wood Village!)

I told the others I would join them later and to tell Flo O'Grady, the local Belle of the Ball, to save the last waltz for me, but of course due to the officer's lateness, I missed the last bus and any lifts that were going to Tonbridge.

By this time, it was around 9 o'clock. So I hung about at the entrance to the camp in the forlorn hope that I might pick up some transport. I was determined not to walk to Tonbridge, although I'd done it on one or two other occasions. It was only about 6 or 7 miles but I didn't want to miss out on the fun. However, it looked pretty hopeless; nothing was going in that direction at all.

Suddenly, I remembered Jacky King's motorbike. Two or three week-ends ago, he had given me a lift to London on the pillion, and after a nightmare ride of slithering and sliding all over the place in the snow—there was no tread on the tyres—we got to Town and returned late and in the same fashion on Sunday night. He kept the unlicensed bike in a hop pickers hut just behind "D" Company Oast house, and he'd said to me if ever I wanted to use it I only had to ask him and help myself—providing he didn't need it himself.

I nipped round smartly to the hut and as luck would have it there she was just waiting to be ridden. I realised I wouldn't have time to find Jacky and let him know, but I reckoned he'd understand and obviously he wasn't going out on it himself, so I skipped that. There was only one other snag, she was empty, there wasn't a drop of petrol in her.

I headed back to the armoury and found the rubber tube which I kept for extracting petrol from motor vehicles, grabbed an empty quart beer bottle, and searched around for the golden liquid. Just as if I'd rubbed the bottle and the genie had done his stuff an Austin utility truck came along the road and pulled up outside the Sergeants' mess, which was just across the way from the Camp. I meandered over aimlessly (well–that was the impression I wanted to give) and walked round the truck twice, as if I was thinking of buying it. There was no sign of the Sergeant driver. He was buying one for the Sergeant–Major, and she just sat there, waiting to be milked. Before you could say "Have this one on me" I had unscrewed the petrol tank cap, dropped the rubber tube inside the neck till I heard a splash, sucked the end of the tube till my mouth filled with petrol, spat it out, and transferred the tube into the neck of the empty beer bottle. Within seconds, it was overflowing! I pulled out the tube, replaced the petrol cap, put the full bottle of petrol into my overcoat pocket and sauntered off. "The Lord helps those who help themselves". We were in business! Once inside the Camp gates, I shot back to the bike and emptied the petrol into the tank. I turned on the petrol tap—titillated the nipple of the carburettor—kicked the starter once or twice, and she roared into life.

In 30 minutes, I was sinking my second beer in our favourite pub in Tonbridge.

It was just about interval time at the dance, and it wasn't long before I was joined by the boys for a drink. I related what had happened, and then conned my way into the dance hall without paying, saying I'd lost my pass-out ticket.

After the dance, which finished at 11 p.m., we repaired to the pub where the landlord, our favourite innkeeper, aided the war effort by serving us with drinks and sandwiches in the sanctity of his sitting room. It was there that I met up with Jacky King, the owner of the motorbike. He had come to the dance earlier, unknown to me, and naturally I told him about my borrowing his bike.

"That's all right," said Jacky "Where'd you get the petrol?"

I told him, and he chuckled, and we both said together "The Lord helps those etc…"

"Can you give me a lift back to camp?" he asked me with a grin.

"You're kidding, aren't you?" said I, "It's your bike, Jacky, you drive and I'll sit on the pillion."

So around about 12.30 a.m., the others having taken off in a taxi and after making our goodbyes in the shape of another couple of pints, we set off along the Tonbridge High Street.

When we got over the railway bridge, I was bursting to go to the lavatory—it was all that bumping up and down on the pillion—I shouted to Jackie to pull up "I want to go to the Gents." He stopped, and I shot across the road to the railway station. It was closed. I hurried back to the bike, still bursting, remounted the pillion, and told Jacky to stop at the lights just up the road (there was a small entry or passageway there which would fit the bill) and when we got there, he braked, stopped the engine, and we both got off leaving the bike propped up against the curb.

Jacky, who had an inbuilt camel-like waterworks, and could go for hours without urinating, lit up a fag and prepared to wait for me. There wasn't a soul about as far as I could see, so I nipped smartly up the entry and was just in the middle of "My Gosh, I needed that" act, when a torch was shone on me. It was a policeman.

"'Ello," he said, as if he couldn't see. "What's all this then?"

"Just watering the grass, officer." I said lightheartedly over my shoulder, slightly embarrassed.

"I can see that," he said, delicately avoiding the stream that was riveting down the incline towards the pavement.

"Good night, officer," I said, hurrying past him, anxious to be away.

"Just a minute," said the copper. "Are you that lot from Paddock Wood—Whitbread's Hop farm?"

(That lot?!) "Yes" I said, and saw to my horror that he was taking out his notebook and pencil!

"Right. Name—Unit—and Army Number." He asked, pencil poised.

"Lance Corporal Kydd; Queen Victoria Rifles; 6896304. But what's the matter, officer?" I asked humbly.

"Committin' a nuisance—that's what's the matter," he answered without looking up.

"But, officer"—it was a call of Nature—I'd had a skinful—and I was taken short." (And then, in a pleading whine) "You can do yourself an injury holding it in, you know."

There was a pause, long enough for me to do up my flies.

"Is that all you're sayin'?" Said the Law, continuing to write.

I was so taken aback, that *was* all I was sayin'—I mean saying. He hadn't finished yet, though.

All this time, Jacky was practically standing to attention, trying to look as if he was a lamp-post placed conveniently so that he blocked out the view of the licence holder. But the Law wasn't born yesterday.

"Is this your property?" he said, pointing to the bike with his pencil, and looking at me.

Jacky, from his sphinx-like trance, spoke, "No, it's mine."

"But I was driving it," I said quickly, "I borrowed it without his permission from the place—er the hut—where it's kept in the camp, and we met here in Tonbridge, by chance, and I was giving him a lift back to the camp."

"Should've been taxed three months ago—the licence is out of date," he said blandly, so sure of himself. "You got the insurance certificate?"

Jacky looked at me and then shook his head.

"It's not insured, is it?" said P.C. Knowall.

Jacky shook his head and said—"Rifleman, King—Queen Victoria Rifles—6896316."

"You're doin' well, the two of you. Licence out of date—No insurance—Drivin' an untaxed vehicle—(he nodded to me)—Drivin' a motor bike, not taxed—not insured—Drivin' without the owner's consent—committin' a public nuisance—exposin' yourself, act of public indecency—anythin' else you want to say?"

I was going to say something about "his promotion" but discretion prevailed, and I simply answered "No, can we go now?"

"Not on that bike, you can't" he said, obstructive to the bitter end.

We had to push it for a quarter of a mile round the bend in the road before we were out of his vision, and then we started her up and sped home to the camp.

I apologised to Jacky when we were inside the hut.

"Oh, that's alright," he said sportingly and understanding, "it was bound to happen sooner or later. Perhaps he was just chucking his weight around and won't do anything about it."

But he did. After about three weeks I was summoned to the company office and was confronted with the charges.

The policeman had thrown the book at me—the list of charges sounded like an indictment for treason! I told my Company Commander the truth, and he was very sympathetic in a court-martial sort of way. after berating me about the good name of the regiment and our company in particular. But he ended up by saying that he would attend court with me at the time of the hearing, to plead on my behalf. I looked suitably ashamed, crestfallen, and grateful—which is not easy—and marched out.

The day of my attendance at court coincided with our evacuation from the district to somewhere else in Kent, so I conveniently forgot about it.

I never heard any more, so I presumed they'd forgotten about it too. But for a while I was always doubly vigilant when doing anything I shouldn't be doing!

Suddenly—almost overnight—we were given the order to move, and a mad frantic rush to finish deals and leave unfinished those that were unpaid, ensued.

Where are we going? Overseas—to the front in France? To join the K.R.R's in Africa in the sweltering heat? To some long forgotten outpost of the Empire—like the Khyber Pass?

No!—to Ashford in Kent.

Not far from Maidstone actually.

As usual the landlord of the "local" knew before us where we were going and when. He knew a bloke who had a mate whose wife knew a butcher who had a shop in Maidstone, who'd been approached about supplying the meat... consequently, that's where we were going.

We made our mass exodus in convoy, sometime in May, 1940, not long after the German army had broken through in Belgium and France, and a brave sight we were, belting down the roads in our M.C.C. 's in F.M.O. (Full Marching Order) plus gas cape and gas mask.

We were preceded by the Scout cars from H.Q. Company, and then following us came the lorries containing the company stores, bumff and soldiers' kit. A brave and impressive sight indeed. I took the wrong road four times.

"D" Company were billeted in a little hamlet just outside Ashford, and the villagers welcomed us with open arms—they kept bringing us cups of tea and home-baked bread and cakes, and told us not to hesitate to ask if there was something we wanted, which was pretty sweeping of them, but very nice.

That same evening, not being on guard or anything, we made straight for Maidstone and the Gaumont cinema. They let us in for half price, which was decent of them. They obviously appreciated and understood soldiers in Maidstone—as they did in Ashford too! Well, we were protecting them in a sort of way because, from now on our job, apart from the normal day-to-day activities and fatigues, was to shoot about the countryside in our M.C.C.'s (Motor Cycle Combinations) with a fellow rifleman as passenger armed with a Bren gun keeping a strict look out for German parachutists dressed as nuns or priests.

We had an interesting conversation with a farm labourer following an "alarm" report that a strange priest had been seen in the vicinity of Charing. Supposedly having floated down from the sky.
Me: "Have you seen a Priest walking down the road here?"
F. L.: "Oi 'ave."
Me "What did he look like?"
F. L. "Loike ee always looks."
Me: "What do you mean?"
F. L.: "Wall, it were Father Dominic. 'ees our local priest."
Me: "No, we're looking for a German parachutist masquerading as a priest or a nun."
F. L.: "Doin', wot?"

Me: "A German paratrooper disguised as... Oh blimey, never mind!"

On reflection, how could a burly German parachutist ever look like a nun, with a machine gun under his skirt or surplice? I mean they walk differently, don't they.

I never encountered one, and neither did any of the others, although Corporal Barker of "C" company met a monk in Maidstone, who he said, had a peculiar habit! Unfortunately this idyllic, roving commission of policing the roads and fields only lasted a short time, and just as we were getting ourselves organised—getting to know the local crumpet and that, we were on the move again. Like a bunch of nomads. This time it was the real thing. We knew it as soon as the words "Embarkation Leave" were mentioned.

I had my photograph taken with my mother in the garden at Chiswick and our farewells were made with a weeping of Irish tears and a lump in my throat.

What lay head? If only we had known. They weeded out the sick and lame to stay behind and they were branded B.2 or C.3.

I, of course, healthy idiot that I am, was A.1.

We entrained and were cosseted by the Red Cross and the Welfare Ladies with chocolate, cigarettes and chewing gum and arrived at Dover on May 21, 1940.

CHAPTER 2
"For You the War is Over"

And so it was on May 21st, 1940, we set sail for—could it be the middle East?—confusingly we steamed around in circles in Mid Channel at Midnight—in the meantime the rumour grew—my informant had actually seen the pith helmets and the mosquito netting in the quartermaster's stores—or so he said. He must have had hallucinations because on the morning of May 22nd we landed at Calais and after unloading our gear and equipment we formed up in our companies prior to marching off. While we waited, a small detachment marched towards the ship—four soldiers, British, with rifles at the ready and bayonets fixed, and four German Luftwaffe prisoners, six footers. The officer in charge motioned them to go aboard and we looked at them curiously, our first sight of the Enemy. The looked big and arrogant but harmless enough, not like the Nazi monsters we had expected. An hour later we were still on the quayside and the ship eased slowly out on its return to England. My pith helmet informant, a sailor, waved goodbye from a porthole. I retaliated with the appropriate gesture and a raspberry for good measure.

We of course were a motorised battalion and had been fully trained as a mechanised reconnaissance unit with scout cars and motor cycle and sidecar combinations upon which a machine gun was to be mounted to search out and account for the enemy—in theory that was —and in practice in England that was. But not in France. All of a sudden we were now Infantry and as Infantry we marched. No more of that scorching around on our 500 cc Nortons—this was different. This was for real. You can imagine the grumbling that went on. But nevertheless, we marched.

Our company—"D"—arrived at a pre-arranged position and then spilt up into platoons. Again we marched to another position—a minor road outside and leading into Calais—and there we awaited the arrival of the Germans. Everything seemed quite quiet and peaceful so naturally we had tea. We mounted a road block in the form of some railway sleepers—the railway track was about two or three hundred yards away to our right—and we took up our positions, one section to the right, one to the left and another dug in behind a sandbag emplacement facing head-on down the road. We settled down for the night and I dozed till it was my turn for guard duty—from two till four. At home I had never been very keen on guard duty but here it was worse. I hated it. It was eerie and scary—one spoke in whispers and a distant sneeze had you on the alert with the hairs on the back of your neck standing up in sympathy. Rifle at the ready with one up the spout you waited, peering into the inky blackness.

But of course nothing happened. It was one of our blokes dreaming of the hop farm or more likely the hops. When one thinks of the amount of adrenalin that one wasted in those days—well it makes one think doesn't it?!

Towards the end of my stint I was just beginning a yawn when I stiffened. I heard a voice singing—drunkenly. It sounded like snatches of Allouette. Well why shouldn't it be—it was France wasn't it? I listened again. It could be a Jerry pretending. I waited. The sound came nearer—more unevenly and more drunkenly it seemed. I went through the procedure and challenged him. "Halt! Who goes there?" I raised the rifle and peered along the gunsight. He had stopped about ten yards away, and was breathing hard and audibly. "Advance and be recognised" my voice sounding an octave higher spoke. Nothing happened. I repeated the question. Nothing happened except for more heavy breathing. I tried in French. "Avance et—what the hell's 'be recognised' in French? "Avance lentement et doucement." He came slowly and sweetly and almost fell at my feet. "Ah—le Tommy—Le Tommy Anglais" he announced to all and sundry. He was French all right. I was torn between interrogating him and telling him to push off. Luckily my oppo had roused the officer and the decision was taken out of my hands. He was led away.

Nothing else untoward happened through the night or what was left of it and the sun came up early and shone fiercely all day. The inebriated Frenchman was a local and after sleeping it off was told to "push off" in English. We bathed in the nearby stream and breakfasted on bacon and beans. With tea without milk. The supplies hadn't come. So far it had been a bit of a picnic and just as we were getting lulled into a false sense of security, the balloon went up. It started with some stragglers—French and Belgian soldiers on foot—I should perhaps say hotfoot—who came towards us babbling "Les Allemands—Les Allemands!" and before we could buttonhole them, had taken off in the direction of Calais like scalded cats. If I'd had any sense I'd have joined them but then I'm British. After about an hour of peering and looking and wondering and waiting—it happened. A heavy German tank lumbered slowly and ominously into view and stopped about 200 yards away. Some trigger happy machine gunner opened up on his own account and all Hell was let loose. The section I was in was deployed away to the right—there to approach at an angle to engage it with our Boyes Anti Tank Gun for the use of. But as we crouched and edged forward gingerly in our best Tom and Jerry style we were met with a heavy burst of machine gun fire. The section scattered leaving two dead and retreated hastily to the main party at the road block where the rest of them were heavily engaged firing at German soldiers advancing behind the tank. The skyline and horizon was filled with wave upon wave of menacing grey uniforms and over to the right two German scout cars accompanied by motorcyclists opened fire on us. The air was filled with whining shells and bullets and it was obviously impossible to hold such a force, so, as they say in the Military Manuals, we disengaged. At first in a dignified manner, in the end not so. In short we ran. We weren't scalded cats. We were scolded kittens. We lost about seven young soldiers. So much for our first baptism of fire—of action.

We retired to a ridge of high ground about two miles away—a place like the banks of a disused reservoir, which commanded a view of the road we had just left. We joined one or two other scattered sections at this position, making in all a couple of platoons defending it. We expected the Germans—naively—to come down the road. But of course they didn't. They left the road and came across the fields. Running, taking cover and firing. I had trouble with my firing at this point, the reason being my gas cape. It was perched on top of my knapsack which was naturally on my back and when I raised my head to fire my rifle, my gas cape knocked the back of my steel helmet causing it to tilt forwards over my eyes. I was firing blind. I pulled the tape to release the gas cape and it billowed around me like a magic cloak. I discarded it completely and carried on firing. We were holding up their attack momentarily because they had to come into the open to reach the next spot of cover and that was when we were doing the damage.

But not for long, for within the space of minutes the air was made hideous by the shattering crack of mortar fire—a devastating and destructive weapon. It certainly put paid to our resistance. One direct hit wiped out a pocket of our chaps and a rain of shrapnel incapacitated several near me. They had certainly pinpointed our position, making it untenable. We withdrew—or disengaged—again. This time to the centre of the Town. The Town Square to be exact. Some other unit had just made tea—the R.A.S.C. (Royal Army Service Corps) I think it was—anyway they very kindly gave us some which was much appreciated. It washed down the hard tack and bully which they also produced. Our platoon had been reduced to practically one section now but we had been joined by some odds and sods who had been split up from their units—some Welsh Guards, Engineers and Rifle Brigade blokes all answering to or under the command of our officer. We were ordered to occupy or man one of the coastal guns along the beach. These—about three of them—were pointing out to sea covering the Channel and they became our next defensive position. Our rag tag and bob tailed unit marched, if that is the word, to its new destination spreading bonhomie as we went. When we got there—to the gun emplacement—bonhomie became even more conspicuous, for the French who had recently evacuated their posts had left it very well-stocked with drink. Mostly wine of course but there were several bottles of vermouth, Martini and rum. Our officer who inspected the location first warned the troops. It was poisoned he said. And everybody was forbidden to drink it. It had been poisoned to fool the Germans. Well it didn't fool the British—they drank it. Poisoned or not. I heard a few belches but didn't see anybody writhing in agony. As we took up our positions the bottles were passed surreptitiously from hand to hand. The Royal Engineers amongst us asked if they could try and get the coastal guns in order and the officer gave his permission. They were supposed to have been spiked by the French before they vamoosed. This was true of our emplacement, the turret had been wrecked. But the number two effort was turreted round so that it was pointing inland. I don't know the calibre of the guns but they were rather like those you would see on a battleship and there was plenty of ammunition about. The engineers got to work and we waited. To the left of us was a huge wood or spinney and I thought I detected some movement through some binoculars that I had acquired. I looked intently and sure enough two or three bent figures were running through the undergrowth from tree to tree. I advised our officer who took the glasses and looked "It's all right," he said, "I think they're our chaps. Don't shoot." I wasn't so sure. I took another look. "Sir" I cried, "they're Jerries. There's a whole mob of them coming through the wood. To the left and away over there to the right," I pointed in the direction.

"God, you're right," he said. "Tell them (our troops) to hold fire till they get the order."

I ran to the forward section positions and told them.

I hared back to the officer and waited for him to give the order. He waited for perhaps a minute or two until two or three figures had cleared the wood and come out into the open skulking and running. Now, I thought. Now. But still he waited.

And then "Right—let 'em have it."

The machine guns opened up as well as a fusillade of rifle fire and the leading Jerries crumpled in the dust—the rest ran back into the wood. The same thing happened with those to the right of the woods —they too did a smart back pedal into the undergrowth.

"Hold your fire," said the officer.

I transmitted the order and they stopped firing.

"Sir," shouted a voice.

It was one of the engineers working on the number two gun emplacement. He was standing at the entrance with his thumbs up.

"I think they've got the gun going, Sir," I said.

"Nip over and check," he said, "and tell them not to fire till I give the word."

"Right, Sir."

I belted over to the gun a distance of about 100 yards. They had indeed got it going with a shell in the breech already to fire. I relayed the order, and nipped back zig-zag wise to the officer. There were one or two desultory shots from our enemy but we were too well hidden to worry. No doubt they would think of something. They did. They must have radioed back for their artillery plane to fly over and mark our position which it did by emitting a long spume of smoke which hung over us pall-like in the sunny sky. The artillery shells followed thudding into the ground with an earsplitting roar—the range this time wasn't as good as the mortars had been but it wasn't exactly comfortable. I mean it didn't encourage you to stroll about.

We kept our heads down and occasionally looked up for signs of the enemy moving. But nothing happened till the barrage suddenly stopped. It became very quiet and one was aware of the birds singing somewhere and then they started to come out—the soldiers not the birds—in single file at first in ones or two's and then as nothing happened they got bolder—and advanced out well into the open. Again we waited till we had more fish in the net and then we let them have it. For some unknown reason the big gun (number two emplacement) fired too, or I should say attempted to fire, because the whole thing blew up whether by accident or design I'll never know. Anyway blow up it did and bang went our number two! But our attention was diverted by the sight of some troop-carrying vehicles filtering down a minor road towards the edge of the wood—from where we were they could have been ours—but if they were there was nothing that we could do to help them. They'd walked right into it. They disappeared into the wood. And immediately the artillery barrage opened up again. This time they were more accurate and were getting our range so much so that our forward positions had to be evacuated. It was at this time that our officer detailed me to take a message to Battalion Headquarters which I understood to be found opposite the Citadel—a tower-like building not far from the railway station—so with all speed I set off. We had no radio communication so a runner was the next best thing. I cut along behind the coastal guns and made my way towards a river which wended its way to the sea. In order to cross the river I looked around for a boat or a log and eventually found a very sodden and rotting raft nestling forlornly in the reeds. I broke off a branch from a tree to use as an oar or pole and got aboard. It was slimy and slippery and difficult to manoeuvre. I kept going round in circles. I discarded the pole and rowed with my rifle which turned out to be much more effective. Possibly not so good for the rifle however. I made a mental note to write a letter to Lee Enfield advising a more oar like design to their future rifles. I had reached the other bank and almost fell in getting off the raft but apart from getting my feet wet and tearing my trousers I was more or less O.K.. I tethered the raft to a nearby bush with a piece of string, which I had for such purpose, for the return journey and squelched off in the direction of the Citadel. I was making my way along a rough footpath when I heard the noise of aeroplane engines.

I looked up and almost directly above me I saw a squadron of German Stukas. You could see their German cross markings quite clearly and they were evidently making for the railway station—or so I thought. But suddenly one of the planes detached itself from the formation, swung round in a wide circling sweep and started to come up behind me. I turned round to watch it and then I couldn't believe it. It was dive bombing straight at me! At first I thought it must be a vehicle or a lorry or something they were after but when the bullets started to spatter around me they'd convinced me! I ran—zig zagged —did the 100 yards in 10 seconds flat and dived into a bed of nettles. Cowering down as if I were a hedgehog. The noise those Stukas made when they dive bombed was terrifying. A sort of high pitched whine increasing in intensity as they zoomed towards the target. It must have cost a few Reichmarks to try and get me. I don't think the Fuehrer would have approved. On the other hand he might have encouraged it, you never know. After a lengthy and hardly daring to breathe pause, I continued my hedgehog act and rolled out of my nettlebed. I tended to my wounds with a dock leaf and continued shakily on my way. I scanned the sky for further interference but all seemed well. The Stukas were on their way to more worthwhile targets. The bastards.

When I finally reached the Citadel the whole place was in, as the Irish say, a state of chassis—there were burned out lorries everywhere

—troops milling about—but no sign of Battalion H.Q. The air raid had stirred things up a bit and I was unable to contact anybody in authority from the Queen Vics, so after some sustenance (a Cognac) I decided to return the way I had come and set out with this in mind.But I had barely started out on my return journey when I encountered the remnants of my platoon on their way back. They had been knocked about pretty badly—mauled would be a better word—and had decided to retire. The next thing was to try and find our Company or Battalion H.Q and acting on a tipoff, our officers sent another of our chaps to a fort-like barrack which was situated near the railway station—to the left of it—looking out to sea that is. I found myself doing quiet a bit of this now—looking and longing for the safety and peacefulness of England. It had been a hectic and chaotic not to mention disastrous three days since we had landed from the "Old Country". I could think of nothing better than going back there and as if in answer to my thoughts the order suddenly came "All Units to group or hold themselves in or around the environs of the harbour prior to embarking for the United Kingdom." We could not believe our ears. It was the Best Order of the Day that I'd ever heard—not that I'd heard many—but it was great news.

Great News. Alas—after a wait of half the night during which it teemed down incessantly to add to our discomfort—the order was countermanded and we were now ordered to defend Calais "until the last man". Quite a switch, wasn't it!

Wearily, in the early light of dawn we took up fresh positions to counteract the lightning advance of the enemy. And again it followed the usual pattern. We retired to the sand dunes near the beach. Soon there would be nothing left to defend.

It was now obvious that the Germans were far superior to us in every way—it's hard to stop a victorious advancing army, a highly professional one, and we were, after all, a very mixed bunch of civilian soldiers thrown in at the deep end, but who at the time tried very hard.

On what was to be the last day, May 27th—the net was closing in tighter. The Germans had taken most of the town except for a large pocket of resistance in and around the harbour—this side of the level crossing.

I was helping a stretcher bearer to carry a wounded man to the railway station—where a first aid post had been set up—when a heavy burst of machine gun fire mowed down the group of soldiers in front of us—one bullet penetrated my water bottle—and scrabbling and crouching and carrying the wounded men we took cover behind a lorry parked close to the wall which ran along-side the railway tracks, there to wait for the firing to lessen. The Germans were firing from the Citadel, from the rooftops and from adjacent buildings. The level crossing was effectively blocked with railway carriages but they—the Jerries—had complete command with heavy fire-power directed over our side of the crossing because of their firing situation. It was hopeless to venture out to the left side of the lorry.

There was only one way to go—over or through the wall, a concrete wall about 6 foot high and 6 inches thick. I took my rifle and pummelled the wall as if my life depended on it and after about 10 minutes a crack appeared and finally a hole. The wall was actually concreted bricks—bricks in the centre and concrete either side. I kicked the rest of the wall down and we were through. We hugged the wall down the other side and eventually when out of range and dodging behind a goods train we cut across the tracks to the station. Just as we made the platform the Stukas came over for the umpteenth time to show off their meticulous dive bombing. They decimated the goods train we had dodged behind, but we were safe in the bunker at the station (or what was left of it). About two hours later I was on the beach near a jetty along with three other riflemen and our officer from "D" Company.

For some unaccountable reason we were digging this slit trench —I can't think why—probably a last ditch effort, when I suddenly spotted some German troops away to our right advancing along the beach. I warned Fee Fee.

"Right," he said "In the trench everybody. Move."

It was about three foot deep you couldn't even squat in it— comfortably. To our horror a similar squad of Germans were spotted coming from the opposite direction. We looked at Fee Fee and all he said was "Oh Christ." He took out his white handkerchief, waved it and turned to us and said "Sorry, fellows it's bloody hopeless."

We were soon surrounded by 30 or 40 unsmiling Krauts, and the toughest looking with close cropped hair came bounding up and bellowed at us. In German of course. They were bellowing and motioning with their machine guns and the awful thing was you didn't understand a word they were saying and they in turn took it for dumb insolence. Our rifles and ammo were thrown into the sea and we were searched for any other form of weapon. By this time their officer arrived, looking as if he had just stepped out of a film—he had two British revolvers in his belt and a pair of binoculars hung round his neck. He sported a monocle and with the effort of keeping it in place his face assumed a twisted grin just like Erich Von Stroheim.

He announced the immortal words "For you ze VOR is OVair!"

He proceeded to make a speech in his best German spy speaking English:

"ZEE Cherman Armee is victorious. NOZING can stop us. Vee vill capture Paris end France vill fall. England vill surrendour—end zee Vor vill be OVAIR."

My arms began to droop a little during the speech but after a heavy dig in the back from a rifle they resumed the "Hallelulia" position for the rest of the propaganda.

"First you vill be sent beck to Chermany und den you vill go home. Vee are not barbarians. Vee are Chermans fighting for Deutschland. Deutschland Uber Alles!

The chorus was taken up and echoed by his choir of soldiers as if on cue—"DEUTSCHLAND UBER ALLES" ending in heel clicks and Hitler salutes. Which was later to become—crudely—in English parlance "How high is the propaganda shit today?" And the answer was—with arm upraised in the Hitler salute—"THAT HIGH!"

To be taken prisoner had never entered my head. I wasn't even aware of the correct procedure when taken p.o.w.—Name Rank and Army Number Only. Not that it mattered. The Germans knew everything anyway. *When* we set sail—*when* we had landed—*how* many battalions—the *names* of our commanding officers—etc— etcetera. Some Fifth Columnist had done his job well. After six frenetic, disorganised, chaotic days our active service was "ovair". Looking wistfully out across the sea the faint outline of England—21 miles away—could be seen. It was more than 5 years later that we were to see it again. But some never made the return journey.

Later that day—forever emblazoned on my mind, the 27th May 1940— round about five o'clock we were herded into a huge field to join hundreds of other newly taken prisoners. There we were interrogated, one by one, by filing past a largish table, answering questions put to us in excellent English by a German Officer. He was a *Sonderfuhrer,* a sort of political relations officer who seemed to know all about the regiments involved in Calais.

After giving him my name, rank and Army number, he confirmed it by reading out my details from my Army Book.

"Kydd. Samuel."

"Lance Corporal. Not yet confirmed."

"Number 6896304."

"Yes sir."

"Born in Northern Ireland, I see."

"Yes sir."

"You're Irish, then."

"Well, yes sir, but I'm British."

"You're Irish and yet you're fighting for the English?"

Not wanting to get involved, I answered "Yes."

He looked at me steadily and curiously and then said "I see."

This curious riddle was to intrigue the Germans many times in the future. Some of them thought I was a mercenary—at two shillings a day! That's rich! I rejoined my section who had been captured with me and we waited for something to happen, but nothing transpired.

Some N.C.O.'s prior to interrogation had stripped off their stripes, demoting themselves on the spot and some private soldiers did the reverse. They promoted themselves with the discarded stripes and then claimed they'd lost their Army Books so no check could be made. When I taxed a Sergeant on why he had done it he said that he didn't want any responsibility under our captors but twelve months later when he saw it was to his advantage, he changed his mind.

Much later that evening we marched or stumbled out of Calais on our way to Germany, and apart from being shelled by the Royal Navy, little of incident happened. My last meal had consisted of five spoonfuls of Keiller's marmalade, but grub for the prisoners didn't appear to be on the German menu.

It was well after midnight when we were halted and ordered to file into a church at a place called Guines where we were to spend the rest of the night and not a night of rest. The candles on the altar were all lit to greet us and the Communion wine had been long finished when we stepped through the portals. The German guards were posted at the two or three exits including the vestry, and the captive congregation, about three thousand of them, or so it seemed, sprawled wearily here there and everywhere. Up the aisles, down the aisles, under the pews, on top. And even on top of the other prisoners—if you see what I mean. Talk about no room at the Inn!

The single lavatory at the back of the church worked overtime and after a while it gave up the ghost. Hundreds couldn't wait anyway (and didn't bother to) and because the Jerries wouldn't let them out they used the gratings which led to the crypt. Consequently there were minor outbursts of rage and threats, not to mention unchurchlike language, when the others lying near the gratings got wet or contaminated. Well they had to go somewhere. I was lucky. I was in a pew. Gradually the "relievers" queue shortened and was finally exhausted and it was then that an uneasy quiet descended on the multitude, broken only by the snoring or the mutterings of sleepless groups.

Reveille took place at four in the morning with guttural German shrieks of *"Los—Los. Aufsten. Los—Los—Los!"* (Come on. Come on. Get up. Come on.) We were to get to know that cry well—and to hate it! We shambled to our feet—I was still with some of my former section—and I noticed that the "Offerings" or "Poor" box had been whipped from its hinges and to add to my indignation my haversack which had been near to my head had gone the same way! It was hopeless trying to find it in that mob. I asked of course but everybody denied all knowledge of it. I had lost my shaving gear, tooth-paste, towel, soap and some personal effects, including my wallet and some precious cigarettes. It was the first lesson I learnt as a p.o.w. To survive you have to look after Number One. Later—much later, it finally sunk in. If the Jerries don't take it—the British will—well, some of them!

The dawn streaks were just chalking the sky when we stumbled into the light to be marshalled into a rambling, meandering column, out of step, out of sorts and, as our bellies told us, out of grub. Enquires of the nearest German soldier about the food stakes or as we were quickly to learn *"essen"* (eating) conveyed in pantomime by rubbing the stomach and much champing of the jaws (imaginary eggs and bacon) always got the same answer—a pointing of the finger down the road in the direction we were taking. It fooled us the first time and the second, but after a while it became a bad joke—in poor taste!

No food was provided. Or drink. So, for that first day we marched—and marched and marched. In circles I think. We were guarded by the front line troops, some of whom weren't too bad, but the majority unfortunately had this awful habit of bellowing in the un-understandable German and unhooking and cocking their rifles ominously if one showed any dissent. Which as the hot summer's day wore on was shown!

But the trigger-happy Jerries had to be outwitted at all costs! When we were passing a field of cabbages one or two of the p.o.w.'s broke ranks and dived for the vegetables. The nearest guards allowed a few to be pulled up and then resorted to their frenzied bellowing and aiming antics. And again the same procedure occurred when we passed a potato field, but this time shots were fired at the avaricious spud stealers. In the scramble, showers of "Le Roi Edwards" spattered the roadway and the scrabbling continued till the road surface was bare! Cold uncooked Murphies aren't bad. Especially when you're hungry. Gives you the shits later, mind you, which isn't conducive to good marching but who cares as long as your hunger's assuaged!

The sun shone fiercely throughout the day giving us a swarthy sun tan and apart from the one spud that I picked up that was all I did get on that first marching day!

I did manage to find a tin which I used as a cup—very good for trailing into a horse trough as you went hovering past, which I and my companions did on several occasions.

At the end of the day's marching I had acquired about five or six words to add to my German Vocabulary—mostly to do with food, I must admit— well?

In order and phonetically they were—Essen (eating) Hoonger (Hunger) Shpater (Later) Kartoffel (Potato) Mittag-Essen (Lunch) Zuppa (Soup) Fleische (Meat) Brot (Bread) Butter (Butter) Englander (English) Verdamt Englander (Damned English) Pauser (Pause or break time) Scheisen (Shoot) and Du Englischer Schwine (English Pigs) and of course the inevitable LOS-LOS-LOS—Jump to it, you English Bastard!

We were led shunted and shoved into a huge field at a place called Marquise and as it was obvious we weren't going to be fed, protests were made to the Senior British Officer amongst us—a Lieutenant Colonel. He listened sympathetically. Demanded an audience of his equivalent in charge of the prisoners. Made his protests. Was listened to sympathetically and was then told that there was no grub. No arrangements had apparently been made for such a vast number of prisoners and besides they themselves lived off the land as they went along. There was no answer to that, so we mooned about the field before we turned in. The whole field was ringed by German guards at approximately twenty yard intervals and one of them called to my companion and myself.

" 'Allo—*Du Kommen zie hier* ' "

We presumed what it was and came. He spoke slowly as if he had difficulty in remembering the words—which he had. He had corresponded with an English pen pal in Sheerness and came from Dresden.

"You—er—knaw Scheerness?"

I didn't, but I nodded.

"Very fine city—*Jah?*"

"*Jah*, I said. "Very fine."

"I—er (he went through the motions) er—*schreiben* wiz er *freund* er Scheerness."

"*Jah?*" said my companion (he spoke German too)

"*Fraulein?*"

"*Jah,*" said our new acquaintance, "*Fraulein*—er Girl. Miss Villiams."

"Oh, a Welsh bit" I said.

"Vat ees bit?" he said.

I ignored it and came straight to the point. "When," I said as if I was speaking to a deaf idiot, "are we going to have some fucking grub?"

"Grab" he said, "Vas is grab?"

"Mangez—Food—Meat—Spuds?"

"Shpuds?" he queried, "Vas is shpuds?"

"Oh for christ's sake. Bread and butter!!"

"*Na jah,*" he said "Bread und Butter. Bread und Butter."

A ventriloquist and his doll had nothing on him! All that was missing was the "gottle of geer!"

He carried on defiantly "Guns bevore Butter." (Big laugh but not from us.)

"Look, Fritz, we want bread, butter, soup. We've had nothing to eat."

"Nozing to eat. Nozing to eat. You nozing to eat. Me nozing to eat. Not good."

"And *you're* not much bloody good either!"

The conversation was exhausted and so were we. We sidled off and joined the others, related the abortive conversation, and then, lying on the ground huddled together, soon fell asleep.

"AUFSTEN" which as I've said is GET UP, greeted us at dawn and shortly after we'd collected our wits—we'd nothing else to collect —we were on our way again. The pattern and way of marching life remained the same. We started out freshly enough, albeit no rations— strode bravely on till midday, pinched a few spuds—a cabbage or two between six and two or three tins of trough or pump water completed the menu. Occasionally when we went through a small village the women would venture out to watch us pityingly and sadly. Occasionally a sandwich or small loaf was thrown to the remnants of the B.E.F. and if you weren't maimed in the rush you might end up getting a crust or more likely a belt in the ear from a rifle or a boot up the rear from a German guard. Sometimes they allowed us to fill water bottles from the pumps—I had acquired an old wine bottle which served this purpose—and all the time the sun burning high in the sky without a cloud to mar the azure blue—shone down on this meandering mob. We got browner and hairier, and thinner and sweatier. That evening we arrived at Desvres and again were led into a field. From the air we must have looked like khaki sheep—rows of khaki sheep asleep in a fold. Not the ones that Mary had but the Whiffenpoof lot —the Yale University Acapella singing act — those "Poor little lambs who had lost their way—Baah—Baah—Baah!"

Again no food or drink was issued and the craving for a meal and my thirst to be slaked even entered my dreams—so much that when I went for a pee (in my dream) I woke up to find it raining! It must have been a hark back to that well known joke—

"I had a dream last night."

"What was your dream?"

"I dreamt I was eating flannel cake."

"Flannel cake?"

"Yeah—and when I woke up the blanket was gone!"

Unfortunately for us we had no blanket, no ground-sheet or raincoat for protection, so our little coterie of Queen Vics—four to be exact—drew closer together and turned our faces to the ground, and the rain, like staircase rods, drilled down as if in spite.

It rained solidly all through the night, stopping only when we started to march again. Luckily the sun sun came out and shone splendidly and we steamed as we walked along. I almost forgot. We had an official German issue of Coffee and the buzz went round the field like wildfire. We dutifully queued up for this doubtful beverage —I used my tin—filing past one of the field kitchens to be doled out a ladle-full. It was ersatz coffee, of course, made I believe, or so I was told, from Acorns! But it was a drink—and it was hot and acceptable. Like most things, you got used to the taste and even welcomed it. Later on they varied it with peppermint tea which looked like a cup of hot urine and tasted as if a Polo mint had been dipped into it—and pulled out again! They always left some mint leaves floating about on top which gave you something to chew. If you closed your eyes you could imagine you were revelling in a Pimms Number 69. That's if you were delirious.

The next port of call according to the signs was named Hesdin, and at least we were sheltered this time, in some stables attached to a Cavalry barracks. It wasn't bad in the straw. It was soft and warm and snug like a country woman or a town woman come to that, but women were furthest from our thoughts. The first priority was food.

I personally had had a good day. Like the forecasting astrologers say "A good day for Aquarians culminating in a successful evening spent with friends!" Not all of them of my own choosing mind you— but at least they weren't all of them unfriendly. Envious perhaps—but unfriendly, never!

To recap—what had happened exactly was —we (our little section or me and my muckers) were at the head of the column and while passing through a small village in the afternoon, a charming old French woman had appeared at the side of the road with a small handcart full of those long French loaves, and before you could say Free French those nearest to her were being showered with the bread. I caught one that had my name on it and stuffed it smartly down my trousers—the inside of my trousers. Two more of my section caught one each which we immediately broke in half and shared out there and then. I was chewing happily and on looking back I saw that the cart had almost disappeared under a melee of bodies kicking and fighting to get at the rest of the bread. The German guards in the vicinity had rushed up and were bawling *Los, Los, Raus*! ineffectually. *La pauvre* —the poor old lady—had been knocked to the ground during the onslaught, and the guards in front of us leading the column, including the *Unter Offizier,* seeing what was happening, halted the column and hastened to the scene of the fracas.

Two of them unslung their rifles, cocked them and fired into the air—that is they finally fired into the air because just as they were about to pull the triggers their rifles were knocked upwards by one of the prisoners. He, the Tommy, was joined by another soldier and they grappled with the Germans! A dreadful five second silence ensued and then all Hell was let loose.

The *Unter Offizier* screamed "Fire! Fire!" and other guards unslung their rifles and proceeded to fire into the crowd indiscriminately. The air was rendered hideous by the cries and shrieks of the wounded. As we waited, my eye was caught by another French woman standing at the door of her cottage who unbelievably was beckoning me over. Moving my head I panned over to the right to take in the scene then back to her and then to the right again. *They* were fully occupied. She was still motioning me to come. I threw caution to the winds and went. I dived sharply into the small entrance hall or parlour and shut the door. She retreated and once I was in she took hold of my arm piloting me to the back of the cottage—the kitchen. I wouldn't have considered the bedroom. She said something about "*mangez*" and I nodded my merci beaucoups enthusiastically. She was about 30 years of age, with high cheek bones, dark hair and a curly mouth and very sympathetic eyes. If the time and circumstances had been more propitious we could have discussed the entente cordiale or I could have told her fortune and discussed our future but wiser counsel prevailed—my stomach! She took a small empty flour sack and filled it with eggs, she handed me an earthenware jar filled with butter and a fat bottle of red wine.

I showed her the bread tucked down the inside of my trousers and said "*Pain, regardez*" just in case she thought otherwise and she smiled. I put the sack containing the eggs inside my battle dress blouse to the left and butter in my hot hand. I practically curtsied— bent over and kissed her on both cheeks, said "*Merci mille fois*!" and retreated to the door. I opened it cautiously to see what was happening and luckily the scene was still simmering. I re-joined the column and tried to look as if I'd never left it. With success!

The two British soldiers who had "come to grips" with the Germans originally had been taken across the road and were heavily guarded, and the wounded of which there were several were being carried to a German wagon.

The wounded were put aboard and the two mutineers were bundled along with them, guarded by two sullen looking guards. Both of them had their rifles at the ready and we expected to hear the worst about their fate, but after we arrived at Hesdin and had partaken of our first civilized meal they turned up unharmed. They had been driven to the local hospital, ordered to unload the wounded and marched to German Army H.Q. then hung about for a couple of hours, waiting to see what was going to happen to them. Fortunately for them the officer in charge, to whom they were taken, wasn't interested so they were marched to the gates of the stables and sped on their way with a boot up the Jacksi. But as for me—the Day of the Aquarian remember?—it worked out at about four boiled eggs each— practically half a loaf each—some boiled spuds in their jackets, swilled down with a mugful of red wine. We never had it so good. It wasn't so bad being captured after all! And to cap it all we were issued with some pork and potato soup, which we had for "afters" instead of "befores".

After Hesdin we "visited" Frevant where we spent the night in a flax factory, to be followed the next day by Doullens prison where ten of us shared a cell meant for two and you had to watch where you sat because of the excrement. It had been occupied by French p.o.w.'s shortly before our arrival, and once the Jerries got us locked in they refused to let us out—for anything.

They did let one man out to collect the watery soup in dixies, and then told us to use the dixies for going to the lavatory. We were glad to get away from that place although it took most of the next day. We were searched, individually, one by one, and with thee two or three thousand prisoners that they had taken, that took some time. And a thorough search it was. I was made to turn out my pockets.
My scout's knife with the multiple blades and all the extra accoutrements for getting stones out of horses hooves etc., was taken from me, but immediately "lifted" from the pile by one of my friends while the guard was distracted and handed back to me once we got outside. Our guards had been changed at Doullens and the new arrivals, obviously not front line troops, and therefore not so amenable or complacent as the others had been, seemed to want to impress their superiors by their overstrict discipline. A point which they demonstrated early on.

As we left the prison and were straggling down the wide main road we came to a cross roads, when suddenly a fleet of military vehicles started to cut directly across the road in our paths. Some of the fellows who were partly across dashed the remainder of the way to get out of the path of the lorries and the blokes I was with stopped. Two of them, unfortunately, dithered as if to go across, retreated and then went again. From our left came this hulking Jerry idiot maniac who exploded into a furious Teutonic fit. He unslung his rifle, bellowing and screaming some German oaths and proceeded to fire at the two hesitant riflemen. They fell in their tracks, and when we went to go to their assistance he swung round on us pointing the rifle in our direction. It's very difficult arguing with a raging Hun pointing a gun at you and this one in particular was almost foaming at the mouth as if he were a hunter who had maimed two young lions and was saying "they're mine!".

I could never understand this trait in their make-up. Even the most inoffensive were liable to blow up—hysterically, like petulant lunatic children. Perhaps it was all those Hitler newsreels—he was always screeching and thumping and waving his arms in a demoniacal rage. Maybe they were encouraged to ape their furious Fuehrer and they should have been pitied. But that wasn't easy to do—difficult with two of our blokes lying in a pool of blood.

CHAPTER 3
"Alles ist Verboten"

The town of Faucvilliers was our next stop, where we occupied another field, soon to be followed by Bapaume. This time a football stadium, on the pitch and in the stands— floodlights and all! Finally, we arrived at Cambrai, a town of some importance.

The civilians—mostly women–didn't seem to worry about the Germans and waved to us sympathetically, and there were shouts of *"Bravo, Tommy" "Vive L'Angleterre" "A bas les Allemands."* They were definitely hostile to the Jerries. Quite a few were weeping. And although we looked like an undistinguished rabble we tried to brace ourselves up a bit and smiled back at them. It was all rather sad really. For them. And us.

At Cambrai we said goodbye to our guards, not literally, but they had to go back for the next lot, and we were shunted into Cambrai barracks, a huge fort-like edifice with literally thousands of prisoners milling about everywhere. There were Belgians and an equal amount of French and British. And, for some unaccountable reason, the French resented us. This resentment was reciprocated by the British, mainly because the French seemed to have come prepared for capture —they carried everything with them, including their little cooking stoves. They certainly had it all laid on. And what the British really couldn't stomach was that the Froggies seemed to have an inexhaustible supply of British tinned foods and English cigarettes. Fights were always breaking out at the drop of a British tin! And some of them got pretty ugly. A fire would be kicked over by the British and a dixie of Ambrosia creamed rice which was being gently heated by the French, would be deposited all over the ground. The Germans would arrive on the scene and we would have the inevitable firing in the air in the end. If the positions had been reversed, and we had had lots of French food and the French had none, would the British have shared with the French? I wonder. No, I don't. They wouldn't. As it was, *A bas les Allemands* soon became *A bas les Anglais.*

Food there was in the form of Soup and Bread. German Military bread—sort of dark brown (sometimes black) very hard ancient "Hovis" which could be kept for a week and got sourer the longer it was kept. Actually, I had already eaten it on one of my scavenging expeditions on the march—I had found some in a dustbin—so I wasn't exactly a stranger to it. So far we had had no approach to registering as prisoners of war and indeed until we got to Germany we never did. Consequently all of us at home were listed as missing—presumed dead. Somebody who did get home from Calais personally phoned my mother to tell her I had been blown up—for lack of food, maybe, but certainly not by shell.

Cambrai—like any collecting centre where stacks of unwilling men are corralled—became a sort of rogues' kitchen, a racketeers' paradise. Goods were bartered, and pinched, and whipped. Nothing was sacred. If, for instance, you'd got hold of some tobacco, you looked around for a bible or hymn book. Because these pages— Ancient and Modern—made the best cigarette papers.

Occasionally, the call came for working or fatigue parties to go outside the camp into Cambrai, and it wasn't long before I got onto this. Anything was better than queueing up for 3 to 4 hours to get half a litre of watery soup and again repeating the process to get a fifth of a loaf and some ersatz margarine. Acceptable as it was to some I preferred to get outside somehow knowing I would fare better in every way.

So, in order to achieve this, I hung about at the huge gates at the entrance to the barracks hoping that a fatigue party would be required. Mind you, two or three hundred others with the same thought in mind hovered there, so there was quite a bit of jostling and pushing and shoving when there was the likelihood of a party being needed.

For three days I got up at the crack of dawn, did my toilet (washed in the trough) in double quick time and hung about the gates without any luck, but on the fourth day it happened. I along with another Queen Vic was chosen. Just the two of us. We were taken by a guard, a corporal from some outside unit who had to sign for us, and marched through the streets to our destination, a huge house in a fashionable square which was being got ready for some high ranking

German military personnel. Or so we were told. I clanked along as we marched. Two dixies were attached to the rear of my jacket and a fairly substantial haversack of unknown vintage hung on my shoulder. These were from my syndicate who would naturally share in any good fortune that I encountered. In other words, for extra grub or chattels of bartering or exchangeable value—within the barracks, that is.

When we got to the house, we were shown what was needed. All the windows had been blown in or out—shattered—and the debris lay all around.

The house was graced with a huge entrance hall with a black and white marble floor and a large glass chandelier had crashed to the ground and was in pieces everywhere. We got hold of two sweeping brushes and started to clear up the debris.

And so we continued until 11.30 a.m., and then it was time for *Mittag Essen* with a big E—in other words, the grub stakes!

We were taken to the kitchen, a large airy room filled with stoves and the usual appliances, and there given our eats. It was a great lunch, consisting of pork chops, potatoes, peas, and sauerkraut, followed by a sort of Dundee cake covered in custard. I had two helpings of each, putting the second pork chop into my haversack. At the invitation of the cook, a German soldier, I filled up both dixies with potatoes, peas, and sauerkraut, squashing it down till the dixie was choked with it. My companion did exactly the same with his.

We finished off with a cup of coffee, the real stuff, obviously French, and I belched contentedly as we walked upstairs. The cook, who came with us up the first flight of stairs kept saying what sounded like "*Schmekt Gute, jah?*" To which I nodded and said "*Jah, danke*". It must have been the right thing to say because he looked pleased. I later found out from a German who spoke English, that it meant broadly "All right was it?" So "*yah, danke*" was obviously in order.

Happily, we carried on with our chores in the afternoon, but suddenly I'd got wise to the fact that we might be able to get another day out of it—the German guard who was supposed to look after us, or guard us, was always missing, chatting up a French piece who was scrubbing the floors so we were left to our own devices, which at my behest meant introducing a go-slow. I went to the lavatory five times, once genuine, and my mate did the same!

Then came coffee break at 4.30—known as *kaffee pauser*—the cook came and fetched us and escorted us down to the kitchen where he produced two steaming cups of French coffee and a wurst or German sausage sandwich each. I wasn't sure whether he fancied us or whether he just felt sorry for us, but whatever it was, he was certainly kind to us. It was difficult to reconcile his attitude with that of the bawling, haranguing, foaming-at-the-mouth brigade. I asked him in my pidgin German if we would be needed tomorrow.

"Jah! Jah!" he said.

Something like a cash register clicked in my mind—"Bring four monster dixies" it registered. At 6 p.m. the Corporal came to take us back to the barracks. He indicated that we would be required to-morrow *"morgen hier"*.

"Jah, danke" I said. My Queen Vic mate did the same.

"Jah, danke" he said.

Not only was he my mate, he was my echo!

We clicked our heels and almost Hailed Hitler. I had noticed one or two knick-knacks in the house—vases—a small clock— candlesticks (I took the candles), that might be of value for bartering purposes in the barracks, but decided to stay my hand in case we were searched on arrival. As it happened, we weren't.

When we arrived at the gates we stopped, and I spoke to our guard—the German equivalent of a corporal—an *obergefreiter*.

"You spracken officer *us here"* (I tapped my mate's chest and then mine) "Us here, *morgen, jah?"* *"Jah, Jah*, good" he rejoined.

He motioned for us to go in. He wasn't a bad lad, quite smart in an *ersatz* sort of way.

My three muckers were waiting for me as if I'd just returned from a goodwill tour of Cambrai!

The mixture of spuds, peas and sauerkraut was rapturously received and rapidly demolished. They had saved me some soup, which I declined, so we flogged it to an Algerian Froggie for a packet of fags which smelt of camel dung. Nevertheless, we smoked them! During the night (we were lying huddled up near the wall). I woke up with a terrible stomach ache and had to make a bolt for the bog. I only just got there! Obviously making a pig of myself had something to do with it, but for ever after I was always a bit wary of sauerkraut!

The next day me and my mate (Little Sir Echo) were at the gates shortly after dawn broke, looking as spick and span as we could under the circumstances. I had shaved with a borrowed razor and so had he. I had also attempted to polish my boots for the first time since we had been captured. I looked very lean—I had definitely lost weight. I had weighed myself on some Frenchman's scales (he charged one cigarette to weigh yourself) and I was now down to 9 stones. I was 10 stones at Calais so I was looking forward to making up some of the loss in the hands of our friendly German cook. We stood apart from the other "workers"—*our* assignation was secure!

At the appointed time for our rendezvous (8 o'clock) we looked expectantly for our new-found friend each time the gates opened. An hour passed. Two hours. And just as we were about to give up hope, he arrived! We greeted him like relieved lovers, or long lost relatives! We waved and shouted. Anybody watching would've thought that we were pro-German. He smiled and nodded, and we did the same.

When we got outside, and we are preceding him along the road, I said to him "you *schlaffen*?" (sleep).

"*Jah*" he replied. "*Schlaffen.*"

"Nix good for Tommy" I said. He laughed.

"Nein" said my echoing mate "Nix good for me, and nix good for him!" He was becoming adventurous.

"*Bitte*?" Said the Corporal.

I gave my mate a withering look to tell him to keep his trap shut.

"Him *schlaffen*, too" I said hurriedly. I put my head on my hands like an imaginary pillow and snored loudly. Then I laughed, cueing my mate to laugh too. The German Corporal joined in the laughter, and that fortunately was the end of the conversation.

It was a repeat performance of the day before with two exceptions. First I had brought three dixies instead of two, and secondly we were closely guarded by a German soldier, who watched us as if we were an investment and even tried to increase the work rate by making remarks like "*Schnell*" (faster) every now and again. And even when I told him I was going to the lavatory, he wouldn't wear that. We all went together! And again, when my mate wanted to go, we all went together.

I stood outside, trying to chat to him whilst my workmate was performing. But he wasn't very communicative—all I could get out of him was something that sounded like "Immer pissen!" "Immer" means always and the second word meant what it sounds like!

Consequently we were not given the opportunity to whip anything as we had planned. Originally, I had thought that by some miracle, we might stretch the clearing up to another foodfull day—and if we had been left to ourselves we might have done—but not with this over-zealous overseer in charge. By 5 o'clock we couldn't find any more work to do—he couldn't, I mean.

Our cookie friend didn't let us down, of course, and as that was the object of the operation, we couldn't complain.

Again, we went through the menu twice—a large dollop of stew, followed by two apples for dessert, plus the usual cup of genuine coffee. For extras, I filled my three dixies with stew and he gave me 4 more apples, and my echoing mate benefited likewise.

Then at *Kaffeepauser* time after the coffee and wurst sandwich he gave us a loaf of bread each and a packet of German cigarettes. They were called "Juno" and on the packet was written *"Warum ist Juno rund"* (why is Juno round?) He was a real toff! The cook, I mean, not "Juno!"

It was when we were leaving that we discovered that the house was being got ready for "Der Fuehrer"—Adolf himself. And that was the nearest we ever got to seeing him, in the flesh!

The following day I hovered at the gates just in case the German Corporal showed up again, but this time there was no dice. For the moment my outing days were over. It was not to be. I hoped the Fuehrer enjoyed his stay. I was certainly grateful to him–in a roundabout way. I offered a little prayer for his car to be blown up with him in it, of course, but the message must have got a bit garbled because he passed through Cambrai unscathed.

In the barracks, the enmity between the French and the British got worse instead of better, and the entente wasn't at all Cordiale.

Apart from the trouble I mentioned before, at the sight of the English tins of food—the NAAFI supplies—and the flaunting of English cigarettes in the hands of the French, over which fights and scuffles broke out about every twenty minutes, the main contributing factor was the fact that the place was bursting at the seams with prisoners and the Germans themselves didn't seem able to cope. Every day two or three hundred more prisoners would roll or totter in and the queueing for soup and bread became more intolerable and more frustrating. The whole day was passed in queueing.

Starting at 10.30 a.m. for a cup full of thin watery vegetable soup, which, after struggling, and pushing and cursing and fighting you eventually got at 1.30 p.m. Then start again immediately queueing for the ration of bread and ersatz margarine due to be issued at 3.30 p.m. This you didn't sometimes get until 8 o'clock, and then the best plan was to eat it right away before it was knocked out of your hand or stolen. The British were the main culprits here, although the Algerian French weren't far behind!

Some fellows exchanged their bread ration for four or five cigarettes. (The exchange rate changed daily—sometimes it went up and sometimes down. One day five cigs—the next four, and maybe next day three.) The extra bread ration then became a bartering asset. If a prisoner was newly arrived and naturally starving, he would be approached by the prisoner with the extra bread ration, and would be offered it in exchange for, say, his khaki shirt. Off would come a shirt in exchange for the bread and the bloke with the newly acquired shirt could change that in another part of the camp for two bread rations, *and* five cigarettes! He was in business, or the "Rackets" as it was soon to be called! I'm not saying I stood aloof, but at least I tried to play fair—which got me nowhere. I was one of the newly arrived prisoners who had sold his khaki shirt for a bread ration.

To him, that hath shall be given" and I wanted to be one that hath, unfortunately there was an awful lot of competition–and pilfering—and stealing—and looting!

For instance, if you had to go to the lavatory or "shit creek" as it was colloquially known (those French bogs, where you squatted down on your haunches over a hole, and hoped for the best!), it was advisable to take your most valuable possessions with you. Even mugs and empty tins used as cooking utensils weren't safe. Going to the bog was another queueing job although the Algerians didn't even bother— they crapped where they sat, which I suppose is all right in its way, but it doesn't make for good public relations.

I didn't give up going to the gates trying to get on to another working party, and after three days I succeeded. This time it was to unload four barges of sugar in the local canal.

50 prisoners were chosen and we were marched to this very large warehouse at the side of the canal, in ranks of fives. Ten ranks of fives was easy to count—you'd think. But not with the Germans. You could always reckon on 30 minutes hanging about while they counted. First, they'd make it 45, and then 55 and then 49. 49!!

The four barges, the largest I'd ever seen, were moored alongside and were packed with the sacks in pyramid fashion. Twenty-four men were detailed to unload the sacks, 20 were given railway-like trolleys, and the other four were detailed to stack the sack once had it been unloaded.

And so we had this chain of worker ants, moving in perpetual motion or so the German *Unter Offizier* (Sergeant equivalent) would have us be, and he was for want of a better word, a proper bastard. He carried a riding crop, which he used unmercifully, flicking the legs or rear of some slow coach, who wasn't going as fast as he thought he should. And, if anybody showed dissent, which one or two did, he did the bawling foaming-at-the-mouth act, undoing his revolver holster, and drawing out the gun simultaneously.

He was imitated of course, by the guards he had with him who also got into the bawling and shouting act, which made life very tedious. We were, fortunately, saved by the bell or *mittag essen*, which came none too soon. And very good it was too. A sort of pork stew with potatoes and the usual sauerkraut, and we were allowed two helpings, that is, if you got in quickly before the fellow next to you had finished and he was unlucky. He had one helping, but not two!

One or two of the prisoners had dozed off after the stew and were lying on the sugar sacks when the order came to commence work again, delivered in the usual "*Los! Los! Pauser fertig*" (finished) fashion, and unwittingly they dozed on.

The *Unter Offizier* took out his revolver, took aim, and fired at just above their heads into a sugar sack. The sack, punctured, oozed sugar like a waterfall all over the recumbent figures. They leapt up with alacrity brushing themselves down and jumped off the sacks only to meet the swinging riding crop across the buttocks, shoulders and backs. It was like a scene from a slave ship and the worker ants scurried even faster than before! But, out of evil, cometh good.

It was the *Unter Offizier* who gave us the idea—I don't say we wouldn't have thought of it—he just accelerated it a bit that was all! The sugar sack that had been punctured rapidly sagged like a pricked balloon, but the problem was how to get hold of the sugar—a great bartering commodity—without Big Chief Riding Crop seeing us. I pondered during my frequent trips to the barge and then back with the sugar sack and then a sweet idea hit me!

It needed the cooperation of one of the prisoners which was readily forthcoming. When he was coming away from the barge loaded with his sack on his trolley, he was to slip (the planks leading to the barge like a gangway were a bit shaky anyway, and one or two blokes had nearly slipped, once, or twice, much to the chagrin and rage of the *Unter Offizier*) and let the sack drop into the canal. He was prepared to take the consequences, providing I gave him half of what I got. It was a bargain. He was on the same runway as me—that is, he passed me as I was on my way back into the warehouse loaded with a sack and going up the ramp to unload it. Luckily, there was no guard near me when he did it splendidly. A shout went up—a curse—and there was a commotion at the barge. There was laughter too. Everybody, including the guards and Riding Crop, converged on the gangway. In the meantime, I went to work. I got out my scout's knife and stabbed the blade into a sack of sugar at the back of the pile (where it wouldn't be seen). The sugar gushed out into my haversack which I gleefully held under it. In addition, I shovelled sugar down the front of my trousers (I wore gaiters) so that I walked with leaden legs.

Also into my pockets and finally into my dixie, which had become my nearest and dearest! Tate & Lyle would have been proud of me.

Unknown to me my conspiratorial friend had gone the whole hog. He slipped as planned, the sack went overboard, so did the trolley, and finally—himself! They got him out with a boathook, and eventually, after about a quarter of an hour, the trolley. The sack sank like a stone, and may still be there to this day—if the fish with sweet teeth haven't swallowed it!

The rest of the afternoon, as far as I was concerned, was spent concealing the fact that I was carrying a platoon's weekly ration of sugar about my person, and working hard at the same time! But the guards and *Unter Offizier,* luckily for me, concentrated on the complete emptying of the barge, which, by 6 o'clock, after much haranguing and crop swishing, was accomplished.

I was glad to sit down. I think I lost a few pounds in gaining a few pounds—if you follow me. Almost at once we lined up in ranks of five. 10 multiplied by 5 = 50. They counted laboriously like a child just learning to count. From the front and the rear—and then "Riding Crop" did it again. It was O.K. Nobody was hiding in the hold of the barge or behind the sugar sacks. Led by "R.C." himself and flanked by his minions, we returned to the barracks.

Again as luck would have it we followed in behind some newly arrived prisoners and were not searched. My new found "diversionary" friend, by now completely dry, stuck to me like a leech. It wasn't that he didn't trust me, he just wanted to make sure that he got his half of the loot! He watched as I emptied the haversack, and then my pockets, onto a newspaper, and finally took off my gaiters, and the last of the sugar cascaded down from inside my trousers. There was quite a good amount of sugar there, a profitable amount. He gleefully took his half and pushed off.

I took off my boots, turned them upside down and shook them, just to make sure I wasn't missing any, did the same with my socks, so that any pinhead crystals would join the others. I told my mates to keep guard and then went and washed my feet!

Before we had marched away from the gates, we had all been issued with ration cards or tickets, which entitled us to collect our bread ration without queueing.

This I did and immediately afterwards set about sewing some extra hessian pockets, out of an old sack, into the blouse of my battle dress.

When tomorrow came, I was going to be well prepared!

The second sugar day dawned, bright and clear as the sun shone earlier than usual. Or so it seemed. I was up before it though, doing my ablutions and eating my meagre breakfast before most of the others had stirred. Accoutred with my extra pockets, dixie and haversack, I was soon down to the barrack gates, waiting for the *Unter Offizier* "Riding Crop" and his circus of attendant guards to come and pick us up.

Sharp at 7.30 a.m. they arrived and calls for the *Zucker Party* rang out loud and clear. Most of the originals from the previous day were there, but when they came to count us—which they did—twice, we were only 42 in number. Eight slaves had defected or slept in or didn't want any part of the sweet life as demonstrated by the Jerries. In the event, as they say, six French (of which four were Algerians) and two unsuspecting British were press-ganged into the party, and we moved off.

"Riding Crop" swaggered about as before, bawling at the top of his voice as usual, but because of the heat, he had turned the cuffs of his tunic back and undone his collar. He really did fancy himself, and when we passed a German officer in Cambrai High Street (well, it looked like Cambrai High Street, although I didn't see a Woolworths!) he flung his arm up in the Nazi salute, shouted "*Achtung*" and then "*Augen Links*" (eyes left). One or two of the prisoners looked curiously left, the others looked right, wondering what was happening, and the remainder just said "Bollocks, and shambled on.

The Algerians were going to be a bother, for already they were apt to lag behind, and were constantly being harassed and bawled at, and "flicked at" with the riding crop, and we hadn't even got there yet.

When we did, we started immediately to unload barge number two and were given to understand that two barges were to be emptied before the day was out!

We started off at a good speed, but as the morning wore on and the sun got hotter and the warehouse got stickier, the pace definitely began to flag, and "Riding Crop" got more and more worked up. He would not leave the Algerians alone, he seemed to have some personal vendetta against them, he lashed them with his tongue and his riding crop.

Most of our fellows felt sorry for them, shouting out things like "Why don't you leave them alone, you loud-mouthed bastard!" and more succinctly "Piss off, you big cunt!" But of course, it was all wasted on him. He got the drift perhaps, but he ignored it. At least he did until I said "Bloody sadistic bastard"—he was upbraiding the Algerian right in front of me at the time, and he immediately turned on me—"*Was? Was? Was? Was haben Sie gesagt?*" (What did you say?) —he didn't understand what I said, but he guessed it was derogatory.

He lunged towards me, grabbed me by the collar, and wiggled the crop in front of my face, and said something sarcastic ending up with… "*Mein Lieber Freund!*" The other guards found it very funny, whatever it was, and laughed immediately. I saw the warning signals and said nothing. It was probably something to the effect that I would get the same treatment. If I didn't watch my P's and Q's—the *lieber freund* phrase was always used in a sinister and sneering manner.

He had enormous energy, I'll say that for him, but it was wasted on the Algerians. They were all on the sugar sack trolley run, and he pursued and hit them mercilessly, laying about them with his crop, as if he was beating an Arab carpet, all to no avail. They didn't go any faster and they seemed indifferent to the whackings and carried on in their own slow Arabic tempo.

Inevitably, as they say, something had to give. And it did.

One of the Algerians was having trouble in manoeuvring his trolley loaded with sugar off the gangplank—the right-hand wheel had run off and it wasn't easy to readjust it, especially as at the same time he was being belaboured by "Riding Crop". Trying to lift it up and half turning to the *Unter Offizier* at the same time, the Algerian missed his footing and toppled over. On the way down, he made a despairing grab at his mentor to save himself, and "Riding Crop" came a cropper with him.

There was a loud splash as they both hit the water together preceded by the trolley and sack, and a guffawing derisive cheer from the prisoners.

The guards rushed to rescue "Riding Crop", the Algerian was thrashing about as if he was learning to swim, and was trying to hold onto the *Unter Offizier* who was trying to shake him off.

I didn't wait to see anymore. I shot up to the back of the pile of sacks and did my well-known act of "Stabbing the sugar sack" followed by "Holding the haversack" and for an encore "Filled the extra pockets" in my battle blouse, and for my finale "Corner the crystals into the pantaloons". The dixie, unfortunately, I couldn't use because I needed it for the *mittag essen*—pork, soup and potatoes.

I dumped the blouse and the haversack behind some sacks near to where my sugar was being stacked, and then blouseless, joined the others at the scene of the accident.

Enthusiastic mickey-taking helpers were proffering useless advice on how to rescue the *Unter Offizier*—somebody was dangling a rope for the Algerian—and the boat hook was being used to extricate the German.

He, apparently, had gashed his hand on the hook, but was holding bravely on and trying to tow the trolley at the same time. Two German guards were heaving and puffing, and pulling him downstream towards some steps. He finally made it and clambered out shaking himself like a dachshund! At the same time, taking off his jackboots, and emptying out the water.

He abused the Algerian in typical bad-tempered fashion, made no attempt to help him and squelched back to the barge to take over the operations. The trolley and his precious riding crop were pulled out of the water, but the Algerian still dangled at the end of the rope too scared to let go. Eventually he was pulled along to the same steps and meandered back to the gangway. Within minutes, the soup, in the shape of a mobile cookhouse, appeared on the scene and the prisoners, more food-conscious than work-conscious, understandably crowded round it.

It consisted of a sort of pork and potato stew and sauerkraut and soon became a memory. The *Unter Offizier* had retired somewhere to dry himself, and the other guards were sitting around near the gangplanks so I decided to take myself off to the back of the sugar sacks for a quiet siesta for twenty minutes. I clambered up the sacks, found myself a spot that was out of sight of the others, laid down, and before you could say "Demerara" I was away in the land of sweet dreams!

I was rudely awakened by somebody kicking me in the side of the ribs. It was the *Unter Offizier*, standing over me in shirt, trousers, and as I can testify—his jackboots! He kicked again, and I got up shakily. His face was contorted with rage and a stream of abuse was flung at me (I had been missing for 20 minutes apparently—twenty minutes past the normal break time), and as I went to go past him he swung at me with a left hook, but I saw it coming and ducked. I wasn't quick enough to avoid the fast right though that followed. He caught me flush on the side of the jaw and that was all I remembered.

I was out for quite a long time or so it seemed, and surfaced only when a bucket of water was thrown over me. I felt very groggy, but was not allowed to recover or convalesce. I was hounded relentlessly with the riding crop, and had in fact superseded the Algerians and become target for the day. Suffering, but surviving, we gradually moved to knocking off time with no chance of emptying the two barges completely.

One was completely cleared but the other was barely started when it came time to finish. Earlier on I had become apprehensive about the sugar I had looted, and hit on the idea of switching my battle dress blouse with a bloke from the Durham Light Infantry (he was the same size as me). He had been unloading the sacks from the barge onto the trolleys, and therefore had little chance or opportunity to steal any. I approached him and offered him half the sugar if he would switch jackets and take my haversack at the same time. He agreed readily—"Why Aye Man!"—and gave me his jacket, and I made the switch with mine.

It was just a precaution but when we came to line up to be counted, my assailant came and found me to deliver a personal *"Mein Lieber Freund"* speech. He ended up by searching me—and the four Algerians. But he found nothing illegal on any of us—to his chagrin, no doubt.

My Durham Light Infantry confederate gave me back my jacket and haversack once we were inside Cambrai barracks, and then followed me to collect his rightful dues.

The usual routine followed with the bread ration and I related the incident to my three muckers. They had swopped some of the sugar from yesterday for two pork chops, and three eggs from some French racketeer so we had quite a useful supper before we closed down for the night. My jaw and my ribs ached but the thought of the loot made up for it and it wasn't long before I was asleep. There was a strong rumour going round the barracks that Churchill was negotiating for peace, but it sounded like wishful thinking on the part of the French. At the same time, I half wanted to believe it. We all did.

The next morning I lined up at the barrack gates for the final day of unloading the barges along with the rest of the party, and when the *Unter Offizier* and his guards arrived at 7.25 a.m. we were paraded in ranks of fives and counted. The Algerians were missing and who could blame them. I was in the last rank to be counted, and when "Riding Crop" came to me he gave me a long hard look possibly examining his handiwork to my face. I thought for a moment he was going to hit me again, but he didn't. Instead he beckoned the *Unter Offizier* in charge of the gates, pointed at me and held a short conversation with him. I was withdrawn and told that I was not wanted on the sugar party. Obviously, he'd labelled me as a troublemaker.

I watched my replacement and the rest of them march out of the gates. Bye-Bye Sugar Bunch! Hail and farewell "Riding Crop"!

I returned to the boys and told them I'd got the sack—but not the one they thought! And then faced reality by queueing up for soup and later for my bread ration. During the morning about four or five hundred Frenchmen were lined up just inside the gates and checked, and checked, and checked…. It took about three hours before they eventually moved off to the station supposedly to Germany. Before they went, I moved in among them like a ticket tout asking if anybody needed sugar—"*Sucre a Vendre*"—and sure enough there were two takers. For about a quarter of a pound of sugar I exchanged or got a tin of English meatloaf and a packet of Gauloise cigarettes and for the same quantity, maybe a little over, a packet of rice and a small container of salt and pepper. Supper and smokes assured.

At supper—chopped meatloaf with rice (boiled) heavily salted and peppered—we discussed and agreed upon a new plan for two of us to go out on the working party, leaving the remaining 2 to be cook bottlewashers and scroungers-in-chief in the camp. Up to now two of them hadn't been very fit, which in this disease ridden dump was understandable.

Thus it was the following morning that Bob Wilson (an old mate of mine from way back) and I paraded at the gates ready to sell ourselves to the highest bidder—well, any bidder—and there were none! Even the sugar party had finished, they had cleared the barges the day before, working very late in order to do so.

For four or five days, we presented ourselves full of hope and anticipation, and on the sixth day, it happened! Which is just as well because our bartering commodities were down to rock bottom.

A party of 36 men were needed to assist (so we were told) a German signals unit—the *Unter Offizier* who came to collect the prisoners had electricity flashes on his arm—but we didn't hang about to weigh up the pros and cons, we were there lining up directly the call came for "*Arbeits Kommando*" (working party). We were duly counted—5–10–15–20–25–30–35—the first guard made it 34; the second 36, and finally 35—they dispensed with the 36th man, it was easier.

We were taken, by which I mean we marched, to a suburb of Cambrai, where we were introduced to our working place—a chicory factory—where their lorries—stacked with signalling equipment— were to be unloaded. Coils of field telephone cable, equipment and phone exchanges, porcelain knobs for Telegraph poles, and boxes of screws, nuts and bolts. There was a vast amount of gear that looked as if it would take a week to clear—which, in fact it did. It was like working for the Post Office and travelling Electricity Board Authority at the same time. The only thing missing were those little conical canvas huts, where they hold the tea parties! Actually, it was a section of the German Ordnance Corps, and the guards, as we got to know them, were very civil.

They were mostly older men—well, thirty-ish, and over—experts at their jobs, although, of course, there were younger fellows sprinkled amongst them.

Most of the working party was split up into gangs or sections of four or fives, and two Jerries were assigned to each group and were responsible for them. It was almost as if we'd been conscripted as part of the set up.

The Germans advised about the gear—where to put it—how it worked etc., but the thing that struck me was they also took a hand physically, helping to unload, and you would find yourself working alongside a Jerry, who was heaving and puffing, and swearing and grinning at you, as if you've known him all your life! Only when the Kapitan in charge came round to inspect did they put on a show and even then they didn't go mad like old "Riding Crop".

Our particular two Jerries came from Austria, and we are both oldish men. At lunchtime (*mittag essen*), we all had the same meal as them and when one of the prisoners didn't have a dixie, they organised one for him. After the soup was finished—thick pork and pea soup followed by an apple and coffee—French cigarettes were handed out all round and they showed us photographs of their wives and children. The British made the right noises and showed theirs. "*Schoen*—"*Gut*" — "*Sehr gut*" —"The wife" —"Vife" —*jah schoen*" "Kids" — "*Kinder*"—"Prima!"

They didn't speak English, but it wasn't long before they latched onto one word in particular.... "*Was ist* "fuckin'?" They would say— "*Immer* fucking"—and when it was explained, they would nod and laugh and say "*Oh jah—nicht gut*" but they still seemed a little bewildered, and if you think about it, why is it used so often? (I've often wondered too!) Fucked if I know!

Towards the evening, we were told that we would not be going back to the barracks, and that a bread ration would be issued, which, indeed it was—half a loaf per man, some margarine (ersatz), and a generous slice of German cheese (ersatz? Went down well nevertheless!) Rounded off with coffee (French), with chicory—naturally!

We were told that we would be sleeping in the factory in order to start work early in the morning, and late that evening, we bedded down in a corner of the chicory factory. The smell was a bit off putting at first, but after a while you got used to it. I browsed around to see if there was anything we could purloin, but there was nothing, except of course, ground chicory, which on its own taste to me like senna pods and you know what that does to you!

The Germans had put some straw down to serve as bedding, and after some desultory chat about our captors, their habits, customs and the food situation, we finally "hit the hay" but not to sleep. Just as we were about to doze off the guards who were supposed to be guarding us came in for a chat—they talked about everything except the war, although they did mention the Polish campaign. They hated the Poles. Later, we were to find that the feeling was mutual as far as the Poles were concerned, and after the way the Poles were treated I don't blame them. Finally we yawned our good nights and were soon in the arms of that Greek Irishman "Morpheus".

I started to make odd diary notes in a small pocket book that I had for the week that followed, and I quote from it: –

6th June. Fatigue party. Ordnance. Chicory factory. Grub good. Jerries not bad. Compared to usual run. Nosed around. No buckshees. Slept on straw provided. Jerries said they were 10 miles from Paris—Propaganda! War over soon—Propaganda?

7th June. Up 5.30. Worked 6.30. onwards. Jerries working harder than us. Soup middle day. Half loaf per man. Cigarettes running out. Me running too. Very loose. Blood with motion. All that soup?

8th June. As before. Jerries say closing in on Paris. True or false?

9th June. Still hard at it. Job for life. During day nipped off several times to bog. Severe diarrhoea. Blood. Did not eat soup. Saved it. In afternoon ventured round behind factory. Not seen. Went into French house. Given three eggs and white loaf by old lady. Took two eggs raw which is how I'm feeling at "that" end.

10th June. Not well. Guts ache. Can't stop running. Lots of blood about. Very sore. Jerry sanitator (First Aid) gave me pills. Did not work. Did no work .

11th June . Felt better. Worked. Nipped out back after midday. Bought milk (1 franc) from estaminet. Bread (3 francs) and Tobacco for rolling fags. French money almost finished .

12th June. Still Chicory factory. Queasy but better. Wakened 4.30. Work 5.30. Change of plan. Now loading instead of un. Unit moving Thurs. or Friday to Paris. (Say they are only 2 miles away). Our oldish guard offered to take me with them? Spoke to Bob. He advised against. Get registered first, he said, anything can happen. Worked till 10.30. Given extra grub, and bread.

13th June. Same as yesterday. Nipped out back of factory. Called French house. Saw old lady. She confirmed imminent fall of Paris. She wept *"Pauvre Garcon"* she said. Gave me bread and packet of "Mazawattee" tea. Gave her a ring as souvenir. Thick pea soup and pork midday. Apple. Worked late to finish loading. Said goodbye to Jerries. Back to barracks 10.30 p.m. Big sweep-out of British p.o.w.'s in our absence. All Q.V.R's & our sugar gone to Germany. Bob and I only ones left. Place looks deserted. Like end shot in film.

14th June. Barracks. Slept in open last night. Rained all night. Up at 4.30. Fried two slices of bread in someone else's pan on someone else's fire. Lined up gates for fatigue. Waited three hours. Nothing doing. Slept all afternoon. Missed soup. Swapped small jar fish paste for rice. Bread ration. Did not sleep night. Counted stars. Thought about home. Heavy rain at 3.30.

15th June. Up 4.30. Breakfast one slice Toast. Midday—ladle full of lentil soup. Rumoured we are to stay here for the duration. Christ! Send you mad. Churchill and Chamberlain flying to Berlin? They should drop a few food parcels here on way over. Paris—surrendered. Official—Jerries. Prayed. Hope Mother and Family all safe.

16th June. Slept intermittently thru' night. Up 5 a.m. Lined up at gates. Call for 15 men. Fatigue for German air force depot. Great! Bob and I are on it. Had to clean out three houses. Food in plenty. Four eggs—three loaves of bread. Wine. Sackfull. Strawberries —gooseberries & red currants. Found pullover—Nazi vest in one house. Wore both pullover & Vest. Bloody great Swastika and Eagle printed across vest. Cigs. in abundance. Arrived back in triumph. There is some justice after all!

The following day, Monday 17th June we got up late—late? It was 6 o'clock and we made no attempt to line up for a job. We had had enough Sunday offerings to last us for a couple of days, although somebody whipped a loaf of ours when we weren't watching; you needed eyes in your backside. I needed something. I couldn't stop going to the lavatory—I ran—continually. Which makes it difficult to conduct a sensible conversation, at any length. I suppose it was not to be wondered at with the goosegogs—and other fruit, and unclean rice et al!—Apart from that, I think I had caught some germ that was to trouble me for sometime to come. Peace rumours were rampant, but the only rumours we were really interested in were.... What time was the soup and bread being issued and when will there be a good working party?

My spasmodic diary listed Tuesday as an uneventful day, except for a kind gesture shown to me by German guard! Yes—a German guard! I couldn't believe it either, at first. Seeing me, crouching over our remaining pieces of kit, like a brooding hen, and looking a bit pale and wan after a recent dash to the bog, and giving him my pleading Oliver Twist expression, I nodded to him as he stopped and looked in my direction. Was he looking for someone to help wash up at a banquet? To help in the cookhouse? Fancied me and wanted me for his own?—No, none of these things—he wanted to *give me* something!

He came over to me, unhooked his dixie which was attached to his belt, and turning it upside down dropped the contents onto a piece of paper at my feet. It was a largish portion of cooked rice mixed with meat. I looked up at him and said "*Danke*" (I couldn't get up because of my bowels, I was afraid to). I told him I was *krank* and returned the compliment by giving him a shilling as a souvenir. In return, he gave me a franc (It must have been "Be Kind To The Prisoners Day") and he wandered off, tossing the shilling in the air like George Raft and looking sideways at the same time!

I bought two cigarettes with the franc and made a note to use the self pity and the *Ich bin krank* ploy again. I was rapidly becoming an "Artful Dodger!" The diarrhoea part was genuine though—I really did suffer with that. Perhaps it was dysentery—there was no one to appeal to, to check. You just had to soldier on..

On the Thursday we were all paraded and marched out of Cambrai barracks, leaving it deserted and devoid of prisoners. Presumably to Germany. We were told we were going to the station, but they didn't say which one. 30 Kilometres later we were still looking for it expectantly, but it never came. Not that day anyway. We ended up in a field by a canal and a place called "Le Cotillon"—I was practically flaked out, I had had to leave the column several times to relieve myself, and the Jerries took a dim view after about the sixth effort.

At first I modestly went into a field to perform, but at the end, I couldn't wait that long, and embarrassing and humiliating though it was, I just dashed to the side of the road stripping for action as I went and behaved like an Algerian in full view of everyone. During one of these forays I lost my pal, Bob, and didn't see him again till the next day. Consequently, I was very low and dispirited on arrival at the field and just lay down for some considerable time, to recover from the fertilising deposits I had parted with along the roads of France.

Lots of the prisoners were bathing in the canal, and I thought perhaps some of the same treatment might do me good. I bathed in the nude and certainly revived myself.

My Nazi vest caused quite a few stares and comments, but I ignored them.

If you can squat down on your haunches at the side of the road in full view with everyone and crap, you can do anything!

I felt slightly better after the swim, till I had to go to the bog again! By the way this time I just had excruciating pains and nothing else happened. I must've been empty by now after all those sessions. I found rocking myself on my haunches like a baby eased the pain a little, and after a while I was back to normal, looking for something to eat.

I came upon three Frenchmen who were cooking what looked like a three course meal on their primus stove, I sat down about 5 yards away and just looked at them and at the grub fixedly. I didn't say anything, I just looked. With a hangdog expression on my face.

They were conscious of me, and looked in my direction several times, and whispered among themselves. In French, naturally. Finally, embarrassed, they gave in. Perhaps I reminded them of their young brother or sister, (or maybe their mother) but whatever it was, they beckoned me over and gave me some of the rice covered with a delicious sauce, and three prunes for afters. They had obviously been one of the first to arrive in the field because they had established their right to a corrugated iron lean-to shed, which was er…leaning there.

They were French Chasseurs and like French picnickers, they had everything—blankets, and a mountain of equipment —and I gathered that they were *not* going to be taken to Germany—I mean, they didn't intend to let the Jerries take them that far. So I presumed they were going to escape. They looked very fit, strapping, great chaps with tanned faces and frowning eyes, caused no doubt my constantly coping with the glare of sun, snow, and ice. I edged in with them when it came time to bed down out of the rain and they edged over. I don't know why they took to me, but they were certainly very kind. Perhaps I reminded them of a saint? A Saint Bernard! I could certainly have done with the brandy! The next day, Friday, I woke early and bathed in the canal for a morning dip. Returning to the shed, the Chasseurs were just "coming to". I offered to get some coffee which the Germans were serving from some mobile kitchens placed at the entrance to the field. I took three dixies and queued up for the ersatz beverage—there was no rush for it, and it was easy to get—but there was no bread issue, only the coffee, and I returned with the dixies full, passed them over and sat down to gulp the liquid down. Immediately I swallowed the hot fluid, I had to rush to the bog to do my well-known monotonous act. Eventually, I came back, and they very kindly looked after my haversack, containing my bits and pieces, and my dixie, but I didn't dare drink any more of the coffee! After a while, I noticed a hubbub going on round the mobile kitchens, and it turned out that they were issuing biscuits in lieu of any midday meal. I nipped over smartly and found that they were ladling out one ladleful per man of very small biscuits—rather like Spratts dog biscuits. I joined the melee, and when it came my turn to be served, I told the Jerry—an oldish man—that my comrade was sick, and could I collect his ration? Naïvely, or maybe he didn't believe me anyway, he still doled out two helpings from the large sack. I sold the buckshee (or extra portion) to a prisoner for five francs, and then bought half a pound of French butter for three francs. On my way back to my Chasseurs acquaintances, I ran into my old Q.V.R, mate Bob Wilson. He had been looking for me since yesterday, and after I told him what had happened, he said he didn't expect to find me "mucking in" with the French! I took him and introduced him to the mountaineer soldiers as "*Mon ami*"—and they gave us a small tin of paste to celebrate the reunion, which we opened and had with the butter and biscuits. They refused anything in return—not that we had much.

But they didn't go short. They had everything. They set up their primus, and before our wondering eyes, they whipped up three portions of macaroni, sprinkled deliberately with parmesan cheese! They certainly "took the biscuit" for the quick-fire snacks—not that they had any (the dog biscuits)! Well, you know what I mean!

It got hotter as the afternoon wore on, and after a quiet sleep in the sun, we decided to have a bathe in the canal. Unfortunately, quite a few others had decided the same thing and the canal began to look like an "Immersion day" on the banks of the Nile. As usual, I had to clamber out rather quickly as I felt the first rumbles and dashed to the makeshift bog for my inevitable "visit"! I laid down and slept for the rest of the afternoon to try to stop the running. Lentil soup was issued in the evening and after a 2 hour queue, we turned in early.

On the morning of the 22nd June, we woke at 9.30 a.m. and breakfasted on the rest of the dog biscuits and butter, and some stale bread that Bob have been saving for a rainy day! No more grub was issued till late evening when some watery rice was doled out— half a litre each. I was still troubled with my "complaint" but slept most of the day to try to counteract it.

During the night, the heavens opened, and it rained incessantly like a tropical monsoon, and we suddenly found our corrugated iron roof being torn down around about our ears by an unruly bunch of British prisoners, leaving us exposed to the elements. Mind you, it was their shed as much as ours, and they wanted to shelter too, and who could blame them (the French did!) but I was too weak to protest. In the morning, following the wet and sleepless night, we were finally lined up and told that we were going to the "*bahnhof*" (station). I'd believe that when I saw it! But we lined up nevertheless. Before we moved, the French, who had paraded with us, were told to fall out, to be segregated from the British. I said goodbye to our Chasseur friends and wished them "bon voyage". We were dished out half a litre of soup (no bread), but I didn't attempt to drink it until it had gone cold —just in case. Four hours later, we started off—shambling through the gate and on the road till we surprisingly came to "Orrs" station, where we were to "en-train"!

We were marshalled into a railway goods train and counted off in batches of 75. Written on the outside of the wagon was S.N.C.F. *40 Hommes ou 8 Chevaux.* (40 men or 8 Horses.)

Whatever the official French ruling for the amount of "*Hommes*" to be allowed to a truck, the Germans were out to break the record. 75 prisoners were squeezed and squashed into that confined space—the sliding doors were snapped shut and padlocked —and at 6.45. p.m. precisely, we shunted off on our way to Germany.

Before long—before we passed through Valenciennes, in a stop and go fashion, as if the driver was a learner—we were exhausted from the intense heat and the rapidly deteriorating airless atmosphere. The Black Hole of Calcutta had nothing on this. There were no windows in the wagons, only slits, about 4 inches wide and 2 feet in length. Even eight horses would've found it uncomfortable—not that the French care much for them, after all, they do eat them! But they surely would have provided hay and water. The prisoners were given nothing. We were parched, cramped, and fed up lying across each other, as if in some nightmare orgy!

To make matters worse—you've guessed it—my stomach began to herald another attack. I gritted my teeth and tried to restrain myself by squeezing my buttocks together; but alas to no avail.

What could I do? Somebody, thank God had used his steel helmet to urinate in and then dribbled the contents out of the slit. I asked him if I could use it, but he was reluctant. On payment of a cigarette he allowed me. I emptied the contents out of one of the slits hoping it would hit a German soldier on the way.

After what seemed an age we arrived at Dinant in Belgium. We came to a juddering stop followed by a long silence and after the prisoners began banging on the doors and shouting insults at the Jerries, they were eventually opened very slowly. *"Alles raus "* said the guard, and everybody got out and took great gasps of air and relieved themselves against the wheels of the train.

We were in a siding or side line which bordered a busy street, and were being curiously and sympathetically watched by a crowd of Belgian men and women. All the men, mostly of middle-age, seemed to be carrying briefcases, which must have contained uneaten sandwiches, because a veritable shower of sandwiches, cigarettes, magazines, newspapers and Belgian money, was flung over the railway fence between us, and the usual mad scramble ensued to grab them. I got three cigarettes and a Belgian newspaper, and Bob got a meat paste sandwich. We could see from the headlines all about the "Fall of Paris" and the invincible success of the German army, led by the victorious German high command. The "Fuehrer" was thanking them, and they were thanking him! Propaganda, but sadly, and unfortunately, true.

By now, the 75 *hommes* from the next truck, were trying to edge up to ours to get in the act—to enjoy the privileges (?) that we were enjoying—but the Jerry guard detailed to our truck, would have none of it, he *"Los—Losed"* them back, even going through the motions of unslinging his bond hook (rifle, madam) and pretending to fire. They fell back like thwarted revolutionaries, yelling obscenities and cursing.

We stayed there for about an hour, by which time the crowd of spectators had doubled, and, in fact, it seemed to me that some went away and came back with white loaves and pieces of cheese, which they hurled over the fence. They shouted to us "*A bas les Allemands*!" And we in chorus answered back.

Us – "*Oui!*"

"*Vive L'Angleterre!*"

Us – "*Oui!*"

Somewhere a whistle was blown, twice, and we were all back into the truck or wagon-lit and the doors were slid home. We continued to look through the slits defiantly answering the Belgian lament until we jerked and shunted fretfully on our way to the "Fatherland."

From then the "stop—"go"—and "just a minute, are we on the right line?" journey stuttered and shunted us till we arrived at Bertrix —still in Belgium. There "we heaved to" in a siding after several spasmodic going forwards and backwards.

We remained in the siding for the whole of the night with the doors locked and bolted, and the conditions became, if possible, more cramped and more inhuman. Like being incarcerated in a confined evil smelling subterranean tomb!

It was Sunday. A day for rest—a day for Christian unity—a day for prayer. I prayed—to no avail.

In the morning, despite our shouts and curses for the doors to be opened, they remained shut, and we moved off in the usual fashion to our next destination—the "Duchy of Luxembourg." By now most of the 75 occupants in our wagon (and no doubt the others in theirs) were past caring where we were going, what happened to the train, the Germans or themselves. Especially themselves.

To lie in the same cramped bodies-overlapping position for over 12 or 13 hours may be O.K. for sardines, but when to add to your misery, there's no grub, no water, and no way of appealing to anyone for help, *If you can keep your head when all around are losing theirs, you'll be a man, my son*. Blimey! "Comradeship" took some hard, straining knocks!

Finally, when we got to Luxembourg, the doors were reluctantly slid open. We stumbled and tumbled out and drank the water which was permanently cascading out of a hosepipe used to wash down the carriages.

Because there was still no issue of food from the Germans, that was all we were going to get— officially—but after a conversation about the bread situation, which I had with a young soldier guard, I swapped my precious 21st. birthday gift, a "Swan" Fountain pen, for a portion of black bread. I had no plans to write to anybody for a long time, and as it turned out—writing home in ink was *verboten*.

Entraining (joke over) took place after a couple of hours break. This time, whether by accident or design, the doors were left unlocked.

Immediately, *en route*, they were quickly and gratefully pulled open and the fresh and beautiful air rushed through.

It was a pleasant countryside if one was in that sort of mood—full of tall, majestic trees—well-cultivated fields, and later, when we shunted into a side line to allow a fast train to go through, we jumped down onto the track to forage around in the vain hope of finding something.

One of the p.o.w.'s found a couple of snails, which he instantly polished off, but our foraging was cut short by the arrival of the guard who rousted us back into the wagon and just as he was about to close the doors, the train started to move off. We cheered derisively as the scuttled back to the guards van, leaving the doors open and we continued on our way.

For your information, Luxembourg, by railway wagon with 75 *hommes* lying on their backs all the way, is 37 kilometres from the German town of Trier and this was our next port of call. It seemed outwardly to be a pretty town.

We were finally over the border, and in Deutschland, and although one would have liked it otherwise, it was my first visit—travelling as a captive tourist!

We were ordered to "detrain" (*Alles Raus*!) outside the station in a siding and paraded and assembled into some sort of column in ranks of five.

We were then addressed by a fat pompous *Sonderfuhrer* (Political or Propaganda Leader). He wore a normal officer's uniform with special insignia to denote his rank or department, and was inevitably a dedicated Nazi Party man. He seemed to have great power and importance and was treated with much respect by the German officers and soldiers. In other words, they were afraid of him.

He climbed up into an open coal wagon and addressed us, like a mini-fat-Füehrer, in English.

"For you, the war is over"—(Yes yes. We've got that).

"You are now all prisoners of the victorious German Reich (trite but true). You will be sent to a prisoner of war camp where you will be well treated (?) according to the rules of the Geneva Convention for prisoners of war." (If the train journey was anything to go by it wasn't worth the paper it was written on!) "If you try to escape you will be shot. Heil Hitler!" (No comment.) He gave the Nazi salute, arm raised and outstretched (like asking to be excused)—and so did the entourage around him, like a Greek chorus, echoing his words "Heil Hitler!" Somebody in the crowd blew a raspberry, and a ripple of laughter swept amongst the ragged ranks, but either he didn't hear, or he chose to ignore it.

We were marshalled out of the station and marched up a very long hill to a huge barbed wire encampment at the top.

As we straggled through the flag-flying town—a red and black swastika flag fluttered at every window—we were watched by a curious and silent crowd, as if we were Martians.

Round a short bend in the road, a man with the inevitable briefcase under his arm, detached himself from the crowd, and took a step towards us as we marched—"English pigs" he shouted, *"Schweinhund*!" He spat at the nearest p.o.w., and a growl of resentment went up from the victim, who was just about to attack the spitter, when he was restrained from behind by two other p.o.w.'s. A German guard strode briskly forward and pushed the man back into the crowd saying *"Nein—Nein. Verboten! Verboten*!" .We never found out what was forbidden—the spit, the shout, or the social intercourse!

The rest of the p.o.w.'s ignored the incident, but it marked the attitude of certain sections of the German public, although up to now, as far as we were aware, they hadn't been bombed, well, only with pamphlets.

The camp at the top of the hill was vast, triple-barbed-wired, well guarded with look-out posts and dog patrols, but at least it was well organised. It had large nissen-like huts with three tiered beds or shelves inside and supper tickets were distributed as we filed into the hut, which everyone immediately lined up for and got, and although it was pretty watery stuff it was very acceptable.

Soon it started to rain—German rain—heavier and more hurtful than a soft and gentle drizzle. As it teemed down it drummed out on the nissen hut roof "For you the war is over, For you, the war is over" —and just before I dropped off, I thought about home, my mother and family and hoped they were all safe and O.K. I felt pretty low, but I was rudely awakened about three hours later by a voice bellowing in my ear that there was an issue of bread and cheese.

I was galvanised into action as if on fire and joined the queue for the rubbery cheese and black bread and coffee.

I slept well through the night without waking and woke at six, only to make my usual dash for the primitive latrines that had obviously been hastily erected. The smell from this long pole over a pit was indescribable, but I was rapidly becoming immune to anything like that. And I was once such a sensitive and delicate flower where things like that were concerned. So—you can change, can't you?!

I queued up again for bread, ersatz honey and margarine, and half a litre of barley and bean soup at one p.m. A German interpreter speaking English came into the hut and announced that we were all to prepare to move at 4 o'clock, but later the order was postponed until the morrow.

Bob Wilson and I went in search of the canteen (*kantine* in German)—I had found a pound note wedged at the bottom of the inside pocket of my battledress blouse and we bought 2 cigars, a box of matches and four lagers. Change from a pound was 5 marks and 50 pfennigs. No food was sold in the canteen—not even cakes or biscuits.

In the evening bread and margarine—four men to a loaf—and coffee were issued and the next day, Thursday, I believe, after being issued with half a loaf, we moved off down the hill through the town back to the station, and once again underwent the same "treatment", but not quite so severe. 60 *hommes* in the wagon this time.They had deducted 15 from the original arrival record of 75!

Again, the doors were kept closed and again it was stifling hot, but the train this time was driven by an expert and in two or three days we arrived at our final destination—Thorn (in Polish Toruna). We were in Poland.

I was very weak at this point having had dysentery or the bug all the way and had reached my lowest ebb. I practically had to be carried from the track, being helped along by Bob Wilson, and another Queen Vic with my arms around their shoulders.

Luckily for me, we didn't have far to go. We marched to an old disused balloon hanger, surrounded by barbed wire and electrified fences, where large tents had been erected in the grounds to accommodate the extra influx of prisoners. I flopped out on the straw, and Bob Wilson went to the German M.O. and got some powdered charcoal and sulphur tablets to alleviate my "condition". They certainly eased the griping stomach pains, and although it worked slowly at the other end, I finally seized up! Thank God. I never want to go through all that again—it was like having perpetual "motion" for three or four weeks. I think the lining of my stomach and several interior parts were swept away too!

CHAPTER 4
"Streng Verboten"

This balloon hangar, we later learnt, was only a holding or transit camp. We were there to be registered and sorted out for work—each man to be set to work at his own particular trade. You had to say whether you were an electrician—a plumber—a bookie's runner—a deep sea diver—I said I was a model for "Don't let this happen to you" photographs! And when they saw my emaciated body, they agreed it could've been true!

It didn't matter what anybody said, it was all a big take-on. In the end, everybody did labouring, regardless of what he'd registered! It was reminiscent of that hoary old army joke

Sergeant: "Anybody 'ere know anythin' about music?"

Unsuspecting recruit: "I do, Sergeant."

Sergeant: "Right. Come and help me move this flippin' piano."

In theory, after registering, you sat around and waited until a call came for 50 or 250 men to be needed in some distant area of Poland, like Warsaw, for instance. There were coal mines there, and as far as I was concerned, they could stay there. Warsaw was approximately 200 kilometres from Thorn as the crow flies. Polish crows, of course. And this was about the limit to the east of our particular Stalag area. (We were known as Stalag 20A—there was Stalag 20 B (Marienburg) in East Prussia). Stalag was an abbreviation of *Stammlager*—Head Camp or Headquarters. They had *Oflags* for officers, but there were very few, if any, in our part of Poland.

When a large working party was needed it usually ended up as doing permanent labouring jobs on building sites or roads or the mines, and small parties of, say, 24, or 50 men could turn out to be a farming party, in which, in a sort of "collective commune" fashion, the prisoners supplied the labour. Some of the prisoners liked their jobs so much and got on so well that they stayed with their farm for the duration of the war and became part of the family. Some had "affairs" with the farmer's daughter or the farmer himself if they were that way inclined.

So, after registering, there would be a more or less constant movement of prisoners (unless of course you were sick or maimed) to these '*Arbeits Kommandos*,' as the Germans called them. They were very fond of the word '*Arbeit*'—it means work. There were three big posters in the Jerry Guard room saying:

"*Arbeit fur Deutschland*"—"*Work* for Germany."

"*Wir mussen arbeiten fur den Sieg*"—"We must *work* for victory." and

"*Kraft durch Freude*"—"Strength through Joy."

We never found out who Joy was, probably some busty Prussian blonde!

And then, of course there were lately captured and newly arrived prisoners arriving about every other day, mostly Scottish units taken at St. Valery and in and around that vicinity. We were told about one company of "Gordon Highlanders" who marched off the boat straight into the waiting arms of the Germans. It may have been true. Everything and anything is true in wartime, and on the other hand, it could've been what was known as a "shit house" rumour (gleaned from the lavatories) and was completely untrue! I didn't know what to believe. Rather, like my daily horoscope—sometimes you believe, and sometimes you don't!

Rumours were to lift our hearts—and to dash our hopes and tended to make one sceptical, like the message that was transmitted to the front—"Enemy, advancing on left flank, send reinforcements" which became "Enemy, dancing on wet plank, send three and four pence!"

On Sunday, we held a church service conducted by a corporal from the Welsh Guards, a lay preacher. We prayed for the safety of our loved ones, and sang "Oh God, our help in ages past" and I was just singing "Our hope for years to come…" when I was ordered to go and register—at once.

This consisted of filling in the usual form—Name—Rank—and Army number. Profession prior to call-up. And date of birth.

What, no Date of Death?

My number was 13745 duly stamped on a square serrated disc thus:

K.R. GFF LAGER
THORN
13745

KR. GFF LAGER
THORN
13745

If you died, the disc was broken in half and one half was buried with you, and the other half was sent to the Swiss Protecting Power to confirm your demise. The disc had to be kept highly polished and was inspected regularly just in case your number came up!

Next came the photograph—you were handed a small black board with your p.o.w. number and name chalked on it which you held across your chest and glowered into a camera while the fussy photographer took the picture of a lifetime for the German *Wehrmacht* records. I had had all my hair removed by a volunteer British barber who could've taught a sheep shearer a thing or two. I had been shaved, minutely, all over. My head, chest, armpits, and pubics. The only hairs I had left were two dark satanic eyebrows, one pointing east, and the other west, and a week's growth of beard. With my thin mahogany face, and no hair on my bonce, I looked akin to a Caucasian shepherd's piebald pony—and there weren't many of them about!

The reason for the dearth of hair was not through any whim of mine, or trying to emulate the squarehead's cult, it was simply because of the hordes of lice, which appeared from nowhere like locusts, to invade the privacy of every prisoner's body. They nestled and hatched where it was warmest, among the lower regions, under the armpits, and wherever there was hair, sucking the anaemic blood from the veins of those who could least afford to lose it. They were German, of course! They had to be.

I've seen some terrible sores created by lice. If the skin was broken by scratching, the lice would concentrate on the easy entry, and the wound would take ages to heal up. And when it did, a permanent reminder would be left by a red-blueish scar, rather like a spreading bruise. In later years lots of blokes pretended they were shrapnel wounds (not unlike), but they weren't—they were a legacy from a louse, and it's lousy mates.

So as I said, in order to defeat the lice, which was impossible, I had all my hair removed, leaving me looking like the original prototype of Yul Brynner, for my happy registration snap.

Darkie Smith, a Scottish black man with a thick Scots accent, always took a lighted candle and ran it down the seams of his battledress, where they loved to lay their eggs.

"Would you look at that" he'd say "Fried Lice – ye canna whack it!"

Bob Wilson my old Queen Vic mate, was carted off to hospital or Lazaret with "Scabies", so for a time I was left without a confidant, but I struck up a friendship with Ronnie Carter, another Queen Vic, which was to last for some time.

It was here at this balloon hangar camp that the first signs of disrespect and gradual hatred for the British N.C.O.'s became apparent; created by their own greed and selfishness. Not all succumbed to the God of Mammon, but they had to be watched. Naturally, they were put in positions of trust by the Germans. For instance, it was two Sergeant cooks and two Corporal helpers who got themselves installed in the cookhouse. The spud bashing, as usual, was done by the other ranks. Sergeants and Sergeant Majors were detailed off to collect the bread and margarine rations, and to dole them out— they practically had a platoon of them to do it! They were guilty in many cases of cheating the soldiers to whom they were supposed to set an example. They became so suspect at cutting the bread—so vital to starving men—that it had to be seen to be done, in the open, fairly and honestly. Oddly enough, the p. o. w. disc was exactly a fifth of a loaf in width, and this became the standard of measurement when five men shared a loaf.

We used to think that it was the Jerry cooks who spoilt the soup, making it thin and watery, but when British Sergeant cooks were responsible at the balloon hangar, it became, not better, but a damn sight worse. We all saw the pork meat being brought in—and the Swedes and the potatoes (they were terribly bad and squashy, really only fit for pigswill). I know the rations they had to play with were meagre for 700 men, but they either didn't seem to get the hang of it or there was a fiddle going on.

Which is exactly what the Germans thought. The cooks were changed twice while I was there, but it didn't get any better. It was rumoured that they were having pork chops and chips, every evening in the cookhouse, and inviting their friends! "Another chop, Jack?" "Don't mind if I do!" Survival of the fittest? You can't win, can you!

We lay around in the straw, itching and scratching, de-lousing, exchanging gossip and exploits, and waiting for the next meal. Tobacco got scarcer and cigarettes fewer, but it became the custom if a man lit up a cigarette, for someone to say "Two up" which meant that person was entitled to a drag or smoke before the cigarette was finished, and just as I was due for my own "two up" drag, the German interpreter came in and ordered us out on parade to listen to a very important speech from the Commandant. All agog we hurried out.

The Major read the speech from a Roneoed typewritten sheet, extolling the virtues and victories of Germany. "The war would soon be over... The prisoners must bide their time and be patient... behave... And they would be well treated, and then sent home in due course." It was all propaganda crap. A nothing speech. And he knew it too. His voice dwindled a bit at the end and his "Heil Hitler" was almost sotto voce.

A low hum went around the assembled prisoners and a high hum came from the latrines.

The German interpreter, who had translated the speech into English, read from another piece of paper:

"Tomorrow, all boots are to be handed into the stores and wooden shoes will be issued to replace them. There will be an issue of overcoats the following day." He stood down.

Somebody said "Wooden shoes this week—wooden overcoats next. God bless the Fuehrer!"

My British boots were finished, one sole was nearly off, bound with string, and the other had a split in the side, which let in water, with both heels at a crazy angle, so I looked forward to the wooden shoes.

They turned out to be Dutch clogs and they curled up in the front to a point like something out of Ali Baba and the 40 thieves. At first, they were murder to wear, the top of my instep was chafed and raw where it caught on the inside of the clog. I tried stuffing some straw in between to ease the pain and that seemed to help, and eventually, after about four or five weeks, I got used to wearing them.

I found out later they were issued to prevent us from escaping. There was no danger as far as I was concerned!

The following day I was issued with a Belgian Cavalry overcoat (no British gear), which was flared all round, rather like a ballet skirt, and a Polish peaked forage cap (Africa Corp style, only khaki) which you could pull down over your ears, similar to a balaclava. I walked so tentatively at first in my new outfit that I resembled an ancient Chinese Mandarin whose corns were killing him.

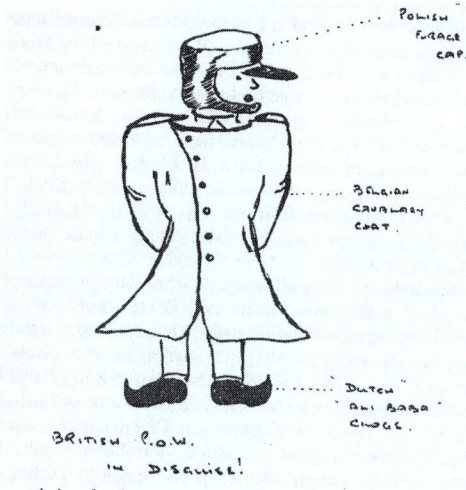

POLISH FORAGE CAP.

BELGIAN CAVALRY COAT.

DUTCH ALI BABA CLOGS.

BRITISH P.O.W. IN DISGUISE!

Every Friday was a meatless day, when the parable of the loaves and fishes was re-enacted. You were lucky if you found any meat in your soup on any of the other days—("I got a bit of gristle"—"You're the Cook's favourite, you are!"), but Fridays became "Klippfisch" Day. It was caught, so we were told (I always maintained it gave itself up!) only in Norwegian Fjord waters, and looked like a tired anaemic haddock, was heavily salted and frozen stiff. They seemed to keep for months without refrigeration, and were stacked in the cookhouse like snowshoes in Lillywhites. In an emergency, it could be used as a table-tennis bat or a canoe paddle. It was like supping seawater and chewing an old Norwegian boot. Even the cats ignored it, and Polish cats "polish" off everything!

Later in the war, as German belts were tightened (and British were unloosened) and pigs were a dying race, we had *two* meatless days a week. Tuesdays *and* Fridays; but by that time, even the Klipp fish withdrew their contributions (or maybe it was the fishermen), and we had to make do with mouldy potato soup, or rotting vegetable soup!

One day we were all ordered to parade for de-lousing, which entailed marching about five kilometres to a shower house— a sort of Polish Public baths—to which was joined a huge oven-baking contraption. We stripped and then parcelled or folded our uniforms up and handed them to the Polish house exterminator attendant, and then entered the concrete bathhouse for our showers. Pipes were criss-crossed all over the ceiling out of which came luxurious piping hot water. We were handed bars of German green soap which had the word "RIF" stamped on them but it was very poor stuff, being gritty, like solidified VIM, and when you rubbed it on your body it scraped. But it was soap—of a kind. "Don't whiff—use RIF!"

We were not allowed or encouraged to hang about because of others waiting to be "done" so after the shower we huddled around in the nude—in theory clear of lice—waiting for our baked lifeless uniforms to appear, which they duly did all lovely and warm, but smelling of cyanide fumes. Unfortunately, the operation was not a success, for after about two days, the bloodsuckers made a counter-attack and reappeared in what seemed even greater numbers! I think the eggs that had obviously been deposited in the seams hatched out due to the baking, and we were back to the usual scratching and eliminating sessions—by hand. Or nail on the thumb to be precise.

Bob Wilson, my old mate returned from the hospital, looking thinner, supposedly cured of scabies, but still scratching! He said you could get white bread there and produced a loaf to confirm his story. It was demolished in five minutes.

On Tuesday the 9th July, 400 of us were marched to a new camp, Fort 17, which was on the other side of the road facing Thorn mainline station. To the West the line went to Berlin and to the East—ominously— to the Russian border. We arrived at Fort 17 to be kitted out etc., in preparation for moving to a permanent working party which became in p.o.w. parlance "Going on Transport".

During our three or four days at Fort 17 we saw train after train carrying German troops, tanks, and massive gun equipment, stopping at Thorn station, prior to continuing the journey to the Eastern Front, although war against the Russians, as far as we knew, had not been declared.

On our second day there, the whole camp of about 1000 men were inoculated against typhoid, administrated by British medical staff (R.A.M.C.) under the supervision of the German Medical Officer, so obviously the danger was prevalent.

Fort 17 or *"Bruckenkopf"* (Bridgehead) which was the name written up on the outside over the arch was one of several forts in and around Thorn. It was solidly built, by the Germans, funnily enough, in 1857 and was surrounded by huge moat.

There was Fort 13: Fort 14 (Hospital): Fort 15: Fort 16 (which was used as a punishment camp) and Fort 17. All containing British p.o.w.'s. There was also a Fort 12, used only for Polish prisoners.

Fort 17 seemed to be well organised and was heavily guarded and was run more or less by the British N.C.O.'s (on the staff!) Who in turn were answerable to *Obermeister Commandant* C.S.M. (Company Sergeant Major) "Lofty" Horner from the Rifle Brigade. It was here that we saw the first issue of a newspaper called "The Camp"—printed in Berlin—with (supposedly) contributions from p.o.w.'s, saying how well they were being treated and all that crap, and although they had photos of planes supposed to be bombing London etc., we condemned it all as lying propaganda! I think the only thing we ever believed in that paper was the football results! It was full of misprints like DUNCSTER RIVERS for Doncaster Rovers and VOLVERS-HIMPTERN for Wolverhampton as if taken down in long-hand from a B.B.C. Sports Report while sitting in a moving lorry.

Friday, the 12th July was our "Red Letter" day—we had our First Red Cross Food parcel issue—67 parcels between 1,000 men.

In our hut we drew lots for the magical treasure of British food. Bob Wilson got a quarter of a tin of cocoa (about four spoonsful) and I drew half a tin of Keiller's marmalade.

The Cocoa was put into our ersatz coffee and the marmalade (along with a white loaf which we recklessly bought from a fellow p.o.w.) was eaten reverently as at a wine-tasters convention, rolling it around the tongue—savouring the peel and the bitter sweetness of it! We also bought some odd looking cigarettes from the canteen called "Junaks". Half cardboard and half tobacco dust which smelt like the latrines on a hot summer's night, and when you inhaled, it was advisable to hold onto your forage cap—otherwise, it would've been blown off! God bless the Red Cross, Fry's Cocoa, Keiller's marmalade, not forgetting Mr Junak. VOOM!!

Anybody see my cap?

On Sunday, the 14th July, as a concession to the workers, reveille was at 6 a.m. instead of 5 a.m. as on working days. Roll call was at 7.30 a.m. during which 200 men were detailed for a working party due to move off to Danzig on Tuesday.

A short church service was held in the open air where roll call had taken place earlier and was well attended. No collection was taken and hymns for those that had the strength were lustily and fervently sung.

On the morning, Monday, after roll call I was detailed along with 59 others for a local working party to carry iron beds from Fort 17 to the hospital, Fort 14. We were taken to a hut which was stacked with iron beds; there must have been over 500 there. It was a strange single line procession that proceeded out of the huge Fort doors winding its way along the main road—2 men per bed—carrying 30 iron beds—2 guards, one in front one in the rear—of the bed-carrying column "doing a daylight flit from the buildings".

We did the repeat journey in the afternoon bringing another 30 beds, having returned to Fort 17 for *mittag essen* (midday soup). I got some white bread at the hospital (they had their own bakery!) which I bore back in triumph. We were counted again at the evening hourly roll call and I retired early to my flea-pit.

The following day till Friday the pattern followed—more bed carrying till all the beds were transferred to the hospital and stacked in the so-called wards.

On Saturday six men were detailed, of which I was one, to do a garden fatigue round the back of the Fort at the side of the moat—cutting the long grass with shears and clearing weeds in order to make it presentable as a sort of sunbathing platz for German officers and N.C.O.'s to loiter, and dally in their off duty hours with their fraus and fräuleins or somebody else's. An old Pole, a gardening expert who was in charge of things (although we had a Jerry guard with us of course) doled out spring onions and lettuce and told us to help ourselves to the elderberries. The bush was denuded within 10 minutes!

I ate some there and then and crammed the rest, including the lettuce and spring onions, into my ever faithful dixie! When we finished, later, in the afternoon, we were given two issues of watery soup for our good work!

The following day at roll call, my name was read out to go away on the Tuesday on a working party to (as we thought) Danzig, and although I tried to get off it or get him on it with me, I was to be separated from Bob Wilson and wasn't to see him for a long time. He did alright for himself though.

On the Monday, our new party of 200 men, which, luckily for me included Ron Carter and Eddie Watson (both Q.V.R's), marched to Stalag XXA Headquarters, which turned out to be a central civil administration building, complete with Co-op stores, to be kitted out. This was the central depot for p.o.w.'s in our area—everything appertaining to prisoners came here.

Letters were censored here by an army of censors—both incoming and outgoing—private parcels, books, educational and fiction, Red Cross parcels, and all official orders from Berlin regarding p.o.w.'s came here. Each department was headed by a German officer of high rank, and p.o.w.'s did the menial work, and in the process achieved positions of power (behind the throne) and the whole was ruled over by an *Oberst*, equivalent to a Colonel in the British Army.

I got a new pair of clogs (less oriental!), but later on each member of the working party was to receive a pair of Norwegian ski-ing boots, a vest, a new pair of pants (Army issue), a water bottle and two pairs of socks—all British. I suppose they must've captured loads of our stuff in France.

But considering the number of thieving hands it must've been through before it arrived there, it's a wonder we ever got it at all. Having said that, clothing from home was beginning to trickle through via the official p.o.w. channels—witness the first consignment of parcels that we'd already had.

Of course, what we were all apt to forget, was the fact that we weren't the first p.o.w's to be captured—only the first bulk—there had been quite a few navy personnel captured early on in Norway (there were three or four from a submarine in Fort 17) also Merchant Navy men plus a few airmen, and of course civilian internees, although they wouldn't come under the same Geneva rules as p.o.w's—or would they?—I never found out. But we were the first British p.o.w.'s of quantity in Poland—unfortunately!

Tuesday, the 23rd July was moving day. At 12.20 hours we left for "the unknown"—supposedly Danzig (another shithouse rumour!) but it turned out not to be.

We entrained in five cattle trucks (40 men per truck) overseered and guarded by 5 German guards who had one truck to themselves, and arrived at a small town called Nertzhal at 3.30 pm precisely. This was no hardship in comparison with our early experiences of 75 *hommes* to a wagon.

We got out and clogged along in more or less orderly fashion for five kilometres till we came to a village called Wirsitz, our final destination. On the outskirts of the village we came upon what looked at first sight like a small factory or warehouse—but was, in fact, the camp. It was completely enclosed in barbed wire (naturally) and round it again was another encirclement of barbed wire—a compound within a compound.

The Jerry guards' living quarters were at the rear within the first compound, and the cookhouse and two small offices were adjacent at the entrance gates, which meant coming out of the inner compound through some more gates to get the grub. Sounds like Hampton Court Maze, doesn't it?

Two-tiered beds like bunks with wooden slats were on the floor and at the rear of the factory (inside) there were some steps up as if the end part had been built up like a stage. Wooden trestle tables were in the alleyways between the beds. It was not unlike the balloon hanger in shape and size, but not so big and slightly better appointed.

After grabbing or laying claim like a prospector to our beds – we were near the doors – Queen Vics, Ron Carter, Eddie Watson, and myself became a threesome, in the nicest way—that is we decided to "muck-in", all for one and one for all, a sort of Three Musketeers trio!

We were issued with white bread – one loaf between three men, or in p.o.w. lingo, three men to one loaf and some ersatz margarine, plus a dixieful of meat and barley soup.

A British sergeant was in charge under the German Sergeant Major (*Feldwebel*) and two cooks and fatigue workers were appointed to do general fatigue work about the camp. At first sight, it wasn't too bad, but of course, these were early days!

On our first day in the camp, we did nothing except to assemble for a speech from the German Commandant. He had with him a civilian who looked Polish, but was in fact, a "*Volk Deutsch*"—a Pole of German origin who after the invasion of Poland claimed German nationality. The Germans called them "*Gummy Deutsch*" (Rubber Germans) and didn't have too much respect for them, but we found that we had to watch out for them, because they were invariably "snide" and would report us to the Germans at the drop of a hat in order to ingratiate themselves with their conquerors. The Poles hated them even more than the Germans, if possible. They were the first to get their throats cut when the Russians advanced!

This *"Gummy Deutsch"* civilian — we were to call him "Snideface" —was apparently the representative of the contractors who had hired us as a labour force. They had to pay the German Army for our services, and we got the equivalent of three marks per week each.

The three marks they paid us was in a special currency called *Lagergeld* (camp money) and could not be used outside a camp.

Anyway, we assembled waiting for the Commandant's speech.... *"Britische Soldaten…"* he started off and waited for the interpreter to translate... (British soldiers...) "you are all prisoners of war (here we go again) and are the responsibility of the German army (really?). We will protect you (from whom?) and see that you get all the privileges you are entitled to under the Geneva Convention, providing you work hard and behave. Intercourse, social or sexual, with Poles is strictly forbidden (What? On these rations?) and will be dealt with harshly. (Give us strength). Escapers will be shot. It is up to you to make this a happy camp. Heil Hitler!"

We retired to our beds to ponder his words, and were called once again to be duly counted, *"appel"* (roll call) they called it, and then retired for the night, wondering what tomorrow would bring.

It was an eye-opener to say the least.

Up at 6.30, which was late for the Germans, we and six guards, marched about five kilometres down the road towards, as the sign said *"Deutsche Grenze"* Schneidermuhl, (German Border) and finally halted outside the gates of a cemetery. A Jewish cemetery. The Star of David was well in evidence above the gates and gave us the clue. The headstones were printed in Hebrew and/or Polish.

We were met at the gates by "Snideface" himself, as if he had popped up from one of the graves, and behind him were three Polish workmen, with patched trousers, each carrying a long spade and a pick. On the inside of the wall which bordered the cemetery, a collection of picks, shovels, and heavy hammers was stacked, and we were invited to choose our own implements. We were slightly puzzled as to what exactly was required of us, but "Snideface" along with two Poles demonstrated what was wanted.

They proceeded to pull down the headstone from one of the graves and then removed the marble board. The headstone was smashed with a pick and heavy hammer, and the pieces were stacked in a corner of the graveyard. Even the small pink chipped stones, or pebbles were shovelled up and removed, leaving the patch bare and open. "Snideface" worked like a man possessed as if he had some personal vendetta to work off, but for all his puniness, he was certainly strong. At the end of the operation, he turned and surveyed us as if waiting for the applause. He was bathed in perspiration. Some wag asked him "Wot abaht the stiffs? Aren't we going to dig up the stiffs as well?"

"Steefs? Steefs?" he queried "*Vas ist* 'steefs'?

"Long cold things like you'll be one of these days, mate."

"Steefs—*Vas ist* steefs?" he went on.

"I'll tell you when I dig *you* up" the wag retorted.

As it happened, there were two or three Jews among our party, but they wisely did not voice any protest, but sank into anonymity. They didn't want to be top of the Nazi Hit parade. I spoke to one of the guards, an oldish man. "*Nicht gut arbeite*" (not good work)" I said, pointing to the macabre handiwork

"*Jah, Jah*" he agreed, "*Nicht gut*" shrugging his shoulders at the same time. I didn't know the German for "sacrilege" but he obviously shared my point of view.

I and quite a few others picked half-heartedly at our first job for our new masters, making our attitude clear that the whole thing was distasteful. The civilian, "Snideface", tried to make us increase our work rate by bellowing "*Los-Los*" at us, but the old guard waved him away with "*Nein-Nein*" and then took up the cry himself, for appearance's sake. He winked as he said it "*Los arbeite-Los*". We had a definite ally in him.

As it turned out, we were soon to put all the guards into categories.

"Not bad" (like our oldish one).

"So-so" (don't take too many liberties).

"Bastard" (pretend to work hard whilst he's around).

"Super bastard" (don't try *anything!*) and

"Shit face" (Trigger-happy. Hates everything British. Especially p.o.w.'s. Usually fervent Nazi!).

Three days we took to demolish the cemetery entirely and a sad reproachful site it looked on completion. We'd actually been used as part of Hitler's pogrom against the Jews. I hope they decorated "Snideface"; perhaps they did eventually—with a knife! Between his ribs.

In the evening, after we returned from the cemetery, soup and our bread rations were immediately issued, that is meat, barley and potatoes and one loaf between three men coupled with one pat of margarine and one spoonful of ersatz honey.

I had just finished off my soup when I was told that somebody wanted me at the gates of the compound. Somebody wanted *me*? *Here in Wirsitz?*

It was our old German guard—our winking friend from the cemetery party—who told me, well, he actually beckoned me, to follow him round the back to the Jerry quarters, which I dutifully did.

He invited me into his *stube* (room) and gave me a glass of lager, and just as I was thinking could this be the start of a very close friendship, he handed me his jackboots and asked me to clean them for him, at the same time handing me the brushes and blacking! I was relieved and delighted and got stuck in doing my-shoe-shine-boy act in double quick time. It wasn't that I was all that keen, but I could see "reward" signs above his greying head and that was incentive enough. And when the job was finished, (and I'd like to say that you could've seen your face in them, but I honestly can't), he gave me a packet of "Junos" (Cigarettes, Madam) and a large portion of Jerry bread. *(Brot —Jah? Jah-Danke!)*.

Just as I was about to go his two comrades who shared the room with him came in and demanded that I repeat the process for them. I set to work with a will and some "elbow grease" and was again rewarded with three cigarettes from each which equals 1 1/2 fags per Jackboot (Bargain basement prices) and a piece of German sausage *(Vurst—Jah? Vurst—Danke!)*.

Elated, I made my own way back from the outer compound to the inner and produced the spoils to share with Ron and Eddie—26 cigarettes, bread and German *Vurst* was a good evenings work. The *"Vurst"* of many, I hoped.

Next day, Saturday, we started on a new project. 40 of us were detailed for what was euphemistically called "The Theatre Party" and although we should've learnt by now, we all had visions of a local theatre and were looking forward to painting the scenery or posters or something equally exotic, but of course it didn't turn out that way. True to form we ended up on a Polish hillside which was to be made into a stadium or amphitheatre for future Nazi Rallies. Theatre Party indeed!

The place was a huge U-shaped hill, which wouldn't have made a bad ski-slope in winter. It was covered in grass, scrub, weeds, bushes and boulders (how *they* got there, I'll never know) and the earth underneath was a mixture of sand and soil. Our job, at first, was to clear or denude the hill entirely, leaving only the sandy soil exposed, and eventually to concrete or cement the steps in a huge semicircle, as in a Roman theatre so that every able-bodied Party man could look down on the central dais or podium from which the pearls of Nazi wisdom were to be spoken.

We started from scratch (yes the lice were still with us) by which I mean we pulled up the bushes at the top of the hill and tossed them as far down the hill as we could. Boulders were easier, you just set them in motion and they gained momentum as they went down the slope, narrowly missing the German guard en route!

On the top of the hill there was a flat plateau which contained the biggest cornfield I had ever seen in my life. As far as the eye could see there was corn waving gently in the July breeze. About two hundred and fifty yards away there were some Polish workers, who waved as well just like the corn, but the guard discouraged any social intercourse by shouting in their direction and shaking his fist. An old goat woman dressed like a gypsy, along with her shoeless teen-age daughter, was watching over some five or six tethered goats who had little clonkity bells round their necks. They too were shooed away by the guards and they tinkled off in the direction of a small copse away to our right.

There was no arrangement for latrines and one had to walk about 200 yards to the copse of small trees for purposes other than urinating. Apart from the two German guards there was also an old Pole whose name was Jadrinski who dished out the picks and shovels and advice about what we were doing, or hoped to do.

It was at lunchtime (we had no lunch) or *30 minuten pauser* (30 minutes break) that I signalled to the guard and pointed to the copse and he nodded and carried on sitting down and smoking while I looked for a piece of newspaper to complete the operation. After performing I was pulling up my trousers when the goat woman's daughter appeared about twenty yards away, and slightly embarrassed I hurriedly did up my trousers, but she seemed totally unconcerned. Whether or not she had been watching me searching for a spot like a dog who has lost his bone and then squatting down I'll never know, but she smiled when I nodded to her and placed a small package at the base of the tree, pointed to me and then to the packet, and then scampered off. I looked around to see if I was alone and then walked over to the tree and picked up the package.

It contained 4 large slices of home-made bread smeared with dripping, a wad of tobacco wrapped in a piece of newspaper and some cigarette papers. Before putting it in my blouse I looked around to see her to thank her but she had vanished. I did hear the goat bells in the distance and presumed that she and her mother were over the other side of the copse. I returned to the party and the guard who was still sitting and smoking another fag said:

"*Gut? Alles in ordnung?*" (Everything alright?)

"*Jah*" I said "*Gut, in ordnung.*"

But we won't referring to the same thing.

I related the incident to Ron and Eddie and we scoffed the dripping sandwiches on the spot. Some of the others looked at us, wondering where we'd got the "eats" from, but I didn't enlighten them. Otherwise they'd *all* have been crapping in the copse.

The following day was Sunday and there was no work.

Lying on our beds eliminating the lice we discussed the situation. It was apparent that even though we were getting just that little extra official issue food compared to early days, we were still *always hungry* and until the Red Cross Food parcels got into a permanent flow (which was a very long way off) we were to remain so. In theory working on a working party was supposed to benefit you, the promise of extra rations was one of the incentives to work, but whether it was the hard work or working in the fresh, open air or what, there was always this *acute hunger*. All the time. It definitely superseded sex, because for each and every prisoner, there was no interest in females, or any particular female in *that* fashion, only—"can we get some bread, sausage or sandwich out of her?" Not that we came into contact with any of them, but you occasionally did catch a glimpse of one or two, strolling down the road past the camp, but they were not encouraged to loiter.

If a presentable or pretty woman had been put alongside a bowl of soup and the choice had to be made "Take the woman or take the soup?" 95 % out of 100 would've taken the soup, 5% were homosexuals anyway and under normal circumstances would've preferred the cook.

On the Saturday two prisoners were seen accepting sandwiches and tobacco from a Pole during working hours at the local Burgomeister's place in *Wirsitz*. They were to be sent back to Stalag XXA—"offences under the social intercourse act with civilians" was the charge. The guard—a "Bastard"—had reported them to the Commandant, and they were to leave the following week. The Pole was reported to the Civil Contractors and lost his job. So far, I had got away with it—so far! When we returned to the 'Theatre Party' on the Monday, I was assigned along with 11 others to dig a latrine pit at the top of the hill, on the flat plateau. "Snideface" our "rubber" German had turned up, and was as usual in charge of operations. He was in his element, dashing from one job to another, upbraiding, and showing his prowess at tearing down bushes. (we very nearly got him with a boulder incidentally, he just jumped out of its path in time!) and then telling us and showing us what to do with the wooden poles for the erection of the bog. We now called him "Snideface" to his face, and he answered to it—I think he thought it was a term of endearment!

"Hey, Snideface, what abaht this bleedin' pole, then?"

"Vas? Vas?" he would say looking round.

"D'you want me to stick it up you now or later?"

"Jah, jah." And he would take hold of it and practically do the work himself, thumping it into the ground with one of those 10lb hammers.

A large pit 30 feet in length by about 10 feet wide and 6 feet deep, was dug and then four smallish poles (made from trees cut from the copse) were knocked into the ground at either corner. Then an arrangement of two trees was knocked together to form a cross shaped cradle and these also were knocked into the ground at either side of the pit lengthwise. Next a solitary pole six inches thick in circumference was placed in the "V" formed by the crossed trees and nailed. The pole on which the p.o.w.'s had to perch was placed about two feet away from the edge of the trench, which meant that it was easy-going for the blokes with long legs, but slightly fraught for those with shortish pins. They were liable to overbalance if they weren't careful! With dire results.

However, there it was in all its glory, and all that remained was to sprinkle it liberally with lime, put some hessian around the poles and declare it open to the "Public". "Snideface" was invited to "perform" the ceremony, but he declined. As a matter, of fact, I can't *ever* remember him going to the lavatory in any sense whilst he was on the job.

In the evening, I went to the Jerry quarters in the outer compound to shine my old guard's jackboots, and was detailed instead to carry the kit of one of the guards to the station. He was going on leave prior to being transferred to another unit. Judging by the amount of kit and junk that he had collected, it felt as if he was taking one of the Jewish headstones home to his wife as a souvenir. I was so borne down that I now know what it must've felt like playing the "Hunchback of Notre Dame" which is what I looked like from the front. I didn't dare to look left or right, my head and back were permanently bent, and all I could see was the road and my clogs!

However, when we got there, he did have the decency to give me a packet of fags for nearly crippling me! And when I walked back from the station with another guard who had come with us, I received some curious and sympathetic looks from the Poles we passed—but unfortunately that was all I did get.

When we returned to the camp I nipped round the back to do my chores with the jackboots and was given some bread and sausage for my pains. What I really needed was some embrocation for my back! But, talking of pain, I had been having some trouble with my left eye for three or four days, it was continually watering and itching, and in the morning when I woke up I was unable to open it. I joined the sick parade—there were about three of us— and saw the English medical orderly who was installed in a little cubby-hole office near the cookhouse. He gave me some aspirins, a piece of cotton thread and a cardboard eye shield and told me to come back at 10 to see the Doctor. (He was a German army doctor, who did the rounds by car, attending two or three working parties in the district. Although my eye was highly inflamed and very sore, he didn't seem to think there was much wrong, but advised bathing it in some powdered solution (probably boracic) and keeping a piece of lint over it under the eyepatch, so that I looked like Captain Kidd, the pirate.

I was detailed along with the rest of the sick to help peel the potatoes for the camp soup, which I gladly did. (Unless you were mortally sick, you were expected to do fatigues about the camp.) I meandered into the inner compound, lay on my bed for a while, and then ventured into the outer compound and ambled round the back to the Jerry quarters. I sculled around for a bit and then, looking through the barbed wire behind their rooms. I saw a very pretty blonde German girl coming out of a large house which overlooked us.

She saw me and walked across the well-kept lawn to speak to me.

"Hello" she said in perfect English "What's the matter with your eye?"

"Oh" I replied "it's inflamed. It just keeps watering."

"Have you seen the doctor?" she asked.

"Yes, I have, thank you" I answered "Where did you learn to speak English?"

"At my gymnasium" she said.

"Gymnasium?" I got a mental picture of wooden vaulting horses, ropes, netball.

"Yes, it means High School in German."

"Oh, very interesting." I said. "In England, a gymnasium means…"

"Yes, I know"…. she was just about to say something else when a well-dressed older woman came out of the house and called her.

"*Ursula, komm hier.*" (Come here.)

She dutifully turned and went to the woman and they both went inside. I could hear the older woman's raised voice, but could only guess that she was warning her about fraternising with the prisoners. I waited for a while, but she didn't come out again.

When my mates got back, I told them of my encounter and Eddie Watson commented "You wanna watch out, they'll have you for social intercourse if you're not careful."

"It's alright with Germans, Eddie" I said "it's the Poles that are forbidden."

"I've heard about these German blondes. Man-eaters, that's what they are".

"Look, she's only about 16—a schoolgirl."

"Yea, they're the worst kind. Jail bait, that's what they are."

"Oh balls!"

"I don't know about balls, mate, but your other eye is goin' all red with lust!"

I threw my dixie at him.

That evening as I was returning from the outer compound the Sergeant cook asked me to carry some water to the boiler for the early morning ersatz coffee. Peculiarly the tap was outside the cookhouse about 50 yards away, and water bearers, Aquarians, naturally, were always to be seen to-ing and fro-ing with buckets full of water. (Later, they had a hosepipe attachment fixed to the tap and they dispensed with the water carriers.)

I toted about 14 buckets to the boiler (about 28 gallons I suppose) and was offered a plate of egg and chips (they were having a fry-up) for my labour on condition that I scoffed it there and then. I did, but I got the promise of two extra soups for Ron and Eddie on the morrow, so my conscience was assuaged.

Nothing untoward happened for the rest of the week, but small extras materialised in some shape or form. For instance, I was making my usual way round the back of the compound, bemoaning the fact that I had had no word from home (one lucky so-and-so had had six letters) when I heard the welcome tinkling of goat bells, and there outside the wire on the grassy bank to the road was our goat woman from the "theatre party" and her six goats. They were eating the grass avidly as if they were prisoners, and she was squatting down as always watching over them. I waved and said *"Guten Abend"* (good evening) and she smiled and nodded, but didn't speak. Seeing her was almost as good as a letter from home—almost.

Half an hour later she was still there, but further down the bank towards the rear of the compound. She tossed a greasy packet over the wire which turned out to be a bacon fat sandwich.

Why why should a woman with so little to give take a chance like this with a prisoner? She herself was practically a prisoner—*all* the Poles were in the hated hands of their conquerors. And all over Poland from the beginning to the end of the war Polish men and women took their lives in their hands by helping and making life more bearable—by their courage and kindness—for the British prisoners of war. No prisoner can refute this. At great risk to themselves at all times, what little they had they freely shared with p.o.w.'s.

I have seen them beaten to the ground with rifle butts for daring to give a prisoner some tobacco.

I have seen them thrown into the icy River Vistula for consorting with prisoners, and still they continued to come back for more.

For guts, courage, and unselfishness, and a great love for anything British, the Poles stand alone. They believed to the bitter end that the British would come and rescue them from the German yoke, and then later the Russian yoke—but it all turned out to be a great let-down. To coin a lousy pun—a sour yoke— on them.

CHAPTER 5
"Ist Verboten! (But not if you're Irish)"

Life during July and August moved uneasily on from week to week and various things happened—the Nazi stadium (Theatre Party) location took on a very business-like look, all of the scrub and natural grass and bushes were cleared entirely leaving a bowl of sand to be sorted and shovelled, and finally the cementation of the place started.

The Commandant and the guards were completely changed and the new replacements turned out to be nearly all "bastards"—discipline became more strict and more rigid. My "old friendly guard" went away in the clear out. The rations were cut, and then on the promise of harder work from the p.o.w.'s, were reinstated. A bout of stealing took place within the camp—among our own blokes, and the culprit was caught in the act by the Germans.

His punishment included six strokes on the bare backside in public from the *Unter Offizier,* administered with his army belt, which had *"Gott mit Uns"* (God be with Us) on the steel clasp, and as a little extra he (the p.o.w.) was forced to almost submerge himself in the evil smelling latrine for 30 minutes. There is no deodorant to combat that. Two days later, he was taken back to Stalag with the guard keeping a respectable 15 yards behind him.

Overnight, I purposely left a haversack hanging on the post near the entrance to the bog on the Theatre Party, and in the morning, when we arrived, it was stuffed full of sandwiches, put there no doubt by the Poles working in the fields. Unfortunately, it was discovered by a swine of a German guard who confiscated the lot and dumped them in the bog, and then tried to find out the owner of the haversack. Luckily for me, there was no name on it, but we weren't likely to forget *his*. A week later, our planned revenge took place.

During our usual 30 minute break at lunchtime, Ron Carter took some French pornographic photos out of his pocket. (we borrowed them for six fags) and while we were "Ho-Ho-hoing" and admiring the impossible positions, the "sandwich confiscator" came up and demanded to know what was going on (Phase 1 had worked now came Phase 2). He was handed the photos and whilst he was looking at them, Eddie Watson, and myself crowded round to jostle him. Lost in admiration for the sexual delights now exposed to him, he was totally unaware of Eddie, emptying a matchbox full of very active lice into the left-hand pocket of his uniform. The lice, no doubt itching to go, had been handpicked for the job that very morning and were contributed by the three of us.

Two of them, eager to get to him, fell to the ground. But were immediately rescued and restored to the neckband of the German's uniform by Eddie, who put his arm round his shoulder and leant over looking at the photos at the same time.

Later in the day, the German was seen to be scratching and clapping his hands to his neck in a gesture well-known to louse hunters everywhere. It was a military offence for a German soldier to be lousy.

Well *he* was—he was lousy anyway!

Fortunately for us, he and eight others were replaced shortly after this incident, but it didn't benefit us any; the newcomers were just as bad. This constant switching around of guards was undoubtably part of German army policy to counteract any leniency with prisoners, but as the years rolled on and German losses became higher, the guards got older, and, unless they committed some blatant active indiscipline, they stayed.

Towards the end of the war (1944) we had to contend with ardent Nazi guards who'd been wounded on the Eastern Front and these types were invariably "trigger-happy" and had to be watched and proceeded against with caution.

Our Rubber German—"Snideface"—was still very much with us, as lively as ever, and his new pride and joy which he fussed over like a member of the *"Partei"* was a "hopper"—a baby truck on wheels which ran on miniature railway lines and was used to dump the rubbish and boulders collected from the site.

It ran for about 200 yards to a place where the stuff was tipped and then trundled back again—manhandled by the p.o.w.'s of course.

It was always coming off the lines, sometimes naturally, but more often deliberately, and as you can imagine it was very difficult to pull it up when there were no buffers to stop it!

They tried putting a railway sleeper across the lines to act as a break but when the hopper ran down the track it hit the sleeper at about 15 m.p.h. and turned a double somersault! Eventually a mound of rubbish was built up to halt it and that seemed to do the trick, but a good time was had by all before we got around to that.

"Snideface" nearly had a fit each time it came off and somebody said he lost two marks from his pay for each derailment. If that was the case he must've ended up owing the company money.

Once or twice when working with Jadrenski, our Polish work mate, he would teach us the odd word in Polish and as usual the first ones were connected with the breadline. Some fellows could conduct a conversation in Polish and could reel off the alphabet and numbers 1 to 100 but I only managed to learn a few words, usually derogatory, and certainly never spelt them correctly. Some of them were, phonetically:—

Caleb = Bread. Crova = Cow. Drinkiyie = (pronounced Jinquiua) = Thank you. Prosser = Please. Dobranous =Good night. Dobra = Good. Dobrivietcha = Goodbye, and the nicest of all—Moya Cohana = My Darling.

Occasionally he would 'cough up' with some Polish tobacco called Marchoka, a form of dynamite, but when there was nothing else to smoke, prisoners couldn't be choosers. He was, understandably, very careful, and when there was a purge on, he would become the original silent stranger not speaking to anyone. "Snideface" treated him like a dogsbody, shouting at him unmercifully and as he was loath to defend himself it was left to us to take the mickey out of "Snideface" to divert him from castigating Jadrinski, which we did.

George Brown, a cockney, was his mentor—

"Hey—Snideface—Why don't you shut your big gob and give your ass a chance."

"*Vass? Vass?*"

"Your bleedin' 'Opper is off the lines again."

"*Vas er Vas* Opper?"

"Nix grass hopper—'Opper—over there! Off the fuckin' lines again!"

"*Immer* fucking. *Immer* fucking." (Always fucking.)

"*You*—Immer fucking—sex mad *you* are. Never off the nest. That's why you're so bleedin' thin. I suppose you'll get the Iron Cross when this is all finished. Hail fuckin' Hitler!"

I think in time it gradually began to sink in that he was being baited and then he learnt one or two words and wasn't so easily fooled.

When he had the guards on his side he could make our lives a misery and uncomfortable which he did on many occasions. One day in a confidential mood Jadrinski the Pole said that "Snideface" was a Pole and that when the war was finished….He drew his finger across his throat as if cutting it. I suppose Snideface just thought he was on the winning side.

During the next few weeks, these were the Red Letter days noted in my diary. Sunday, the *18th August* we had our second issue of Red Cross parcels—one parcel between 18 men. We got a tin of sausages and a small packet of Weetabix. Swopped the cereal for a tin of marmalade.

27th August – issued with four American cigarettes, cocoa (loose) and two Ovaltine biscuits each.

Sept. 14th. we got our first pay – 4 Marks each in camp money, Lagergeld, but couldn't spend it – there was no canteen.

On *Sept. 15th.* we got Red Cross Cheese, Frankfurters, and a tin of Quince jam. Everybody got a dose of the shits—take your choice. I don't know what caused it, all I know is the bog did a roaring trade. More Lime for the Limeys.

As an afterthought, we were given a bar of Swiss chocolate each —I gave mine to the goat woman.

Each month, we were allowed to write home, one letter-card and two postcards which were taken to Thorn (Stalag XXA), censored and then forwarded, presumably, via Switzerland to England.

I had written my quota religiously each month since registration as a p.o.w. mostly to my mother, but so far, had no reply.

What worried me, and most of the p.o.w.'s who came from London was the graphic accounts and details of bombing that were written in the German produced paper "The Camp". Places that had been bombed were itemised, like Victoria, West India Docks and Central London, and although we scoffed and continued to dismiss the whole thing as propaganda, we reluctantly began to believe that there was some truth in it. And not hearing from home increased the anxiety and added to the uncertainty. The daily bulletin on the German radio always spoke of the intense bombing and listed the targets on how many planes the "enemy" lost (always a large total) and how many planes failed to return (always a low figure).

To refer to my diary:—

September 22nd 11 letters from England arrived at the camp during the week. Recipients were all low numbers in the 7000 area— Consoled ourselves that any day now we'd be hearing. My number 13745.

September 24th. Roll Call announcement. We are going to new camp. Laughingly called Winter Lager but still in the same area. Somebody said a castle. Newcastle? Elephant and Castle!?

October 7th. New guards arrived – all very young. New commandant also installed. Usual speech. Crap.

October 13th. Ron stricken down with sore throat and shivering —sweating – flu? 30 others very sick returning to Fort17. Eddie got job as assistant to assistant Cook. In the cookhouse—natch! O.K. for buckshees! Weather suddenly bitterly cold. Winds from Siberia.

October 15th. Inspection by new Commandant of uniforms etc., Given Norwegian ski boots to replace clogs. Going mountaineering at Winter Lager resort!?

October 17th. 3rd. issue Red Cross Parcels. 1 between 2—yeah—1 between 2! Celebrated with bacon and dried egg for breakfast! For past kindness, gave goat woman bar of Cadbury's by flinging it over wire. Following night, she threw small package, containing small scarf, one pair gloves, one pair socks, all hand knitted. How did she know my size?

October 20th. Ron had parcel of six Penguin Books. Fiction. Great reading. 15 new p.o.w.'s arrived to replace very sick.

October 27th. Red Letter Day. Had a letter from my mother. Heavily censored in England and here. Apparently not notified of capture till August 5. Wrote at once. All well.

November 13th. Parcel of clothing from home. Vest-Pants-Mittens-Socks-Khaki shirt-Balaclava. 4 large bars of chocolate ruined by camphor balls. Maybe alright for Polish moths but N.G. for Polish myths!

November 30th. De-loused again at Bromberg.
We came out full of hope
We had a shower and then a scour—
And some sod had a grope.
Two weeks later so did the "crawlies".

December 3rd At new camp—very old house; large rooms. Recurrence of eye trouble More severe, this time. Hospital – Bromberg. Marked "return to Stalag". Wrench leaving Ron and Eddie, but as they said "you can always come back—We'll meet again…"

December 4th. Arrived back at Fort 17 Thorn. Reported sick. Eye bathed in saline solution, nothing more.

It was very disheartening coming back to Fort 17. Things were much worse than when I'd been there before. The place was bulging with prisoners, it was extremely cold, snow had begun to fall, and sleeping conditions were deplorable. I had found a place in a three-tiered shelf to serve as a bed and although it was only a short distance to the bog many didn't bother to go, especially at night, they just urinated where they were. I didn't undress to sleep and I couldn't get warm. I determined that as soon as my eye was better I would make every effort to get back to my old working party.

The rations were the usual one loaf between five men and half a litre of watery soup every day. There were more "rackets" there; you could get most things at a price, and I kept myself going by flogging most of my clothing parcel for bread and cigarettes. It was rather like coming back to some huge institution after an endurable way of life had been established. And to make matters worse I knew no one. I was very much a lone wolf hunting on my own. After a couple of weeks, my eye, in spite of medical inattention, got better and I made an application to go back to my working party through the British Company office which was situated on the square where roll call was held. The Germans said it would be O.K. but I would have to mark time until replacements were needed which might mean a month or three months or six months wait. In addition they could not guarantee I would not be put on another working party, going to some other part of Poland.

I could see the way the Siberian wind was blowing, but I still clung to the hope that I would manage it.

The following week, being declared fit, I was detailed to join a local working party of 200 men operating from the Fort, unloading telegraph poles from barges on the river Vistula. It was round the clock shift work and I was on the 6 pm till midnight shift.

When I lined up with the other 199 odds and sods, it was snowing hard, and I thought to myself we'll be alright for a white Christmas! We marched through the town of Thorn, guarded by eight guards—two in front, two along either side, and two at the rear, slipping and sliding on the tramlines, avoiding the single decker trams which were now choc-a-bloc with homecoming Polish workers. I was wrapped up against the cold with a scarf, my Polish Afrika Corp style hat, Belgian overcoat and hand knitted (goat woman) gloves. I carried my haversack and inevitable dixie and had had to take a chance with leaving the rest of my kit in the hut, hoping it would be there when I got back.

When we got to the bridge that spanned the Vistula we turned left and marched along the road which ran alongside the river. After about 30 minutes we arrived at the dock, where the barges—about 15 of them—were moored, wallowing in the water like top-heavy ducks.

They were packed with long, thick telegraph poles—-painted black—and they all seemed to glisten as we approached. There seemed to be enough telegraph poles to cover communications all over Poland—twice—although unknown to us, another 15 barges were chugging their way up river for us to unload.

Eventually, of course they were to be used on the Eastern Front, but we weren't to know that then!

I was part of a 12 man team or gang who carried each pole on their shoulders about 200 yards and dumped it on a rapidly growing pile. After about six hours of this divertissement, I was completely dejected, disenchanted, and fed up with the whole pole situation!

I was wet through, very cold, and miserable and my shoulder was developing a "U"-like cavity where the pole had rested. We finished at about 12.15 a.m. tired and dispirited and sloshed our way back to the Fort. The snow which would never let up all night was beginning to lie in drifts all over the place. I don't know how many trips we made from barge to pile but our barge was empty just before we finished. I didn't care if I never saw another telegraph pole as long as I lived but the following night I was back on it!

On this occasion it wasn't snowing, it was freezing—hard. I had to put my fingers to my nose to make sure the end of it was still there. I didn't dare urinate, just in case it broke off!—well you never know! I pulled my scarf up over my mouth like a yashmak and my breath froze on the outside! Even the Jerries were stamping their jackbooted feet in a German gavotte and rubbing their hands together to help the circulation. Finally, one sensible lad from the Royal West Kents collected some wood, of which there was plenty lying around, and started a huge bonfire. It was a haven to come back to after each pole-carrying trip, and the guards themselves stood with their backs to the fire, shouting and encouraging the p.o.w.'s like spectators at a "Carrying the Caber" contest.

It all got out of hand at the end—more people warmed themselves than worked—and I was among them (the non-workers I mean!).

Then the guards in a fit of conscience would harangue everybody away from the fire, back onto the job, and 30 minutes later, like flies to a dustbin, we were all back at the blaze.

At 11.45 p.m. I made a token appearance with another pole-carrying gang, making sure that they were all taller than me which meant I went through the motions of carrying but in actual fact the pole was just brushing my shoulder, not lying on it!

I was with the telegraph poles job until it finished and lost not only weight but all desire to be a Post Office worker after the war.

Later on in my p.o.w. career I became a "shaver" of small telegraph poles for a local factory which was rather pleasant but it still didn't alter my vow to give telecommunications a miss at the end of hostilities. Pigeon Post—well maybe. Telegraph Boy with a Motor Bike 'Umm? —Telegraph Poles. NEVER!

I went to my first concert on the Sunday before Christmas held in a disused hut in the Fort. The main item on the programme was a sing-song. A p.o.w. with a mouth organ played the tunes and we all joined in, and then somebody got up on the hastily erected platform and told a few jokes. Somebody else recited a piece of poetry, then another joke teller ended up with a well-known ditty:-

"Round and round when the bloody great wheel.

In and out went the rod of steel

Till at last the maiden cried

Darling—I am satisfied."

Some chap did a number "Pennies from Heaven" with a comb and a piece of tissue paper—then a whistler, then a bird call imitator ending up with a sheep being hit by a golf ball producing the usual raspberry. A final sing-song—"Roll out the Barrel"—"You are my Sunshine" and "When you're Smiling" and the evening rounded off with "God save the King". I thought it was a brave effort in view of all the circumstances and whilst I was enjoying myself at it some bastard stole my haversack, and some tins of Red Cross food. It was the week before Christmas— "The Lord giveth and the Lord taketh away!" But to compensate we were all issued with ONE Red Cross parcel for ONE man AND 50 Gold Dollars Cigarettes each. Christmas Day was free—No work. So I treated myself to three Red Cross meals for the day!

On the following Sunday roll call was held in the morning and C.S.M. Homer, the British Sergeant Major in charge of the camp (under the Germans), asked for anyone wishing to perform at the camp concert that evening to see him after the parade.

I handed in my name. When it came to my turn to perform, I did my impressions and a few jokes and seemed to go down quite well. C.S.M. Homer liked it and told me so. I had taken the precaution of bringing most of my belongings with me this time, leaving only my Belgian overcoat where I slept. And of course, somebody whipped it. Perhaps they'd seen my act!!

I reported the loss the following day to C.S.M. Homer, and he arranged for me to go to Stalag (the supply stores) along with a party to get a replacement and this time I got a good old British one.

At Stalag XXA I ran into Eric Hobby, an old Q.V.R. mate of mine, and he told me that he and Bob Wilson were employed in the Red Cross parcels department—stacking, unloading, collecting from the railway and sending the parcels out to the working parties. Unfortunately, (for me that was) they were billeted at Camp 13A just up the road from the Stalag building. It was good to hear that they both had done well for themselves. I was slightly envious of course, but that's the luck of the draw—at the moment I was getting a British overcoat and that for me was a step in the right direction.

When I got back to Fort 17, there was a letter from my mother dated November 23rd, which wasn't bad going—just over five weeks to get there! And the next day, I received a parcel of six books (Penguins). For a loaf of white bread and ten cigarettes, I flogged two of the books, which were "The Decline and Fall of the Roman Empire" and "A Tale of Two Cities" and some wag had made the "C" into a "T".

On the on the 1st. February, 1941 (I remember it well) my name was read out along with about 50 other Irishmen to stay put after roll call as we were needed for interviews.

I couldn't, and neither could the others, think what the hell it was all for, and although a lot of suggestions were bandied about, such as setting us free, which in a sense wasn't wide of the mark, we had to wait till the next day to find out.

We were all shepherded into the outer compound which was Jerry Guards' quarters just inside the Fort gates and told to wait until we were called.

When the first Irishman, Dick Kelly, came out after having been inside in some room for 20 minutes or so we all crowded round him to enquire what was going on. He replied:—

"They want ye all to fight for Germany."

"Ach c'mon Dick, stop muckin' about, what did he say?"

"It's true, I'm tellin' ye," said Dick. "They'll offer ye a drink and a smoke and put ye at your ease, and then get around to askin' ye why are ye fightin' for England when Ireland isn't at war with Germany. They're all so bloody thick they think Ireland is a tight little island and we all joined up to get away from the poverty. They think we're 'Soldiers of Fortune.'"

"Bloody misfortune ye mean. What did ye say to them?"

"I took their drink and their fags, and then I told them to get stuffed!"

Each one as they came out confirmed Dick's story and then it was my turn.

I was ushered into what looked like a conference room—there was a huge portrait of Adolf Hitler on the wall and two furled Nazi flags were crossed above the picture.

I was met by a *Sonderfuhrer* (Political Officer) and shown to a chair placed in front of a large table around which were grouped four important-looking German Army Officers. It looked like a Court Martial Tribunal.

I was offered a drink of schnapps which I accepted (the first since I'd been captured). Then a packet of "Juno" cigarettes was pushed towards me and I was told to help myself. I did. And the Sonderfuhrer lit it for me. He then took a buff document from a pile which obviously had my particulars on it and spoke to me in English with an American accent.

He sounded like John Wayne.

Sonderfuhrer: "Samuel J. Kydd. 6896304. 1st. Batt. Q.V. rifles?"

Me: "Yes, sir."

SF: "What's the "J" stand for, Samuel?"

Me: "John, sir."

SF: "How do you like to be addressed, Samuel or John?"

Me: "Sam or Sammy, sir."

SF: "You don't have to call me, sir—Sam."

Me: "Yes sir. I mean, yes."

SF: "Well now, Sam—lemme see—Kydd. That's not a very Irish name."

Me: "I think it's Scottish."

SF: "Oh—well now, Sam, have another drink. Help yourself to another cigarette. Perhaps you'd like a cigar?"

Me: "No, thank you."

He poured me another drink, and I lit up another "Juno" although I hadn't finished the first one properly.

SF: "I take it you know why you're here, Sam?"

Me: "Well, no. I've no idea really."

SF: "Well, now, Sam—these gennlemen and myself and a lot of my Government colleagues are wondering how an Irishman like yourself got to fighting for England against Germany?"

Me: "Well—It's a long story…"

SF: "I mean, Sam, that Germany has no quarrel with Ireland. Ireland has *not* declared war on Germany, neither has Germany declared war on Ireland."

Me: "No – I know, but it isn't as easy as that. You see, I'm British really."

SF: "British? But it says here, you're Irish. Were you born in Ireland?"

Me: "Yes."

SF: "Your parents were born in Ireland?"

Me: " Yes."

SF: "Well then Sam you must be Irish."

Me: "Well, in one sense I am and in another I'm not."

SF: "Oh how come?"

Me: "Well you see the part that I was born in belongs to England—the United Kingdom….. Could I have another drink please?"

It was very warming stuff, schnapps, rather like honey whiskey.

SF: "Sure, Sam sure."

He poured me another and one of the officers coughed and looked at him meaningfully, but the *Sonderfuhrer* quelled him with a look that said "I'm in charge".

SF: "Now, Sam, tell me, what would be your attitude—supposin'—just supposin' Ireland declared war on England?"

Me: (playing for time) "Well, I'd have to think about it. I'd need time to consider it." (A vision of another interview and two glasses of schnapps.)

SF: "I see Sam. Are you saying that in that eventuality, you might find your allegiance torn? Your sympathies might be elsewhere?"

Me: "Yes. Yes. You could put it like that." (I was beginning to feel a very mellow fellow!)

SF: "Germany, as you probably know Sam (I didn't) has great interest and sympathy for Ireland, and is anxious to repatriate all Irish nationals. In the event of repatriation, Sam, would you be prepared to co-operate with the German Embassy in Dublin?"

Me: (Pause) "Well—um—well, we're all interested in— repatriation."

SF: "Tell me Sam, did you ever hear of a fellow countryman of yours —"Sir Roger Casement?"

Me: "Yes. He was executed for treason."

SF: "A great man, Sam."

I finished my drink, but didn't have the nerve to ask for another, and looked at him. He returned the look for about ten seconds as if he were flirting with me and then stood up and came round the table and extended his hand, which I shook.

SF: "It's bin a great pleasure to meet you, Sam. See you again soon, I hope."

Me: "Yes. Thank you. Yes."

I wanted to say "What time does the boat sail then"? But I didn't, instead I came to attention, half bowed to the officers—stumbled into a right turn (it was heady stuff that schnapps) and made my exit.

When I got outside, the remaining few asked me what they'd wanted. I said "They're setting us all free by landing us by submarine in Ireland and all we have to do is attend roll call at the German embassy in Dublin!"

The next day the "buzz" was all around the camp. I heard it in my hut "Those bastard Irish are all going to be free in a couple of weeks. They're forming an Irish Legion at the German embassy in Berlin and they are being sent home in a flotilla of submarines!" Schnapps—Craps!

The call to defend Ireland, by being put ashore on the Irish coast, never came. It might have been seriously considered mind you, who knows—perhaps they were just biding their time, or ran out of schnapps, or sacked the *Sonderfuhrer*; whatever it was, I'd forgotten all about it, until at the height of the British and American bombing of Berlin in 1944, they raised the whole stupid business again by collecting the "Sons of Erin" from far-flung working parties all over Poland—plus newly taken Irish p.o.w.'s. It was really clutching at straws at that stage of the war, more like a "Wake" really, at the beginning of the slow death of Deutschland. It was almost the death of some of us, because we were right in the bombing path of our own bombers (especially the Yanks!) at a place called Luckenwalde—36 kilometres from Berlin. But that's jumping the gun. For the moment, the present was all that concerned me, and I was carving out a career for myself, in p.o.w. parlance, at Thorn, in Fort 17.

It was suggested by C.S.M. Homer, that we should be allowed to follow the line of German p.o.w.'s in England, that is to be given the privilege of establishing a Concert Party that would be recognised as such and allowed officially.

The logic of his proposals was seen (it was good propaganda) and official permission was given to select 20 p.o.w.'s as the nucleus of a Concert Party whose members would not be sent on working parties, but would stay and perform in the camp. They were not exempt from work and were expected to work locally, though the first call on their services was to be the Concert Party for the entertainment of the captive audience!

I was one of the "chosen few", and the "going" especially as far as I was concerned, became easier. The Thespian God had waved his wand.

A building to the right of the Fort gates was occupied exclusively by British staff p.o.w.'s including C.S.M. "Lofty" Homer (well, he called me Sam!) who did jobs in the camp like company office clerks, Sergeants in charge of Bread Store, rations, etc., In other words, the "civil service" administrators necessary for the running of the camp. Each of the rooms in this block had proper iron beds, two tiered, one on top of the other (they were actually identical to the beds that I had carried to the hospital, when I was at Fort 17 earlier), and a couple of permanent orderlies saw to it that the place was kept clean.

In due time, I, along with other active members of the Concert Party, was installed in one of the rooms, which was to become known as "that Concert Party lot". I teamed up with a Hampshire feller—one Stanley Noake from Bournemouth, nicknamed "Knocker", who was in love with a girl called "Angela" and told everybody so. (He made an honest woman of her—eventually!)

Another very active member of the Concert Party was Vic Thompson who could write funny material (verging on the vulgar), tap dance like Fred Astaire's mother and was a very talented actor. He specialised in comedy. He was always having trouble with his feet, apart from not washing them. His right foot was size nine and his left size ten which made for complications, except when wearing clogs! The clogs came in three sizes – Very Small (Chinese), Medium (Normal) and Large Boot Size (Hello Sailor!).

He and I got on well together, and we usually played opposite each other in sketches, I would be the straight man and he the comic and vice versa. The costumes at first were not elaborate, the imagination had to be stretched for women's gear for instance, but as time went on, they improved tremendously. A Polish Army uniform jacket obtained from Stalag XXA stores could be turned into a reasonable lounge suit jacket, and many women's suits were tailored out of Army blankets.

We did a succession of shows which were mainly "end of pier" concert party efforts all related to our circumstances and conditions but finally we did a three act play—a thriller—written by Vic called "I spy…"

I forgot to mention (how could we ever forget!) that keeping pace alongside the concert party was a dance band. It was devised and directed by Pip Howe and was at first a seven piece affair. Musicians were two a *pfennig* and he had a wide choice to choose from—it was the instruments that were more difficult to get hold of.

"You are all prisoners of war and are the responsibility of the German Army. We will protect you providing you work hard. Intercourse with Poles, social or sexual is strictly forbidden. Escapers will be shot. It is up to you to make this a happy camp. Heil Hitler!"

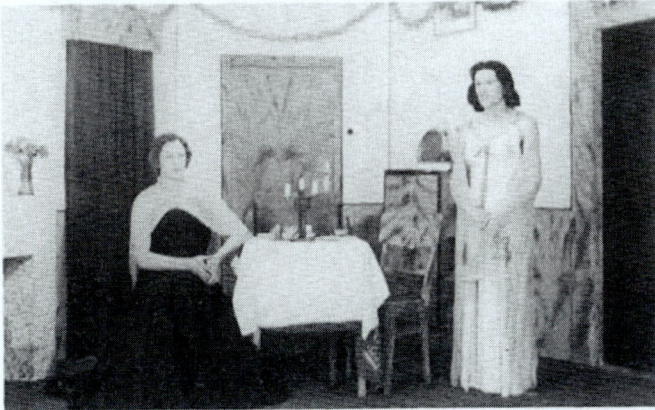

Long before Danny La Rue. Remarkably effective drag by Norman Brown (Left) and Johnny Gaskin.

"Anyone for a Theatre Party?" said the orderly. But *this* was the Theatre and the labour on the normal rations of 1940 at Wirsitz.

The author acting as pall bearer at the funeral of Scots drummer, Danny Faulds.
"All that was lacking was a Scots Piper"

"Out of the blue, I was offered the Editorship of the monthly p.o.w. magazine, *Prisoners' Pie*."
A very David Nivenish Sam in the editorial office with Jimmie Woolcock (right) and Alf Gosling. January 1943.

Sam, not singing Hallelujah, but compering one of the many musical shows.

PRISONERS' PIE
STALAG XXA

OCTOBER 1943.

Top Hat Theatre
FORT 13

Theatre for a captive audience!

GEORGE & MARGARET 1941

Sam, second from right, as Alice the mother.

"and though I says it myself I looked like Whistler's
Mother's Mother. . . ."

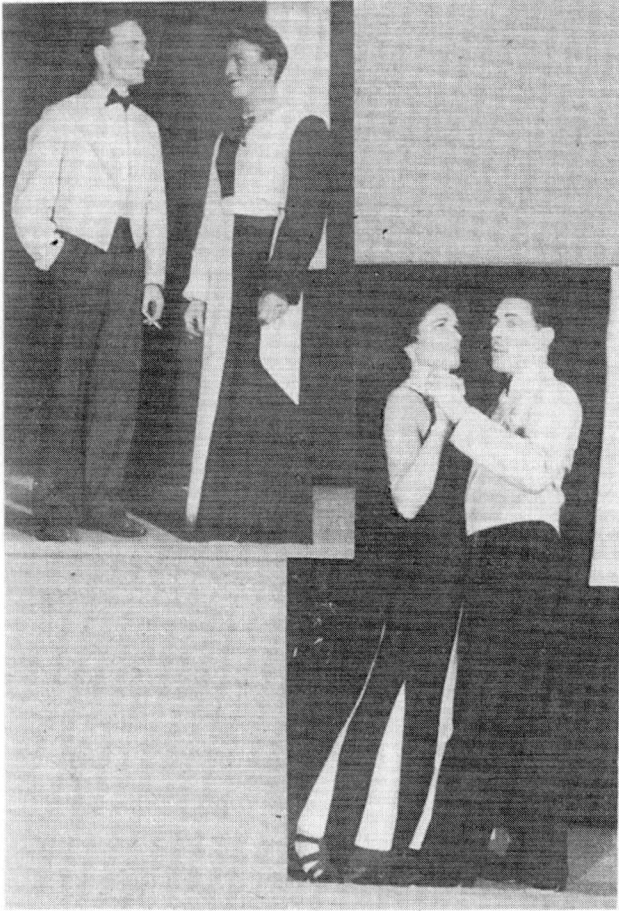

Savoy Ballroom at midnight? The Casino at Cannes?
Gowns by Hardy Amies? Suits from Savile Row?
Actually Fort 13 in Poland, coats and costumes from
sheets.

Britta Luukannen. A brief encounter in the book store.

I did one or two local jobs like unloading coal or swedes on the railway, and clearing the runways of snow at the airfield for the German Luftwaffe. When we pointed out that we were assisting the German war effort and that was against the Geneva convention, they simply said that it was Civil Airport and some Luftwaffe planes just happened to be there—refuelling! We continued to clear the runway!

Around about this time—March—Fort 15 became the home for a large number of British Officers and a party of 50 men were sent daily to Fort 15 for general fatigue purposes, clearing up, washing up and keeping the place ship-shape. Two R.A.F. officers, hearing of our snow clearing runway party, decided that this might be a good way to try and affect an escape—in other words playing it by ear.

There was no set plan but the idea was to try to get into a plane and take off (in which direction, I never knew— Russia? Sweden? Or England), hoping for the best. The first requisite was to switch places with two of the fatigue party, who arrived daily at the fort.

This was duly done one day and the two fatigue privates assumed the identity of the R.A.F. officers, and took their places on roll call that same evening.

By this time, the officers were safely back at Fort 17, in the guise of two privates, intending to go out on the snow clearing runway party at the local airfield on the following day. The British officers in charge were all aware of what was happening. They may have thought nobody else knew, but all the other p.o.w.'s and especially the 200 bods on the snow-way were all in the know!

On the day in question, the 200 strong snow clearers marched the long trek to the airfield and took up their accustomed positions at each end of the runway.

We worked in teams, pushing against the snow a long stout flat piece of wood, to which was attached a long pole. In theory, it should have the same effect as a snow-plough–but only in theory.
The snow spills over, and then you trample on it, and it freezes, and you have to do it all over again. Actually we were not unlike those fellows who clear and clean the ice rink to make it shine for the guest appearance. And that's what we were doing, waiting for the guest to arrive! It was a long and tedious process—we would go over the same

piece of runway several times until the concrete showed through, and then crude salt would be sprinkled on the exposed runway to prevent it from freezing. It was a complete dead loss when it was snowing—a nightmare job that was never ending. What they needed was a Force 10 gale blowing down the runway! Even the guards got cheesed off. Our two would-be-escapers at first joined in with the work and seemed to enjoy it, but after about two hours we noticed them sidling off behind the airport buildings, which were about 150 yards from where we were working.

For three quarters of an hour we were on the constant look out but disappointingly nothing seemed to be happening. Had they been caught already?

In front of the airport buildings stood three Messerschmitt fighters, and almost out of our vision several Stuka bombers were lurking away over to the right behind the buildings.

Suddenly, we saw two figures bent double running like hell for one of the fighter planes—the one in front vaulted onto the wing of the plane and climbed into the cockpit. The other officer tried to do the same, but slipped, fell to the ground, then picked himself up and clambered up successfully.

The situation was tense—several blokes were looking in their direction, and I called out "For Christ's sake, don't all look, or you'll give the game away!" Our guards were all around us and we didn't have to add to the escapers' danger by gawping and gesticulating.

There was a noise of an engine turning over—stuttering and then stopping. They tried again—"Vrum—Vrum—Vrum—Vrum—Vrum…" The engine was too cold. The plane wasn't going to move, let alone take off.

I looked up to see a squad of Jerry Luftwaffe blokes rushing down the airport building steps and belting over to the plane, brandishing their revolvers.

The two officers climbed out reluctantly and were marched into the airport buildings. We marched back to the camp and recounted their exploit. It was a pity that the brave and cheeky attempt hadn't succeeded.

I was asked by Pip Howe, the band leader, to compère a band -show of his. I enjoyed this immensely. I did my impressions again, told a few gags and sang a number with the band. Vic Thompson and I did the "Little Nell" routine, "Can't ye see by my tool, I'm the constabule" which used to be featured by Louis Stone and his Orchestra on radio, and for an encore, we gave them "Barnacle Bill" ("Who's that knocking at my door?" cried the fair young maiden. "It's only me from over the sea." said Barnacle Bill the sailor). At the end of the show the band played "God Save the King". But unknown to us, outside the Fort, the traffic stopped and a crowd of Poles collected, cheering and clapping, thinking the Marines had landed! From then on it was banned. We were not allowed to play the National Anthem, but as a substitute had to make do with "Rule Britannia" which, if anything, was more fervently and defiantly sung and certainly gave vent to nationalistic feelings!

For me life in Fort 17 at this time in comparison with the early days was becoming quite bearable. The Red Cross parcels weren't all that consistent—mind you some weeks went by without any at all and then we would have one parcel between four men but we managed to jog along. I was able to "engineer" a few things occasionally when I was on a local party (except the snow clearing party—you couldn't even engineer snowballs on that job!) But being occupied in entertainment gave me a great kick and fulfilled me a helluva lot. I enjoyed it tremendously. The p.o.w.'s seemed to like what they saw and in a way I felt that we, the members of the Concert Party, were all contributing to their well-being in this confined and unnatural existence.

I had been transferred to a local working party (mainly because a member of the Dance Band was in charge of it and I was heartily sick of the sight of snow!) doing various fatigues on the platform of the mainline Thorn station. Our main job on the railway was to transfer personal parcels intended for the Eastern Front, from a good's train onto one carrying the troops. One would've thought it would've been easier to hitch the whole wagon to the existing train but for some obscure reason this was not done. They took a chance because we were in the unique position of being able to sabotage the parcels, which on many occasions was taken advantage of. We had only one guard as overseer and he couldn't possibly be everywhere.

What the p.o.w.'s wanted most was tobacco and they seemed to be able to smell out those that contained the German weed. A parcel, usually a small one, would be deliberately broken and any tobacco taken out. Then the parcel, minus the tobacco, would be hidden at the bottom amongst the others to look as if it had been squashed by accident. If the damage was too obvious, the remnants of the parcel would be stuffed into one's battledress blouse and later shoved down the station lavatory.

The looting didn't go on every day, only when the time was propitious—if the guard was away with some other fatigue or just resting in the guardroom. (Actually a regular guard had been in charge of the working party for some considerable time and he was what was known as "a tame one".)

Another good thing about the party was that one had the opportunity to conduct "business" (or barter) with the Poles who were doing menial jobs in and around the platform etc….For instance—a small bar of chocolate was valued at half a dozen eggs, which was equivalent to 6 meals for the two of us. Soap was a great bartering agent (even the Jerries couldn't get it)—I got two pork chops for a bar on one occasion. A packet of real coffee was at a premium and was greatly sought after by the Poles (and by the Germans too!). I got 24 eggs for a packet of English coffee once. Tea went well too, but the p.o.w. was very fond of his cuppa, consequently it was hard to get hold of. We did find a way around it eventually. What we did was this. We would use the tea in the normal manner, save the leaves, dry them in the sun and then re-pack them and flog them to the Germans as brand new packets. Well, they prefer their tea weak on the continent!

But even after you'd concluded a successful deal the next step was to get the "Goods" past the *Unter Offizier* in charge of the guard at the Fort gates. Some were bastards, and searched everybody coming back through the gates and if you were unlucky your "deal" of the day might be found and confiscated, but after a while we got to know which *Unter Offizier* always searched us, in which case it was best not to risk it that day, and which one was easy and never searched. Then there were those who sometimes did and sometimes didn't—Well like the Customs, you just had to take a chance with them.

I found that a favourite place for eggs where they never looked was in my Polish forage cap. With a piece of cardboard shaped like the inside of the cap to flatten it, and 6 eggs underneath, it just raised the cap by about half an inch. I used it many times until one day one bastard *Unter Offizier*, suspecting me or maybe it was just by chance, slapped his hand on top of my cap causing the yolks to rivulet down my face giving the game away. He did have the grace to laugh, but I didn't. I cursed!

One evening, after roll call, C.S.M. Homer came in to the Concert Party room and announced that he had managed to get hold of a copy of "George and Margaret" by Gerald Savory, a highly successful play which was running in London. He suggested that it would be worthwhile considering it as our first "all stops out" (his quotation) production.

It was read by each member of the Concert Party and they all agreed it was an ideal choice. It was a domestic family comedy—had only one setting (the lounge)—with a small cast of eight. As it happened, we hadn't any choice. We had nothing else in mind, and we knew that Camp 13A were already rehearsing an Edgar Wallace play "The Case of the Frightened Lady" after having produced a highly successful pantomime, "Cinderella"—words and music all their own work! And there was an element of rivalry developing between us! In actual fact they were well ahead of us in every way, having a better equipped theatre, solid sets built by carpenters, excellent lighting and access to a good wardrobe due to their proximity to Stalag XXA Headquarters where nearly everything was available. And if it wasn't, they had the wherewithal to obtain it, namely Red Cross tins. Well, you know how easily these parcels break open accidentally—on purpose! I wouldn't say they were better actors (or actresses!). They had a boy called Frankie Coburn (from Rochdale) better known as "Phyllis". I ought to tell you that he was also "mentioned in dispatches" and was the possessor of a citation to prove it. He made good as an Air Hostess (I mean steward) after the war!

We were all agog, but there was a lot to be done. The hut we used as a theatre was being occupied by over 200 p.o.w.'s , and they would have to be rehoused. C.S.M. Homer approached the Germans to see if we could use the hut exclusively as a theatre and they gave their permission. An army of volunteers descended on the hut, repainted it inside and out, and within a week it began to take shape. A new stage was solidly built—where the wood came from I never knew; I expect Homer organised it.

He did a helluva lot of good work, unknown to others, although there were lots of people about who hated his guts and accused him of being pro-Nazi and all that crap!

An expert in lighting "Lofty" Martin (R.E.M.E.) was enlisted to re-organise the equipment (what equipment?—There wasn't *any* before he came on the scene!).

He got the footlights working properly (on a dimmer), fixed new house lights (had all the windows blacked out) and did a first rate job. Front curtains, suitably weighted were made out of blankets, and the floor was swept and disinfected and forms and chairs installed.

Each evening the cast religiously rehearsed, under the producer Ray Beal, and a Roneoed programme was typed out in preparation for the great day. Later, we were to have proper printed programmes, done for us by the local German printers in Thorn, but on this occasion we made do with the typewritten ones.

I was playing "Alice" the mother of the family and Vic Thompson played opposite me as my husband "Malcolm". We had to watch Vic as he was inclined to deviate from the script, as he did at one performance. A very tender scene was set closing Act 2 when he's talking to his daughter in front of the fire, reminiscing about his past life, wistfully, and the actual line reads: –

"Two years before I married your mother" and he goes into a long story about an affair he nearly had with another woman, but didn't, and when Tommo delivered his line he said "Two years before I *had* to marry your mother!" Stan Hobday, playing his daughter, with her head on his lap, nearly fell into the fire!

Other members of the company were "Pony" Moore (a submariner from Southend), Derek Lunn (excellent as "Dudley") and

Bert Little, from Ealing. He was tattooed all over and when stripped could so control his stomach muscles that it looked as if the ship tattooed there was sinking! And finally Jimmy Davies, a commercial artist in Civvy Street, who played "Beer" and C.S.M. Homer who played the boyfriend.

I had to have a dress made out of a sheet suitably dyed. Well, actually it was the covering from a Turkish mattress called a "Stepdeka". We had several thousands of these kapok-stuffed, one-inch thick mattresses sent to us from Turkey and they resembled thin eiderdowns covered with white sheets. I wore a wig made out of horsehair (it sweated up nervously every time I put it on—or was it me?) suitably woven and threaded with loving care and though I says it myself I looked like "Whistler's Mother's Head Groom" —hot from the stables!

Suits were made out of blankets—a battledress blouse made to look like a wind-cheater and a dyed army overcoat like a "Crombie". Actually the men in the cast were easy to cater for. It was the "women" who presented the problems—and there were four of us! In the end every obstacle was overcome. There were last minute scares of course. Make-up ordered hadn't turned up, but it did at the last minute. Bert Little, who was on a local working party, working late on loading something or other on the railway, was specially fetched by a guard, by permission of the Commandant! All the civilian gear had to be checked, listed and cleared by the Jerries and handed in immediately after the performance in case anyone decided to "take off" in it.

The German officers and Staff were invited and occupied the two front rows, with all the ceremony of visiting dignitaries. The band started with a roll of drums. Everybody, including the Jerries, stood up thinking they were going to play the forbidden National Anthem. Instead they went straight into "In the Mood"!

Backstage there was a slight feeling of panic. Everybody wished everyone else "Good luck", the curtains opened successfully and "Alice" made her entrance, checking her shopping list and at the same time checking that her home-made jockstrap was doing its job properly!

The show was voted a great success. One or two minor things had gone wrong but there was no great disaster like the lights failing or the stage collapsing. And although the majority of the Jerries didn't speak English, they applauded vigorously at the end.

We were asked to give several performances, of course, in order to accommodate all the p.o.w.'s (the theatre only held about 300), and then several outside working parties—radius 50 miles—were invited. Also Camp 13A, who came to see if there was any danger to their reputation of being the "best in the field"! An official German photographer took photographs of the show, ostensibly for personal records, but mainly for propaganda purposes! It ran every night for a week. Not wanting to rest on our laurels, we looked forward eagerly to the next presentation. Unfortunately, alas, it was to be the first and last full-scale production at Fort 17.

Not long after the last performance the Fort was closed down and all personnel transferred to Fort 13, or to Camp 13A, there to await being sent out on a new *Arbeits Kommando* (Working Party). The time was June, 1941.

131

CHAPTER 6
"Better Plead Guilty!"

June 1941. Like a battalion on the move, we evacuated from Fort 17. After a march of about four miles we arrived at Fort 13 which was a short distance up the road from camp 13A. Fort 13 was not unlike Fort 17 except that we had access on to the top of the fort where one could walk around and look out over the flat and heavily wooded country of Poland.

The moat which completely surrounded the Fort was drained entirely of water and was known as the Roll Call platz. Roll Call Parade actually took place in the drained moat.

Situated on the outside wall of the moat facing the Fort were four or five punishment cells or "bunkers" as the Germans called them— solitary confinement cells in which one day I was to find myself.

The Englishman responsible under the Germans was R.S.M. Seivers of the Royal West Kents, a kindly inoffensive man of the "old school" who never seemed to lose his temper, perhaps not quite so "full of beans" and vital as C.S.M. Homer but obviously efficient at his job in a much milder way.

Competitively speaking—Fort 13 lived in the shadow of camp 13A, where everything happened. 13A had an almost full size football pitch in the centre of the camp, which was in constant use every day, and it seemed as if every other p.o.w. was a Scotsman, or maybe the Scottish accent just seemed to predominate. There were quite a lot of

them there; like the Irish they get everywhere. And as one of them said to the guard

"Lang may your rum leek"—

"*Vas ist* leak?"

"Ye ken Scotch Whisky"

"*Jah, Jah "Viskey.'*"

"Whisky makes you frisky."

"*Visky frisky? Vas ist Visky frisky?*"

"Puts hair on your bollocks."

"*Bollocks? Vas ist bollocks?*"

"Ach run awa an' play wi' yerself, man, or we'll be here all bloody night!"

Fort 13 had no theatre of its own, but used the facilities of Camp 13A which, as I said before, were pretty good.

After the first two weeks of July 1941, at Fort 13, I was sent "on transport" or "*Arbeits Kommando*" to a brand-new working party, at a place called "Weiclestal"

Among my 300 companions were Micky Bain (Accordionist) and Danny Faulds (Drummer) from the Fort 17 Band and we "mucked-in" together, sharing everything—grub, that is!

The Camp, or "Weiclestal Lager" (these words were emblazoned on a wooden board above the heavily barbed wire gates) was about the size of a football pitch, and we were housed in wooden huts each with a stove and two-tiered bunkbeds. The huts lay alongside the double barbed wire posts which encircled the square (or squared the square!).

There were also four Guard's Towers or Observation Posts. They seemed at first to be quite a reasonable lot—not the Towers, the guards! Our job was to initiate building an autobahn (motor road) which would eventually link up Danzig with Berlin or as the Jerries kept saying *"Berlin mit Danzig".*

But first, the senior British N.C.O., a Sergeant, was appointed as Leader of the Camp and two of his cronies became his staff. A First Aid bloke, usually R.A.M.C., or *Sanitator* as the Jerries named him, was also appointed, plus two cooks and two fatigue men to work with them in the cookhouse.

The cooks had assistants, the assistants had assistants. There was no stopping them. They were all hard at it—cooking up something, for themselves no doubt!

Never mind, we were ready to go. When the 270 or so marched to work on the first day we were met by a gang of civilians consisting of the foreman or Chef (*Gummy Deutsch*, Rubber German), Polish, Polonais (in French). Polski (in German) or Polack (in Polish). We liked using the last one *Polack* because it got confused with Bollock!

A certain amount of early work had already been done by the experts. Strung out in the forest were lines of rope attached to stakes, like gardeners' guides, leaving a wide channel or lane in between. Everything in the channel or between the ropes had to be uprooted and carted away.

There were quite a few trees in the path of the road and they were pulled over quickly with ropes or sawed in half by a manual two-handed saw, leaving the stump to be attacked later.

Within three weeks a reasonable impression had been made. About 300 yards of basic earth roadway had emerged from our labours.

The rations were fair, good soup and one German issue loaf between three men, and we were dealing extensively with the Poles, organising white bread, meat and eggs. All these deals the Jerry guards saw but didn't seem to object to, although of course, they knew it was forbidden. Red Cross parcels continued to arrive at about one person per week, although occasionally they would be varied with what was known as "Argentine Bulk Issue". Everything came from the Argentine—large tins of butter, of stew, fine bacon and meatloaf, powdered milk and excellent coffee etc..

The Canadian Parcel issue of which we also had many, compared favourably with the Argentine and in the majority of p.o.w.'s views were superior to the British. So you can see how more contented the prisoners were getting. They were now starting to criticise the Food parcels! Six months earlier parcels of pamphlets were welcomed. Now they were making comparisons!

We erected a sort of outside stage in the centre of the field and on Sundays we gave a pot-pourri of entertainment, consisting of sketches (Tommo from Fort 17 was with us so we did "Little Nell") and Micky Bain and Danny Faulds organised the musical sing songs. In other words, an entertainment known as alfresco (brother of the Arabian juggler "Al beseeinya" in all the old familiar places!).

Cold water showers were fitted to the wash-house and a decent shower after working was a great luxury after months of nothing.

We were still faintly troubled with our old enemy the louse but as our physical condition improved and all my hair in every place got longer and stronger, I had the confidence to declare myself free from the blood-sucker's curse!

From my bed and after lights out I declaimed in Panto fashion:—

"And now that I am clean and free
A fresh-faced youth for all to see
With hair so dark—so lush—so bright
Who dares to sleep with me tonight?"

Chorus: I will – I will!
F.F.Y.: Then name your price.
Chorus: A box of fornicating lice!!
F F,Y.: On second thoughts I'll sleep alone,

And that means I'll be on my own!
Chorus: That means that you'll be on your Tod!
You tantalising, teasing sod!
F.F.Y.: Do you know what you can do tonight?
Chorus: What can I do for my delight?
F.F.Y.: Get knotted!

During the heat of the day, most of the p.o.w.'s stripped to the waist and acquired quite a splendid Polish tan.

Dynamite had been introduced to blow up the troublesome stumps of trees, and, although only knowledgeable civilians were first allowed to use it, it wasn't long before the p.o.w.'s were dynamiting as well with great zest, and not a little abandon! It was not uncommon to be warned after it had been touched off, and you fell straight on your face and put your hands over your head to save yourself from the inevitable shower of bark, roots and earth which rained out of the sky.

The German Commandant was a reasonable man—he had been active during the Polish and French campaigns, got wounded, and was the equivalent of a British Sergeant major, an *Ober Feldwebel* in their lingo. Unfortunately, after a short time, he was replaced by (you've guessed it) a proper "Bastard".

The new Commandant was not satisfied with one roll call a day, it had to be two—A.M & P.M.

He was to be saluted at all times by everybody. Well all right, but when he's inspecting the showers and you're soaping yourself? Where do you put the soap?

P.o.w. discs were to shine so bright that they would reflect the coming of their Lord and Master—the Commandant.

He started off by censoring every Red Cross Food parcel, having some miserable minion on fatigues open them for him, and then going through the contents looking for compasses and coded messages in Fry's Cocoa or Lyons Blue Label.

The p.o.w.'s protested strongly, especially when the parcels were dumped unceremoniously and some of the contents spilt. Tea and cocoa with bars of precious soap cut in half or mixed together was a bloody nuisance—and a disgrace!

After a week or two he received a wrap over the knuckles from Stalag XXA and this behaviour ceased. Prisoners could look for their own messages. And find their own compasses!

Occasionally he would come out on the job inspecting everyone's work as if the Fuehrer had personally assigned him. The *Polacks* (Poles) were naturally very wary of him, and were not their usual Polish friendly selves when he was around. He could get them 10 years for "insolent breathing" so you could hardly blame them.

To us he was a pain in the neck as well. I mean, he didn't stop the deals—it just took longer and we had to think of means of overcoming the search when we arrived back at the camp.

One evening there was a snap search and he made a great haul of white bread, eggs, meat and wine. He confiscated the lot.

The following day we thought of one way of eluding him but it could only be worked on one occasion. We had some pork chops and a bottle of wine to collect and the thing was how to get it past him at the gates, normally round about 6.30.

So—at 5 o'clock I collapsed as if I'd been poleaxed, over acting madly, moaning, and groaning, Micky Bain moved over to me a bit sharpish and then made off towards the camp, shouting *"Sanitator"* Out came the *Sanitator* carrying his stretcher and a blanket. A guard, luckily a bit of a ditherer, asked what was going on and Danny engaged him in conversation saying I was very sick and had a fever (all lies of course) and during all this Micky was putting the pork chops under me on the stretcher and slipping the red wine between my legs. The whole was covered with a blanket and I was carried in state through the camp gates, accompanied by the ditherer, with me still moaning like a banshee! The Commandant never even saw us coming back let alone searched us!

I stayed in the *Sanitator's* hut for about 10 minutes but Micky Bain took the spoils over to our hut, dumped them and then returned to the job to make it look authentic or less suspicious. The *Sanitator* was promised a chop for his sterling work, well he seldom got out, poor chop, I mean chap.

At roll call next morning, the Commandant read out the old instructions about punishable military offences, laying great emphasis on "social intercourse" with Poles, ending the tirade with *"streng verboten!"*

Unknown to him, of course, Thursday was our egg day. I had arranged with a Pole to bring in 18 eggs for three bars of chocolate this very day. And despite the warning from the commandant I carried on with my original "business" plans.

The Commandant also said that henceforth he had forbidden haversacks to be taken out on the job, knowing full well that they would likely be used to bring some "loot" in. So in order to obviate this I carried the three bars of Cadburys in the outside pocket of my battledress blouse, hoping to find a way to bring the hen fruit in, if only in the last resort as a "giant" omelette!

I was digging away legitimately at some tree stump when I spotted our new unpopular Commandant and four soldiers coming down the virgin highway searching jackets individually for contraband or bartering material. They were about 50 yards away. I half looked round and then bent down and quickly dug a hole in the earthy sand with my spade, bent down again on one knee and scooped the chocolate out of my blouse which was lying down beside the stump, dropped it into the hole and hastily covered the bars with sand and patted the top to flatten it out. I was just about to straighten up when I was kicked forward by a jackboot from behind. I sprawled over and turned around to see a German guard looking at me with his rifle at the ready as if about to shoot.

He scrabbled with his foot, kicking the sand away like a dog looking for his bone, and eventually the three bars came to light. I bent down to retrieve them, and the guard stamped his foot on my hand. He ordered me to hand them to him, which I did, slowly and reluctantly. We stood there, me blinking at him as if I'd just been captured again, and he, with his rifle in his hand, and the evidence in his other, calling out to his Commandant, who was now about 20 yards away. The *Unter Offizier* (I always fell foul of them!), along with his other barter searchers came towards us: –

"What have you got there?"

"Chokolade, Herr Unter Offizier," said the guard.

"What are you doing with this chocolate?"

"I brought it out to eat on the job" I said.

"Three bars?"

"Well, there are three of us altogether. I look after the food."

"Give me the chocolate" said the *Unter Offizier*.

The guard handed it to his superior, and I made a grab at it from the *Unter Offizier's* hand.

"That's mine" I said "You are not allowed..."

Before I could finish the sentence, I was hit on the back of the head by the guard's rifle butt and fell to the ground like an axed tree. Later I was marched back to camp and stayed there till I attended my Court-Martial Tribunal.

Whilst I waited I was ordered to do menial fatigue jobs in the camp. Cleaning the bogs—cutting the grass with a large pair of scissors—and unravelling Red Cross string.

Two days before the Tribunal I was permitted to see my Military Defence Counsel whose English was adequate—just.

"You are charged with contra-wention Article 6, relating to *Kriegsgefangenen* (p.o.w.'s) Military Law. Para.. Three." He listed my offences.

1. Deliberate disobedience of Commandant's Orders. Article 6. Para. 5. (Fair enough).
2. "Social Intercourse" with civilians namely Polacks in defiance of Commandant's warning. Contravening *Deutsche Wehrmacht* order.
3. Slovenly and lazy work on party. Unco-operative and undisciplined. (that was a new one on me). And finally, "The Clincher" :-
4. *Inciting Mutiny.*

He asked me to tell him what happened in my own words. (who else's?) Which I did.

"Guilty? Or not guilty." he enquired, taking notes.

"Not guilty." I replied.

"Better to say "guilty.""

"How could I be inciting mutiny with three bars of chocolate?"

"That is possible." But he didn't enlarge on it.

"What happens if I plead guilty?"

"Perhaps you get warning, or perhaps a short sentence in Graudenz." (Hard Labour Camp).

"And not guilty?"

"Anozzer new trial Tribunal. At Graudenz or Berlin and Prosecutor ask for heavy punishment at a Hard Labour Camp. Better to say guilty. It is only a minor offence."

"*Inciting mutiny* is only a minor offence?"

"Not like Treason, Murder, Sabotage or Rape. Except with Poles."

"I sleep with a Polish girl, it's not rape, but if I sleep with a German fräulein, it's rape—yes?"

"*Jah.*"

"Find me a Polish girl? It's worth three bars of chocolate!"

"*Bitte*?"

"I'll see you in two days time." I replied.

The day of the trial arrived, and I spruced myself up looking very spick and span and not at all mutinous. I was marched into the hut, which was laid out like a Court and came to a halt in front of the table, which was draped with the Nazi flag. I saluted the *Oberst* (Colonel) in charge of the court and stood to attention.

The charges were read out in German, and then in English by the Adjutant (another officer) sitting on the right of the Colonel and I was asked:

"How do you plead. Guilty or not guilty?"

"Not guilty, sir."

I caught my defence counsel's shake of his head and heavenwards look as if to say "obstinate fool".

The *Unter Offizier* was called and gave his highly coloured version of the events which neatly fitted all the charges. At the same time, he added additional touches about my being a malingerer, a malcontent, a non cooperative, being always last on roll call and in his opinion a bad influence in the hard-working camp. He particularly pointed out that when discovered with the chocolate, I had flown into a rage and was about to attack him and would've done if he'd not been saved by the vigilance and alertness of one of his guards.

Then it was my turn.

I gave my version, bent a little at the edges, but in the main fairly truthful.

It was perfectly true that I had taken three bars of chocolate on to the job, but only to eat not to barter with. If I had got the chocolate with me to pay for—say—nine eggs (I wasn't going to give them the official rate!) where was I going to put the eggs? The *Unter Offizier* had banned haversacks on the working party. If, on the other hand, assuming one had carried out a "transaction" what would be the point of hiding eggs about one's person when the *Unter Offizier* searched the working party assiduously as it came in and all contraband so found was confiscated.

Referring to the non-co-operation charge, I refuted this entirely. I admired the facilities of the camp, the showers, the beds, the working and food conditions. I enjoyed blowing up trees with dynamite, and here I had been given that opportunity. Witness the length of the autobahn we had cleared. Any "social intercourse" that I or any of my comrades could be accused of, could only appertain to the job with these road civilian experts. (Liar.)

The prosecution council then asked me "Have you ever given anything to Poles?"

"Well—individually, I've given them cigarettes to smoke just as one give cigarettes to anybody, even German guards, who smoke them."

Pros. Counsel: "I mean, have you traded tins of Red Cross food for gain?"

"Not here, exactly, sir. (Liar) At the last working party I was on I exchanged some coffee for some eggs and bread with a German civilian, but there was not much Red Cross food to exchange."

"Do you wish to alter your plea to "guilty"?"

"No, sir."

Defence Council then got up and more or less repeated the rigmarole I had trotted out the day he'd come to see me, adding the plea that I was an only son, was captured during the fierce fighting in Calais, was Irish, and therefore inclined to be hotheaded. (Only after standing in the sun and when you've been whacked on the bonce by a rifle butt!)

He asked me if I was sorry.

"About what?" Said I.

"About attacking the *Unter Offizier*."

"But I didn't—oh, if I gave the *impression* that I was going to attack him, then I'm sorry about that."

"And you will promise to be a model prisoner from now on?"

"Well, I'll do my best to keep out of trouble and knowing that German justice will always respect my rights as a prisoner of war according to the Geneva convention...."

I caught his well-known heavenwards look and stopped.

I was marched outside to wait while they cogitated or smoked, or had a word with a firing squad, and twenty minutes later they marched me in, and again I halted in front of the table, saluted and stood to attention.

The Adjutant stood up, cleared his throat and read out my name and p.o.w. number. He then paused dramatically before he carried on —"Under the powers laid down by the *Deutsch* Military Law, you have been found "Guilty" on the charge of "Inciting Mutiny" and you are hereby sentenced to 28 days of solitary confinement with bread and water in the punishment cells."

"Blimey!"

Early next morning, after collecting my goods and chattels, I said "goodbye" to the rest of the boys at Weiclestal and returned by train under escort to Stalag XXA. My kit was taken from me and put into store and I was led to the "bunker" or punishment cell in Fort 13 which was to be my fixed abode for the next four weeks.

It was very damp in the cell and there was no window, only a slit in the door to catch any light coming in. There was no electric light and no other means of illumination. A slatted bed board jutted out from the wall and there was a lavatorial bucket to satisfy my bodily functions. I was given one blanket and my faithful dixie. It was very, very cold at night, no doubt due to the position of the bunker, deep in the outer wall of the drained moat. I found it very difficult to sleep, constantly twisting and turning, and trying to get warm. Obviously, I didn't undress. I could hear quite a few rats scurrying about which didn't help matters, but as time went on, I got used to them. Almost directly opposite the cell was the lower entrance to the Fort lavatories, that is to say, the cement floor where the excrement and the urine fell and accumulated, and the smell and atmosphere were, to say the least, not conducive to healthy living.

On that first night, I dozed and woke up, and dozed and woke up, and eventually a single shaft of light appeared to denote the coming of morning. I could hear the sounds of activity as the prisoners went about their ablutions and early morning toilet. I had had nothing to eat or drink since midday on the previous day, so I got up and did a few exercises and then paced up and down the cell.

The walls of the cell were covered in pencilled names reminding me of a Leicester Square convenience, both Polish and British and dates and notes like "Love to Mum"— "Fish and Chips—"Thinking of you Always" signed "Wanker", uncomplimentary messages about certain warrant officers and finally one graphic "Double fuck the Fuehrer! And all who sail in him".

I added mine "Sam Kydd, almost slept here August, 1941."

Round about 10:30 a,m., I heard the plod-plod of the German guard's jackboots as he came slowly down the ramp from the drawbridge, and he finally arrived and opened the door. He seemed an affable type. "*Schlaffen gut?*" He said. "*Nein*" I replied "*nicht gut, Sehr kalt!*" "*Jah*" he said as if he'd felt the cold as well. He motioned for me to take the bucket, which I proceeded to do, taking it over to the nauseating opening of the bogs and emptying it. I had to be extremely careful as some fellows were occasionally relieving themselves, and I didn't exactly relish the "raindrops fallin' on my head".

It seemed that I was the only occupant of the bunker. At that time there were four or five other cells, but there was obviously nobody in them. The guard told me to march up and down for exercise, so I walked about 20 yards up the moat, turned and came back again, nodded to him, turned and did the same again.

I was allowed half an hour for exercise, and finally, the guard ushered me in, telling me that he would be back later with some bread. I played noughts and crosses with myself till I tired of it. I played a naval game called "Destroyers". I smoked a cigarette. I lay on the slatted boards which served as a bed. I thought about home, and wondered if they were alright. And wondered if they thought about me, and *I* thought about me. What a bloody place to end up in? I should have gone with the Jerries when they asked me to go with them to Paris. What a chance I missed. "Get registered first" Bob Wilson had said. I should've gone regardless. I wonder how long the war will go on? What'll happen if Germany wins? They won't win. If they do we'll never get home—that's for sure. We don't seem to be having much success, not at the moment anyway. Might be an idea to get myself a cushy working party like a farm, for instance, small group of blokes and become like one of the family. Or take off and make for Danzig and Sweden. Certainly not the other way, I didn't fancy the Russians. Maybe I'm basically a coward and just fancy the sweet life —like the one I was having now! I had met one or two blokes who had been prisoners in the Great War of 1914/18, and now they were prisoners again in this one. Christ, I couldn't have survived that or could I? They usually swapped their bread ration for five fags. They could do *without* bread. I don't think I could've survived that way. My musing thoughts came to an end as I heard footsteps approaching my cell door. The guard unlocked the door and the cell was flooded with light. He had a companion with him, another p.o.w. who was carrying my bread ration and a bucket containing some water. I said "Hello" and he said "Hello, Sammy. I hear you got 28 days. Don't worry, we'll look after you." He turned out to be one of the carpenters from Fort 17 who had helped to erect the stage. He put the bread on the bed and poured water into my dixie, and at the same time he palmed a bar of chocolate under my Dixie. Whether the guard saw it or not, he didn't demur, he must've been pretty cross eyed not to. However, Jimmy Ormerod, for that was his name, said "Don't worry about him, I give him the occasional fag to keep him sweet, it's when you take it for granted that he's a cunt that he objects, and then he can be a bit barbary."

"Thanks" I said.

"Tomorrow when you empty your bucket round about 10.30. hang about for a bit and we'll lower some grub for you, down one of the toilet pans, O.K.?"

"Yeah, O.K. Great. Thanks."

"See you tomorrow then."

The guard shut and locked the door and I had bread and water for the main course, followed by half a bar of chocolate for dessert.

As I lay munching my bread, I noticed two English names that appeared twice on different dates, mentioning that they had escaped twice and been recaptured and had spent their punishment time in the same cell. Both were in 1941. Jackie Chance and Peter Crosby were the two names and they were part of a coterie of about ten prisoners who were constantly escaping and harassing the Jerries, and so far they had all, inevitably, ended up in the bunkers at Fort 13.

There were two schools of thought amongst the prisoners concerning escapes. One school (quite correctly) considered it a right and duty to attempt to escape, and the other school considered it a nuisance and a burden that had to be borne.

For instance, of the attempted escapes that took place from Fort 13, I would say that only a third were properly organised and the sufferers unfortunately were always those who were left behind in the camp. Immediately after an escape, the Germans always reacted in typical Jerry fashion. Everybody was punished in niggling ways. Any privileges that had been won would be instantly withdrawn. If two blokes escaped from a local working party, and at the same time an entertainment had been created, rehearsed, and a helluva lot of effort put into the show, it would without any appeal be cancelled.

Getting civilian clothes, which became possible for the shows and was a great boon, in future would become impossible, at least until the Jerries relaxed their attitude of rigid discipline.

Walking from Fort 13 to Camp 13A without a guard was disallowed, and an official chit and guard would have to be obtained to interchange. Home comforts were cancelled out. Roll calls which under inclement weather conditions would be taken in the rooms, were strictly back to the moat, no matter what the weather. Mere trifles some people would say if the blokes got away, and I agree. But, in the main, after two or three days "shacking up" with some Polish women, they would be picked up and returned—sentenced—do their time and then return to the Fort. Too many were just joyride escapes.

Nobody was against authentic escapes but I would have thought that the best place to escape from would be from a working party out in the country, already halfway to Danzig which was the general route, a place to aim for, and thence to Sweden.

Later on quite a few blokes did make it from Stalag XXA (about 28 altogether) on what became known as a "Cooks Tour" Organisation, but more of that later. No doubt lots of fellows escaped on working parties because (a) they were fed up with the conditions of work (b) got bored and fed up anyway and (c) just fancied a woman, or a week out!

The following day everything went as planned and just after 10.30, when the guard came to let me out for exercise, I shot over to the bogs to empty my shit bucket. I emptied the contents and then put the bucket under a running tap, which was adjacent, and finally sprinkled some lime around, of which there was quite a pile lying there. Looking up, I could see the rows and rows of porcelain lavatory pans, as if they were the funnels of a ship, and down one nearest to me, dangled a small sack, like a Xmas stocking, attached to a piece of string. I pulled gently, and the string fell into my hands. Then I put the sack into my blouse and carted the bucket back to my cell. The guard, unconcerned, had wandered a little way away from the door but he didn't stop me even if he suspected or knew what I'd been up to. I put the sack under the blanket and came out again to exercise for the rest of the half hour.

Exercise over, I returned to my kennel like a good dog, and immediately after the door was shut got to work on my tin of dog food —in this case a tin of pilchards in tomato sauce. I had two of the fish for delayed breakfast and saved the rest for my late afternoon bread and water tea. Also in the parcel was a tin of meat loaf, some Jerry biscuits that looked like Bob Martin dog biscuits—they were just as hard—and a tin of Lingfo cocoa which was a concoction of pre-sweetened cocoa and powdered milk all mixed together. For lighting purposes they had included a small nightlight made out of ersatz fat which had been melted down and hardened again, with a piece of pyjama cord inserted to serve as a wick. When lit it spluttered as if apologising for the frail light. But it certainly worked!

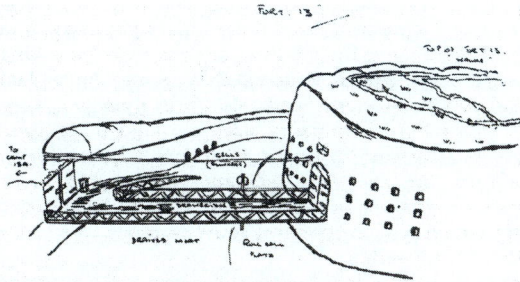

The same procedure followed faithfully day after day until the end of my bunker sentence, except for the days when the "shit cart" came—in all, about three times.

One day I heard the rambling wheels of a cart trundling down the ramp, and the unmistakable tones of the Polish driver shouting "*Zuruck*" (Woa—get back) and "*Brrrrr*" (Giddap) to the emaciated, long-suffering horse as he manoeuvred it round to its best advantage —to get at the crap, that is! For it was the "shit cart" —a long cylindrical metal contraption (rather like a shrunken petrol lorry container) and in charge was this dour and taciturn Pole known coyly as "*Herr Crapmeister*".

He wore a constant "screwed up phew!" expression as if to say "I *must* get another job, I *must* get another job" but he never did. All the time I was at Fort 13 he turned up regularly!

I did get a few words out of him, at a distance, and found out that he went round all the Forts, performing the same ritual, day after day, week after week, and month after month.

He collected the shit by means of a bucket-shaped scoop, which he laboriously lifted into the container, and then departed taking it to various farms in the surrounding districts (where it was in great demand), and unloaded, and spread fertiliser-fashion over the Polish fields. According to him, we were top of the shit parade! I never found out who paid whom for the privilege, but it was obviously profitable to someone. How true it was I don't know, but I did hear of a p.o.w. officer who stowed away in a shitcart in an escape attempt but after getting in through the evil smelling aperture was overcome by the fumes and had to give up. What guts! Even to try it!

The stench from the disturbed shit was even more horrific and the guard—understandably—almost refused to let me out whilst it was there, not from any regard for my health, he just couldn't stand the "pong".

He kept spitting and saying *"Ach– Shisen!" "Mein, Lieber Gott!"* and we went about 50 yards upwind, for my exercise period.

When we returned, the Crapmeister was still hard at it and the guard looked at him—and shouted *"Los! Los! Du—Shiser du!"*

The Pole looked at him witheringly, and pityingly, as if to say

"Look Freund, where there's 'muck' there's marks or where there's shit there's zlotys!" He certainly had the market for manure in his pocket! There was absolutely no competition! Where there's muck there's brass!

In the afternoon the guard let Jimmy Ormerod come down on his own with my rations, whilst he loitered on the drawbridge. Jim had brought my daily parcel hidden in his blouse, and some books. Not that the guard would've made any comment, he never did, and he was fully aware that something was going on.

About three days before the completion of my 28 days I received a visit from the German doctor (Medical Officer Stapbartz) and was examined for any signs of disease or malnutrition due to my confinement. He asked me if I'd lost weight (I had) but as I had no means of weighing myself, I couldn't tell him exactly. I told him I thought I had. He made notes in a little notebook but didn't confide in me what he had found or not found.

However when I told Ormerod of his visit, he explained it was the normal procedure, and an examination by an English Doctor would follow. Then, probably after two or three days in the sick bay for observation, I would be marked fit and ready for *arbeit*. I was counting the days on my home-made calendar because the isolation and awful conditions were beginning to get me down. In any case, if it hadn't been for the boys looking after me so generously, I would've emerged from the bunker looking skinnier than the "Crapmeister" and his horse put together and probably in a worse mental state.

Having done my time, as they say, I collected my gear and was taken to the sickbay in Fort 13, where I was told to undress and my weight and height recorded. (My height? Had I shrunk too?)

I was then told to have a bath before going to bed which I pleasurably and languidly took and finally sated with luxury slipped between the sheets (acknowledgements Red Cross) like a young bride awaiting her Lord and Burgomeister.

And before long, in the shape of Captain Bob Moody, a lanky New Zealander from Dunedin, he turned up. Moody seemed to possess the secret of eternal youth, he was more like a young student than a doctor, and was certainly a most pleasant man to have around. He told me that due to my condition (condition? Perhaps I was more unwell than I thought — I ultimately discovered that I had TB) he would recommend making me (or marking me down as) a permanent indoor worker, doing only light fatigue work, and this of course, being subject to the German Doctor's confirmation which, apparently, was never unreasonably withheld.

The staff of the sick bay, all English R.A.M.C., were a civilised lot and they certainly had things organised for the benefit of the troops. The really serious sick were taken to Fort 14—the Hospital camp where the facilities were superior, but the Revier (German) as it was called, dealt with day-to-day injuries, like flu, infections and the walking wounded, so to speak.

I found it a bit like a club—you could always get a cup of tea and have a chat. Plenty of good books to read. Special meals or diets were cooked, for which the Red Cross were again to be thanked. They despatched also, in addition to the normal food parcels, thousands of invalid parcels destined only for sickbays in p.o.w. territory. These contained a mixture of medical supplies and Bovril and other medicants guaranteed to make a p.o.w.'s mouth water—a sick one, of course. At Fort 13 were two Doctors to tend to the halt and the lame, and two Padres to preach the religious game. It seemed a good set up and I was becoming part of it.

For unknown to me, the plan of keeping me available in the Fort was (in addition to looking after my welfare) to make sure that I was not sent away again, so that I could play a more consistent part in the

Fort entertainment activities! When I heard about it later, I couldn't believe my luck. Although the majority of the old Fort 17 enthusiasts had been sent away, one or two were still around, including Pip Howe, Derek Lunn, Stan Hobday, and Ray Beal (the producer).

After four weeks "solitary" the dark clouds had rolled away, and here I was having already savoured a bath, wearing pyjamas, sleeping between sheets, enjoying cups of tea on tap, and dallying in bed—plus four Red Cross Food parcels. Oh death where is thy sting? What more could a man want? Freedom? Sex? For the time being I would settle for this!

After a week or so I was moved into a room earmarked for the Concert Party.

The majority of the fellows were new to me but it wasn't long before we were on Christian name terms.

In room 6 at that time were, Basil Sweet—a Sergeant from London with a ready wit. George Tyler, a K.R.R.C. man who when dressed as a girl made you look twice! Norman Freebury an old Q.V.R., Richard Davies, the sax and cello player from Bournemouth, Jimmy Woolcock, from Barry, a very fine cartoonist and German passport faker second to none, and Jimmy Davies the commercial artist who had been with us at Fort 17. Also Stan Hobday, Bere Cranston, Pony Moore, Jack Goyder, Ray Beal, Derek Lunn, Pip Howe, and my old "mucker" Knocker Noake.

When I joined them most of them were in the throes of rehearsing for a show called "It Pays to Advertise" and the leading players were Basil Sweet, George Tyler, M.D. Lyons and Pat Delaney, the last two being R.S.M.'s.

The play was to be staged at Camp 13A in late October, and I volunteered to be a member of the Stage Staff, helping with the sets and selling programs etc..

It was a successful show, with Basil Sweet outstanding, and ran for a week to accommodate the other Forts and outside working parties who were conveyed and convoyed in lorries.

The next venture was to be the "Pantomime,"—which was yet to be written and at the latest (apart from set designs etc.), should go into rehearsal a month or so before Christmas. A writing team of five writers was suggested, and they included Basil Sweet, Stan Hobday, Derek Lunn, Norman Freebury, and myself.

We called ourselves, optimistically, "Gags Unlimited!" And set to work. This time, the production would be in Fort 13 in a newly converted assembly room, next door to the library, now named "The Little Theatre". Because of its size, it would only hold 250 which would mean giving more than a fortnight's performances, but it had to be there, mainly because Camp 13A needed their stage for themselves.

We met regularly at night in the fort 13 Company office from 9 o'clock onwards, usually till two or 3 a.m. and gradually the show evolved. When the ideas crackled along it could be fun, but when we came to a full stop, which happened frequently, everybody got tired and irritable, and that was the time to give up. We were stimulated, of course, by numerous cups of tea, but they at times failed to kindle the flames of ideas, sequences and dialogue. However we struggled manfully on and the show gradually began to take shape. It was to be called "Pantomania" and was a conglomerate of all the Pantos that had ever been. There were about 30 musical numbers, (most very short) some original, but mostly old favourites, rhyming couplets, dances and choreographical pieces. The opening scene, in front of the curtains, had Jack and Jill coming home from a late night party on Christmas Eve.

Outside Harrods they bump into Father Christmas, hot from his last minute rounds for Xmas. Some funny dialogue showing disbelief on their part and he transports them away—cue for music of "Somewhere over the Rainbow" very quietly played—curtains open slowly revealing secondary curtain made out of thin gauze (from Sick Bay plaster bandages), 15 seconds of blackout to allow for flashes, explosions, demoniacal laughter. Then orchestra rises to crescendo assisted by chorus, and finally stops—to show that we have arrived in "Pantoland" (Lights Up) and to prove it we have on stage the Seven Dwarves (from Snow White and the Seven!).

Jack and Jill were left on stage with the seven puppet dwarves. Puppet in body size but with heads of p.o.w.'s as "Dopey", "Sneezy", "Grumpy" etc.. They go into their 20 minute act of dialogue, gags and finally "Hi Ho—Hi Ho it's off to work we go". Knocker Noake looking very virginal in a gauze diaphanous outfit makes a short appearance as Snow White him/herself.

As the dwarves exit right they are followed on stage left by Ali Baba and his mate Aladdin dressed (Aladdin that is—and me that was) in navy blue dyed pyjamas, with Eastern hieroglyphics and Chinese Dragons painted in yellow paint on the jacket. They are arguing about something (it changed from night to night—usually something derogatory about our hosts!) When "Ali" suddenly says: "You've done it again. You've left your lamp behind. Your genie is going to hate you."

Aladdin answers: "Have no fear oh Ali dear
Wher'ere I go my lamp is near
Just hang about and you will see
The friendship of my lamp—and
Me!!'"

He claps his hands and says:
"Oh Genie—Gene my handsome pal
You're needed by your lovely Al!
(Come in on a wing and a prayer!)"

Lamp, lit by own small battery and bulb, seemingly floats through the air till it finally arrives in Aladdin's hands. This cute trick was achieved by simply wrapping a strong piece of cotton thread around my index finger just before I went on, and at the other end, Jack Goyder was poised standing on a ladder off-stage, ready to send the lamp off in motion on the cue. Sometimes it stuck halfway, which called for a good deal of ad-libbing, but when it worked first time and floated through the air, it was most effective. I then sang a number appropriately called "Confucius, he say..."

"Very long time ago a sage man say
Lots of things that still look good today.
Confucius say—a boy a girl—hooray
Make wedding bells ringing in month of May." And so on
This was followed by a cod Chinese dance for half a chorus, ending on final singing of chorus. Lamp, which had been left lying on stage during dance seemingly floats up and follows me off. (Same

trick—Goyder lets out thread during dance and then reels in and lifts up on ladder and lamp seemingly floats up into air and slides along cotton thread into wings to be collected by Aladdin (me) who pops his head round wings to show audience it has arrived!)

Widow Twankey and the Ugly Sisters were then introduced, followed by Robinson Crusoe and his man Friday and we were almost at the end of the first act, which, with everybody on stage, ended on a sentimental and dramatic note. After some interchanged, appropriate dialogue, Jack (of Jack and Jill), launches into the "John of Gaunt" speech from Shakespeare's Richard 11.

"This Sceptred Isle….bound by a silver sea... This England" and in the background was heard the strains of (at first very quietly) "There'll always be an England... And England shall be free, if England means as much to you as England means to me!"

The chorus was taken up and swelled into a tremendous climax in that little Theatre. The cast no less affected than the audience gave it everything and sang their hearts out and were joined by the emotionally hooked and lapping-it-up audience. I'll never forget seeing so many grown-up men standing there with tears streaming down their cheeks! It was a magic moment. They stood up like Believers at a Revivalist meeting shouting "Encore!! Encore!"

I know being English, Irish, Scottish, Welsh or whatever the hell these islands consist of—we are supposed to hide our emotions, and in fact have that stiff upper lip reputation but it was not so at this very moment in the pantomime.

The well of suffering, humiliation, and frustration and loss of pride that everyone had experienced since capture was thrust behind them culminating in this "tear-letting" public emotion. Faith in themselves and in all things British had been restored. The floodgates were open.

If some fool had stood up and announced that we were going to take over the Jerry guardhouse at that moment, they would have roared back "Yes!" "Yes!" "Now! Now!" At such moments are Victoria crosses earned. As it was, as the curtains closed they settled for a standing ovation!

We realised of course that in a way we had made a mistake. We couldn't possibly top that ending in the second half, the set up was different and wouldn't allow it, so we had to leave it as it was. We were a bit awestruck and taken aback when it first happened, but after the first night, we blatantly traded on it and were not a little disappointed if we didn't reach the same state for each performance. Ah, well that's Show Business!

The Pantomime which was easily more than two hours in length ran for just over a fortnight and was seen by quite a few Jerries and over 5,000 prisoners.

Christmas came and went through this period but we managed to have a communal spread with everyone contributing and toasting each other in beer and some German wine that we got hold of. Most of the speeches with the same—".... let's hope that this time next year we'll all be well away from the Fort—the Fuehrer and his fucking Fatherland, reunited with our own kith and kin…" etc. That was 1941.

It had been on the cards before, apparently, but at a committee meeting shortly after the pantomime production, it was decided and agreed upon that the theatre should be pulled apart and rebuilt and redecorated with the stage at the opposite end, which would give not only more room, but easier access from an actual large dressing room. (Before it was only a curtained off recess in the corner of the library.)

A pit was to be dug for the Orchestra, the floor sloped, and permanent seating installed to give better vision. Having agreed upon it and after the "Dark Company" production—the attack was launched, and the Little Theatre became no more to make way for the greatly improved "Top Hat" Theatre. All the people devoted to the cause took part—carpenters, labourers, actors, designers, and anybody who just wanted to lend a hand. The pulling apart took no time at all; it was all the building up, refurbishing, and wanting everything to be just right that seemed so long. In all, it took about six weeks or more to do the job properly, and a helluva good one it turned out. It didn't actually hold more, well, maybe about 10 or 12 more. (We were limited by the length of the tunnel.) The biggest advantage I would say, was the sinking of the orchestra pit, about three or four foot deep and 16 feet wide—clawed out of the concrete with picks and shovels and bare hands. The theatre really was something of an achievement and my affection for it grew over the years that I knew it. It was my lifeline to sanity—my haven, my hobby, and my lover! Just consider the amount of entertainment that went through that theatre in various guises—for instance, there were not only ordinary shows with music, etc, but also light orchestral concerts (thanks to Rodney Bashford and Bob Hilling), Dance Band sessions, Variety Shows, Poetry Readings, Drama, Thrillers, Farce. All of the "Aldwych Farces" were done— "Cuckoo in the Nest", "Turkey time" "Rockery Nook", "Thark". It was a permanent part of possibly 5,000 to 6,000 men's lives and as for me I just revelled in it. I suppose you could call it my first real "affair" with the Theatre. I loved the preparation, the rehearsals, the setbacks and the way it kept me occupied. The opening night, if a success, gave pleasure to the audiences and set up a strong feeling of communication. I know they were a "captive" audience, but I would say that among all the p.o.w.'s, who never under any circumstances, went to the theatre in civvy street, many developed an appreciation, and in time a super hypocritical appreciation, formed and initiated through our prancing and singing on the stage. I'm not saying it sharpened their intellect in *any* way. We didn't set out to do this; well, I didn't—the object was to entertain, and to my way of thinking the enforced confined conditions of captivity demanded some light relief, hence, my constant plugging for Comedy shows.

In the meantime, during the completion of the "Top Hat" theatre, it was decided to undertake a combined 13A and Fort 13 Variety Bill, each supplying half the programme. The high spot or climax or *piece de resistance* was to be the combined orchestras playing together some known patriotic piece. They chose Eric Coates' "Knightsbridge Suite" and they played it wonderfully and awe-inspiringly!

I, with Topper Brown from 13A, was asked to compère the Fort 13 contribution whilst he looked after the Camp's offering. Bill Thompson, a dour de-hydrated but amusing Scot from Edinburgh (a brilliant pianist) masterminded the combined orchestras under, of course, the leadership of Bob Hilling, K.R.R.C. My personal involvement consisted of four or five acts, kicking off with two pianists and a drummer—George Parry, Bill Emery and Les Bryan. I remember Derek Lunn and Stan Hobday as "Freda & Freddie" an "Old Charwoman" sketch featuring Norman Freebury and Ben Lyon, and odd blackout sketches. I also combined with a close harmony group which sang with the 13A Dance Section of the band, and did "Hey Little Hen" and another "Easter Egg Hen" song (it was round about that time) and then I told a few gags before introducing the next item. Finally, I appeared in a sketch called "The Green Eye of the Little Yellow God", an old and well-tried comedy routine that I had seen on many occasions at the Shepherd's Bush Empire, in London. Briefly, the compère would come out to announce the next item and then be interrupted by someone from the audience:

Compère : "Can I help you, sir?"

Interrupter: "Well, I would like to make my contribution to the success of this show, but I'm no good without some help."

Compère: "Oh, perhaps I can be of assistance."

By this time the interrupter has come up on the stage. He pretends to be very shy and says "Well, it's like this. I would like to perform this poem but I'm no good at synchronising the actions and I don't know what to do with my hands. So if you could help me in some way I should be very grateful. The poem is called "The Green Eye of the Little Yellow God" but I can't co-ordinate the actions. Now if you stand behind me and I'll put my arms around behind you and you put your arms under where mine would be suiting the actions to the words, we'll be alright. O.K.?"

He then went into the long poem about "Dangerous Dan McGrew" from Kathmandu. A product of the Rudyard Kipling jingoistic period, and very good it was too. Anyway, Maxie Maxwell, as he was known, played the interrupter. He was an R.A.M.C. sanitator who in Civvy Street had been an attendant at Epsom Mental Hospital and behaved in prison camp exactly as one would have expected a mental patient to behave! The beauty of it was he invariably got away with it. We had rehearsed the act of course, but I had one or two surprises in store for Maxi and the audience. When he said: "He returned before the dawn with his shirt and tunic torn—And a gash (!) across his forehead, dripping red!" I ripped his shirt for the "tunic torn" line (to which Max reacted beautifully, muttering implications, not in the script about my over-enthusiasm). Then he tried again... "He returned before the dawn with his shirt and tunic torn"... This time I pulled the shirt right out of his trousers, but he continued... "And a GASH! across his forehead...." On the word " Gash" across his forehead I slipped two eggs which I had concealed in my right hand pocket into my hand and crashed them onto his forehead.

It couldn't have worked better and he carried it off swingingly. The two yolks and whites of the eggs literally coursed down his face as if on a roadmap and a long dribble hung down from his nose for about 15 seconds and as he swung his head gently from side to side so the dribble swung in time! I thought the audience would never stop laughing. I couldn't actually see all that was going on (being behind him of course) but I heard about it immediately the act was over.

Maxie had come to us via Fort 15 which was now becoming a Non-Working (N.C.O.'S) camp, mostly full of Aussies and New Zealanders captured in Greece. The Officers had long since been moved onto Officers' Lagers, but somehow Maxi, complete with trombone, which he played adequately, arrived at Fort13. He gave us a lot of laughs and I immediately took to him and he to me—which is another way of saying we got on well together.

The Germans were completely at sea with Maxie. They thought he was a nutcase, an amusing but always impeccably correct nutcase. Consequently, he got away with murder. Soon after the arrival of a very high up German *Oberst* (Colonel) and his entourage from Berlin to inspect Fort 13, when they were walking across the drawbridge in the usual military fashion, with the sycophants heiling Hitler and bowing and scraping, there was a commotion at the Fort gates and who should dash out but our friend Maxie. He clicked his heels in exaggerated fashion, made the "Heil Hitler" salute, put his trombone to his mouth and proceeded to play "Colonel Bogy" much to the amusement of the British and the bewilderment of the Germans. They saluted and walked hesitantly on while Maxi carried on until the bitter end.

He—Maxie—looked like a constantly surprised Harpo Marx, with vivid red hair, and had his own brand of amusing goonish language , one of his favourite expressions being "Oh Brax and Daybos take it, if they're not interested in my hassens and coosens they can lump it." To which inevitably the listener would say "What was that?" And Maxie's reply always was "Oh, well if you're not interested in what I'm saying I'm certainly not going to repeat it!"

On another occasion when the Gestapo made a surprise raid searching the Fort for a radio (which we had) Maxie donned a white coat to do his Surgeon act, complete with mask over his mouth, and when the men from the Gestapo knocked on the door of his room adjacent to the sick bay, Max appeared with a notice in his hand which read: "Entrance Forbidden—Fever Contamination. Highly Infectious." It only needed Maxie to add in his best sepulchral voice bordering on the lunatic "Positively No Entrance Black Fever. Death. *Nein. Eintritt Verboten*—Nix allowed." He gave the Nazi salute, and they hurried away. Needless to say that's where the radio was hidden.

I was still pursuing my indoor worker routine, which meant that I certainly didn't overwork, and didn't get up too early, but if bread or swedes or potatoes needed to be unloaded, I was one of the gang always around to help. In addition, the indoor workers helped to unload the Red Cross Food Parcels which were now in full flow, that is, one parcel per week per man, by far our most important item.

By now—1942—the German supremacy was very slightly on the skids and continued to slide downwards until the end. I mean, of course the attitude between prisoner and German soldier.

Things were getting tougher for the Jerry and easier for the *Gefrangenen*. All down to the Red Cross. Barter. Food. We were not so completely dependent on the Jerries. There were occasions when we didn't even bother to collect the German soup, but demanded our rightful ration of potatoes in lieu of (usually most of them were rotten but you could salvage three or four) in order to make a few chips for a meal of egg, bacon, and chips.

During my solitary sojourn in the bunker I had read "The Scarlet Pimpernel" by Baroness Orczy and suggested, along with Basil Sweet, that it might make a good musical. It was looked at by Derek Lunn and Bere Cranston and Ray Beal and it was agreed that it would fit the bill. Consequently it came about that Sweet, Lunn, Bere Cranston and myself (Plus Dave Hawley, a newly recruited enthusiastic member who at that time was coming up to be the new editor of the Stalag magazine "Prisoners Pie") took it on ourselves to make the adaptation and the usual late night procedure ensued. Actually, it was written in less time than previous shows, and Norman Freebury had the best part as "Chauvelin" which he later demonstrated in the show! There were no original lyrics, no specially written numbers, but there were 14 musical items and the high spot in Act 3 was where "Chauvelin" was guillotined, which was very craftily and effectively done.

Prior to production, I was rushing along the corridors one day and, taking a corner faster than I should, I keeled over on my right ankle and fractured it. I was immediately hauled off to sick bay and a fracture having been confirmed, my leg and ankle were instantly enclosed in a plaster cast. That, or so it seemed, put me out of the running for the "Scarlet Pimpernel" in which I was to play "Claude Foulkes" a silly-ass type, so Jimmie Davies, our scenic artist for the show, very nobly stepped into the breach and rehearsed my part. However as the show was still five or six weeks off, anything could happen—and did. Jimmie had obviously taken on much more than he could cope with, what with the various sets and the rehearsing, and two weeks before the show he developed a very heavy cold and croaked his way around, and in the end I took over and hopped about on my plaster cast!

On the second night the Germans refused to allow the show to be performed! The reason? Baroness Orczy was apparently on the list of banned (censored) authors, she was Jewish and even worse a Jewish "Revolutionary" and anything appertaining or referring to her was "out!" Or more appropriately "Not on!".

We renamed the show "The White Daisy", removed the author's name from the original posters and programmes and after a couple of nights the show was on again. (In view of the fact that several copies of "The Scarlet Pimpernel" in book form had obviously slipped through and were circulating in the camps some of the censors were at fault somewhere!) Mind you the same reverent tones came a little amiss when in place of "The Scarlet Pimpernel" (bated breath) one had to say "The White Daisy." It's not the same is it?

"They seek him here
They seek him there.
Those Frenches seek him everywhere.
Is he in Heaven or
Is he in Hell?
That Demned Elusive, White Daisy *fell*-ow!!"
(It's not the same, is it?)

The guillotine scene, which I mentioned earlier was a very effective one, and was created by Stan Willgoss, George Tyler and Gordon Butler.

Right in the middle—centre stage—there was our guillotine perfect in every detail and the Executioner (George Tyler) showed an unmistakable likeness to the Hunchback of Notre Dame!

Prior to the beginning of the show a complete plaster cast of Norman Freebury's head as "Chauvelin" was taken (It meant wrapping his head completely in wetted plaster bandages, leaving a small slit for him to breathe through, and then moulding the plaster into the nooks and crannies of his eyes and nostrils finally producing, after make up, an awesome looking replica) and in the final act, when Chauvelin gets pushed on to the Guillotine—the blade falls and with a mighty whoop the dripping head—spotlighted of course (red ochre paint as blood)— was raised by the hair by George amid great cheers. Very macabre and very effective.

CHAPTER 7
Un-Finnished Censor Business

The mail situation by now was falling into a regular pattern—some letters from England only took three weeks to get to Poland, but others took two months, due, I think to the dilatory way the censors behaved —holding onto them longer than necessary. On the whole, however, the mail route seemed to be well established.

The same applied to private parcels. Clothing parcels arrived with fair regularity adding to the pool of bartering chocolate. Book parcels were at a bit of a standstill, mainly due to a hold-up in the censoring. Too many books and not enough censors. We were always very interested in the arrival of books, mainly from the "plays" point of view. Up to now most of the plays we had been sent did not measure up to our requirements. Well, not to mine. Mind you, I wasn't the final arbiter, it was a committee's job to veto or say yes, whether we did a play or not and although there was a place for a thriller I went completely overboard for Comedy. It was what I liked doing best, and what I thought I was best at, and in addition because of our conditions I thought we had enough drama in our lives, and what the boys wanted was laughs. The next play scheduled was ironically enough entitled "Happy Days" and although I was in it I had not had much to do with its production.

There were really two book departments at Stalag H.Q., one for General and Public library use, mainly educational and reference (sent mostly by the Red Cross) and private books (fiction) sent by relatives or friends for private consumption.

Sometime after the "Scarlet Pimpernel" alias "The White Daisy" I received a note asking me to go down to Camp 13A to see "Tiffy" Chase, which I did. He was in charge of the private (personal) books department, and he asked me if I would like to come and join him and Smudger Smith in working in the department. They needed another man to deal with the backlog of books which had been held up because they were rapidly being snowed under. I accepted, of course, and then took steps to have my name taken off the indoor workers list and transferred to local work, which indeed it was.

Being a Stalag worker meant that I only had to travel about half a mile from the Fort or Camp.

Came the time when I paraded and marched down to Camp 13A to join the bulk of the Stalag Workers, as they were known and I had now become what was considered a member of the "Elite".

Anybody who worked at Stalag was given this label, and in some ways I suppose it was true. I think it stemmed mainly from the early days when things were in very short supply, and the Stalag workers had this air of never being short of anything, and they always looked cleaner and sharper and fatter and slightly superior. Which indeed they were, being on the spot where everything was happening. After all, it was the hub of the German war machine as far as p.o.w.'s were concerned and you got to know what was going on. There were always unkind rumours about Red Cross Food Parcels being broken up deliberately to accommodate the "special" workers. It was not true, of course, but nowhere is more susceptible to wide misinterpretation than a p.o.w. receiving depot for Red Cross Food fostered no doubt by those twin sisters (or should I say brothers?) Messrs Envy and Jealousy, whom we all know so well.

I looked in vain for the high living when I got there; in fact I even had to bring a quarter pound of tea for the early "elevenses" and "three-thirties". So much for the broken parcels!

Our office was a tiny one off the main entrance corridor in the three-floored Stalag building, and adjoined the German Censors Room which was a very large room indeed, about the size of a decent ball room or huge conference room. Prisoners were not allowed in—well only occasionally to collect and return books, but they were closely watched. What they were going to do I can't think—pass messages in code to England? What about? Everybody at home knew where we were, well they should have done with all the references to Poe-land not far from Uncle Joe—(Stalin) Hot in the summer—Snow in the Winter—coming from Siberia! Some of the letters we got from home were a bit disconcerting too; the British Censors had a peculiar sense of humour, for example one letter read out in the room went:

"Dear George,

"… I had just got into bed when the…. And when it was over, I went into the kitchen…… and that's the sort of thing George would have said……and I had to borrow next door's…. " It became a game trying to fill in the blanks, it was probably an air raid that took place but censored carelessly and out of context it could be anything!

Unfortunately as the months went on there were quite a few tragedies conveyed via letter, mostly about wives' infidelities, either from the soldiers mother or friends or in lots of cases from the wives themselves who had been to a dance, got drunk and been seduced and were now pregnant. Well, that was the usual story. Then there were others who had quite genuinely fallen in love with some other fellow and were asking to be released from the bonds of matrimony. Some fellows were terribly cut up, but others just seemed to pass it off. I knew of one p.o.w. whose wife had given birth to a child, ironically by a member of the Polish Free Corps, and she wrote to the p.o.w. and confessed all about it, asking for his forgiveness. At first, he was torn apart and wanted to institute divorce proceedings through the appropriate channels, but after a while he relented and cancelled the application. Blow me, a couple of years later, the same thing happened, and again he was a father without any of the fun. This time he just shrugged his shoulders resignedly, and said "it's no good, I love her. Anyway at least this time the father's British instead of a bloody Pole!" He, himself, wasn't doing too badly with a little Polish girl in the German barracks!

Of course we had to be allowed into the Censor's room in order to collect the books that had been censored. Occasionally the wrapping paper got lost or mixed or mislaid and the right person would get the wrong books and the wrong person would get no books at all—not even a label! Towards the end of the Censor's room was another large room, manned completely by British p.o.w.'s who were responsible for sorting and re-addressing letters to their rightful recipients.

Also situated at Stalag were the offices of what was known as "The Man of Confidence" or in German the "*Vertrauensman*" a sort of British ombudsman to whom all complaints were submitted by both the Germans and the British. Mainly, of course, the British. In our case this position of immense trust and power was held by Colour Sergeant Grainger, an old Queen Victoria Rifleman. Not that he favoured us, the other Queen Vics—on the contrary he bent over backwards and went out of his way to prove that he didn't.

"Tiffy" Chase, my immediate superior in charge of the Book Dept., was quite a character. He was in the Royal Army Ordnance Corps and was about 6 feet 4 inches in height and well proportioned with it. He was very enthusiastic about photography and possessed a camera to prove it! He like to associate with the Theatrical set, and that was probably one of the reasons why he asked me to join them.

"Smudger Smith" his ally, compatriot and fellow worker came from Birmingham, and as far as I could see did most of the work. He was very conscientious, hard-working, and a very fair footballer.

The job consisted mainly of collecting the books from the centres, making sure that the wrappers were the right ones for the books (and of course, some of the Censors were just downright careless—deliberately so it seemed to me), wrapping the books and then re-directing them to the appropriate camp or working party having previously checked the prisoner's whereabouts from the mail section. This department had a record of every prisoner's address and was run by a character called Sergeant Turver—known as "Topsy" (Topsy Turver—get it?!) whose same job it was in Civvy Street.

Every parcel sent or re-directed had to be entered in a large register book so that a permanent record was kept.

There was a tremendous backlog of books over several weeks to be dealt with. Apparently there had been a huge influx of letters from England and the German censors had been told to disregard the books entirely and to concentrate on the mail, which they did. Consequently the books had mounted up, and up, and up and were now in a near chaotic state. Tiffy asked Smudger and me if we would mind working an hour late each night in order to break the back of the pile-up and of course we said yes.

We worked pretty hard for about five days, and on the Saturday in order to ease the burden still further, we decided to work right through the afternoon. (Usually everybody returned to camp round about 1 p.m.) On this particular Saturday I went to the Gents lavatory at 4.30 p.m. which was frequented by the censors and which lay alongside the lavatories used by the lady censors of which there were a few at Stalag XXA. In other words the Ladies lavatories were on the other side of the Gents. (I mention this because it has a specific bearing later on.)

When I came out I bumped into the (well, I presumed she was) daughter of the old Polish crone who was the charwoman for our particular area. (There were others all over the building.)

She, the mother, was always on the cadge for soup or coffee or chocolate and I had given her a tin of pilchards, some tinned dried egg powder and some chocolate during my first week there.

Normally all the charwomen would come to work about half an hour before we usually left, but I had never seen the daughter before.

She was quite a charmer, about 23 years of age, diminutive, dark haired, and very attractive. She was carrying a bucket and a mop and was obviously helping her mother.

I apologised for bumping into her, and she smiled and went on her way down the corridor, looking back, shyly, I thought, to see if I was still there. Which I was.

To my surprise, I felt a stirring in my loins for the first time since my capture. It was obviously "lust at first sight". I limped back to the office and told them of my encounter.

Tiffy said "She wouldn't say no to a reasonable proposition."

"She's not like that, is she?" I said, disappointed, but at the same time hopeful.

The hunger pangs had finally worn off, and sex was at last rearing its dark Polish head in the shape of a diminutive figure carrying a bucket and mop.

I said "You mean she'll play ball if I ask her?"

"She'll play with more than that if the price is right" said Tiffy. "It'll cost you, though."

"On the other hand," said Smudger, "You could have the mum for a tin of Fray Bentos and she'll go down to you Polish fashion."

"Polish fashion? What's that?"

"She takes her teeth out!"

They both fell about in laughter, as I recoiled visibly.

"No, seriously," I said, knowing they were putting on an act. "Is that right? Will the girl do it?"

"Well, I haven't sampled it personally," said Tiffy "My friend wouldn't like it!"

"Your friend?" I echoed. "Yes — my friend Smudger here. Isn't that right Dear?"

"Yes Dearest" said Smudger in his thick Birmingham accent, and giggling.

"No, seriously," I said.

"Well," said Tiffy, "you've only got to speak to Neil Mackintosh. I believe he had a session in the dark room, two or three weeks ago when he was working here late on a Saturday."

I had to wait till Monday to find out if it was true, and Neil confirmed it. He had had her. In the dark room lying on the floor, she hadn't worn any knickers, and it wasn't very good. She had pushed him off so that he had to withdraw just at the crucial moment. The terms were arranged before the act, and he had to pay her first. A tin of corned beef (she and her mum were partial to that!), two bars of soap, and three bars of chocolate. The whole operation lasted about 48 seconds. ".. And it wasna worth it" he said. "Even a wank takes longer." Being a Scot he had asked her for the return of the chocolate, but he had about as much chance of that happening as being repatriated. She actually scoffed a bar of Cadbury's whilst he was pulling on his trousers, much to his Scottish chagrin!

Nevertheless the flame of desire having been lit, I set out to make the assignation through the Polish mum.

That same Monday evening, I approached the mother rather diffidently. I mean, what does one say on these occasions?

"May I borrow your daughter for half an hour on Saturday afternoon?"

Or

"Do you think your daughter would be interested in a project I have in mind?"

Or

"Tell your daughter. Four o'clock. Dark Room. Saturday. No knickers and bring a bag for the loot. O.K.?"

In actual fact, I started off by saying "Hello—I saw your daughter last Saturday and she is very pretty, not unlike her mother."

"Oh, do you think so?" she said, "She liked you too!"

"Oh—I didn't know she noticed me." (Liar) "Yes... (cough)... er I wondered if er..."

She went straight to the target, no beating about the Polish bush for her. Through her loose dentures, she said,

"You would like to make love to her? She likes you. You must give her meatloaf (that was my intention!), four *stucks* (pieces) of soap, and four bars of *shokolade.*"

The price was going up, and I trembled at the thought that maybe I was too!

I felt like a priest about to break his vows after my long imposed virginity.

And then she said "You are Catholic?"

I wondered what the trap was, but I half nodded and crossed my fingers. Actually, I'm not.

"That is good," she said, "we are Catholics too!"

I was a bit puzzled over that, but the rendezvous was uppermost in my mind.

"Where are we going to meet?" I said.

"You must arrange," she said.

I couldn't think of anywhere, except the photographic darkroom.

"I find out," I said.

I nipped down to Neil's place and asked him. "Ach, ah'm verra sorry," he said "Ah'll be working all over next week-end, developing some publicity pictures."

"Are ye after stoking the fire?" he grinned.

"Yeah" I said.

"God, ye'll need a bloody good poker to get that one goin'… How about the followin' Saturday?"

"Thanks" I said "I can't wait that long."

I could have, but now that I was on the scent, I didn't want to lose the quarry! There was simply nowhere that I could think of where the girl (and I) would be perfectly safe from discovery.

You see, apart from the other charwomen about, there was always the odd German guard likely to be trundling around and then there was also the danger of a casual soldier or officer visitor.

I tried in vain to find a place for my love tryst but without success and finally in desperation I suggested the Ladies lavatory which adjoins the Gents. The old lady agreed but apparently had trouble in getting the daughter to agree—or so she said. It may have been a ploy to increase the remuneration stakes; anyway it didn't work. So, on the Thursday, I gave her the tin of meat loaf and the soap and two bars of chocolate. I withheld the other two bars just in case it didn't happen. The crone said her daughter would be there at 4 o'clock on Saturday afternoon.

Tiffy and Smudger had been kept informed of the negotiations. They had in fact offered to keep watch once the lusting of the flesh operation took place—in the office, if I couldn't find anywhere else, and they were delighted that I had more or less succeeded in finalising the event.

Came the Saturday—the Day of my Fulfilment—and I was as nervous and apprehensive as a bashful bridegroom.

At 3.30 with much winking and thumbs up from the boys, I went to the Gents bog for a practice run. I entered the third cubicle along from the entrance, closed and locked the door and stood up on the seat, at the same time grabbing the top of the wall with my hands and pulling myself up. I put my leg over, drew up the other and dropped down on the seat of the Ladies loo. It was quite easy. I repeated the process and returned to the Gents side where I sat on the seat and smoked till the appointed time. Four p.m. came and went. I stood up and waited. Nothing happened. I looked at my watch—it was five minutes past four. Perhaps I was fast compared with Polish time. I sat down on the seat and lit another cigarette. I looked around at these most unromantic surroundings. Well, romance had nothing to do with this really, it was just a sort of offloading at a peak period as far as I was concerned. Period. "Period! Menstruation," I thought to myself, "that's it. She's got her period and can't come." I looked at my watch again. (it was 4.15 p.m). Then at the floor, where somebody had left a copy of the *Volkischer Beobachter* —the German *Daily Express.* "Total Victory is in Sight", says the Fuehrer.

I wished I could say the same. It was now 27 and a half minutes past four. There was a noise of the Ladies loo door opening, and a bucket being put down noisily on the floor. I started trembling! I heaved myself up gingerly on the wall, and there she was, standing at one of the washbasins, washing her hands. Hygienic with it, I thought. Then, as I watched, she took out a lipstick from the pocket of her smock. I waved with one hand to attract her attention and nearly fell off the wall! She turned. I pointed to my cubicle, and then motioned that I intended dropping into the one directly, facing me, the one where she should go.

Climbing over, and in my haste, stepping on the seat, I nearly slipped off into the actual pan and in order to save myself I made a grab at the chain, which immediately flushed the closet! I held my breath and almost hit at it to keep quiet. It gave its last "*Arghshise*" (that's what it sounded like in German) gurgled and stopped. I finally made it and stood waiting for the consummation to take place, with the cubicle door half open. She was taking her smock off to reveal her hidden Polish delights which showed up quite well through her black sweater. Around her neck was a chain with a small golden cross. She had good legs, no stockings, and was wearing Dr Schollski clogs. She looked quite pretty in a dark gypsy fashion, with her hooped bangle ear-rings. (For me to swing on, I flippantly thought!) She started to move towards me, very slowly, wobbling her body and hips as if disjointed. I watched fascinated, and ran my tongue over my dry lips. Suddenly, somewhere, a door banged. She froze instantly like a Polish statue, and looked at me as if I was responsible! I wasn't feeling too brave myself, but the imminence of desire cast away any thoughts of danger. "Nix" I said, shaking my head impatiently from side to side. I stretched out my hand to touch her, to welcome her in. And she put out hers almost at the same time. I made as if to clutch it but she withdrew it hissing—"*Shokolade*" (Chocolate) "*Noch zwei stuck.*" (two more bars). As my hand fumbled in my battle dress to get them out, one bar of Cadburys dropped on the floor. I bent down to pick it up and she motioned "Quiet" and cocking her head as if hearing some distant sneeze or a dog barking. I waited transfixed in the half bent position and then stood up in anticipation.

She slipped the two bars down the front of her sweater with one hand and with the other groped at my trousers where my John Thomas was straining at my fly buttons! I nearly swooned on the spot. I said to myself "I don't care if I do get caught!"

She guided my hand under her skirt and left it just below her navel. Neil McIntosh was right! She was knicker-less! I traced the silky line of pubic hair, as if it were a country road, and finally arrived at her Mount of Venus. It wasn't much different from an English one, if my memory served me right, except that there seemed to be much more fungus about, obscuring the orificial target. By this time she had succeeded in undoing my two fly buttons and John Thomas himself, having nosed his way out, and wearing what looked like a German helmet was elevating himself, like an artillery gun about to fire.
In other words, I was as erect as a Sandhurst Sergeant Major and was very much on the point of introducing her to my splendid kidney wiper when there was a hell of a commotion outside the Gents bog. The door was kicked open, and some jack-booted idiot entered the cubicle opposite ours. He urinated noisily, splashing everywhere, farted twice sharply, as if in Morse code, spat into the pan, and then finally coughed his heart up, as he lit and inhaled a cigarette, and stamped out of the lavatory, leaving behind a broken dream and a trail of disillusionment. Whilst I was still exploring her possibilities, she was "off" and I was left with my finger poised like an umpire giving the batsman out, and I hadn't even batted yet! It was hopeless. I tried to restrain her. To get her to stop. All in frantic mime of course. But it was no good. Knickerless and with bucket and mop, Cinderellaski departed, leaving her smock lying on the wash basin. As for me, I never even got to the Ball myself, which was a pity. I was looking forward to it! Immensely.

Mind you, if she'd been caught in what is laughingly described as a compromising position with me it would have meant a very long time in clink for her. I'd probably have got another 28 days bunker—renewing acquaintance with the Crapmeister, and that would've been that.

After the fateful interruption, I sat on the Loo in the vain hope that she might take a chance and come back again. But after waiting 20 minutes I gave up and climbed back over the wall to the Gents. For appearances sake I pulled the chain and marched out. I wandered back to the boys and told them what happened and they sympathised, suggesting that I should try again, but I was too deflated to attempt it.

As it happened, my lusting after the flesh was not to be realised —that time—so I was forced to bury all normal carnal activities in the face of my disappointing non-event with Wadjia (for that was her name) and resort to the Prisoner's Friend—the Hand Job. To the uninitiated—masturbation. To those in the know, "Wankers Doom" or "99 change hands—I don't care if I do go blind!"

For this, I have to confess, was what the majority of p.o.w.'s resorted to. And why not. Who is to blame them? They were all young virile men bursting into the flower of manhood, and now that the primary urge, in the shape of food, had been assuaged and assured, it was natural to seek out the female of the species, or in some cases, the "she-male" of the species. Quite a few liaisons flourished in the camp and Fort, and naive fool that I was (and still am), I always thought they were very deep friendships, not knowing that they were penetrating ones!

Many many husband and wife relationships abounded in the Fort. On location (the working parties), and especially the farming ones, liaisons with women were peculiar if they hadn't happened. There they could pick and choose. Also, in some factories where our blokes worked alongside the fair sex—there they could choose and pick. But back at the Forts if they were that way inclined they just had to make do and bend.

When I first went to work at Stalag XXA headquarters in 1942 I was still wearing my original battledress blouse, much mended trousers and the Norwegian Skiing boots issued to me on my first working party. Tiffy Chase told me to present myself at the clothing store which was under the command of R.S.M. Macintosh, a dour Scot, who for some irritating reason only known to him, dished out the clothes as if they were his personal property and your asking for them was a complete inconvenience. The clothes came, I was told, via the Red Cross from the British Government and from captured stores in France but wherever their source the recipients were very glad to have them.

I was eventually kitted out with a brand new battledress uniform complete, and a new pair of boots and gaiters. Finally, a forage cap to finish off the ensemble. (I still held onto my Polish titfer, partly for luck, and partly for the fact that it was a damn sight better suited to the climate than a forage cap.)

I managed to get hold of (managed to get hold of!—I paid for it with cigarettes), a "Black Badge" from another Queen Vic and two stripes to denote my unpaid acting Lance Corporal status and there I was as good as new—well almost. Let's say that the blood was coursing through my veins again in the right proportions! Most of the German staff, both officers and guards alike at Stalag XXA headquarters had been there from the beginning. Well, one or two had been transferred for official reasons, some for misdemeanours, but in the main the bulk of them were as well known to the prisoners as to the other German staff.

For instance: we had a good relationship with *Hauptmann* Gerdeker (a German captain who looked like Lionel Barrymore) and *Sonderfuhrer* Wolvermann, who had most to do with the Red Cross Food etc.. They were scrupulously correct in their handling of it, were both very well disciplined pleasant officers of the old school and to say the least, were very pro the British prisoners.

I remember Sergeant "Smudger" Smith (the place was littered with "Smudgers" and Smiths!) who was a very likeable Sergeant from the Rifle Brigade responsible for the collecting, storing and distribution of all Red Cross Food Parcels that arrived in Thorn—I remember him telling me that one afternoon he was commanded to be at the *Hauptmann's* office at 4 p.m. for a conference. When he duly turned up, a bottle of Scotch whisky was produced and sunk without trace, and without conferring. As Smudger unsteadily got to his feet, another bottle was produced and that too went down the hatch. Later that evening when schnapps took over from the Scotch Schergean Schmugger Scchmiff wash shupported all the way back—burp—pardon to the Camp13A and the Camp Commandant was told that he'd been working late with *Hauptmann* Gerderker and had been taken *krank* (sick!). End of conversation.

On another occasion he told me a story about *Sonderfuhrer* Wolvermann who limped slightly and always reminded me of the Irish film actor, Barry Fitzgerald. He had that same sort of puckish face and he rubbed his hands together like a Boy Scout starting a fire with two sticks and when he laughed his shoulders went up and down in time with the Ha-Ha-Ha! Well, this particular morning Wolvermann called Sergeant Smith into his office and said "Smudger…" (His English was perfect) "you'll never know…" (Hands rub-rub, rub-rub) "You'll never know who I heard on the radio last night?" (Quick look around, rub-rub, big grin, shoulders shaking) "Our old friend... Churchill! He was very good! Very interesting! It won't be long!" Rub rub! Big grin. Shoulders heaving as he padded off! It was strictly forbidden for German personnel, no matter what rank, to listen to foreign broadcasts, especially Churchill. They could be hung, drawn *and* quartered for listening to him.

I suspect, although I don't know for certain, that when searches of the camps or Forts to find radios or other incriminating evidence were instituted by the Gestapo, advance warning was always supplied by these two worthy German officers, dropping a discrete hint into the flapping year of either Harry "Smudger" Smith or one of his cohorts!

As the weeks went by, the pile-up of books gradually began to diminish and about three months later the backlog was finally conquered, the situation being back to normal.

One day I was sitting idly in the office on my own; Tiffy Chase was in another part of the building conducting a deal and Smudger Smith had gone to see a pal of his who had arrived back from a working party, so I leisurely set about a parcel of books addressed coincidentally to my old Queen Vic friend, Ronnie Carter (who, you may remember, was with me and Eddie Watson on my first working party), when the door to the Censors' room opened and a very attractive female, dressed in a light grey flannel suit, said in English "Would you please come and collect some books which are censored. I mean they are clear!"

I got to my feet and stumbled over the chair in my haste to follow her. She was quite petite with, I thought, slightly Slavonic features (not unlike Simone Signoret's as she would have looked then!). She had grey-green limpid eyes with some laughter lines around them. She had blondish hair with dark streaks or dark hair with blondish streaks—whatever it was, it suited her.

She was new to me, and apparently (as I learnt later) had just returned from a month's leave. She was a full time Censor, working on both incoming and outgoing letters and books. She had got the books and the wrappers from the two parcels hopelessly mixed up, and naturally I took much longer than necessary to sort it out. She was very shy and not too communicative and seemed to be very conscious of the *Feldwebel* who was in charge, and who once or twice looked in her direction, somewhat reprovingly.

Not wanting her to get her into hot water on my account, I gathered up the books, wrappers and labels and string, and carted them out to our office.

I waited till Smudger came back, and then asked him how long she'd been a Censor.

"I don't know much about her," he said, "She hadn't been here long before she went on leave. Came from another Stalag, I believe. She's not German, I know that."

"Not German?" I said, "Well, she must be *pro* German, wherever she's from."

"Not necessarily," said Smudger sensibly "She's probably come from an occupied country, and because of her knowledge of English, got the job as Censor. I mean, they do have to have stringent examinations before they can become Censors, and besides she's got to live, hasn't she?"

Well yes, she did have to live, I was glad to say. And later I found out where. She was Finnish and came from Helsinki. Her name was Britta Luukannen. She wasn't pro-German, so she said; she just had to work with them to earn a living and although she was semi-engaged to some foolish Finn, I like to think that after our friendship together she became very pro-British. I was certainly pro Finnish before I'd even started!

At first the progress to get to know her never "got off the ground". She didn't come into the office again for two weeks in spite of my utilising every visit to collect the books and to simper and leer in her direction. By this time she was back on "Letters."

Finally she got the message (well, she got it before but she hadn't dared to come into our office. She waited until the *Feldwebel* was away on official business) and came tentatively to ask us the explanation of a certain phrase in a book. It was Cockney rhyming slang and she didn't understand it. So she said. It was something about ".... Racing up the apples and pears" (stairs) and referring to someone's face as "His boat race." Also—"She's a bit of alright" came up for scrutiny. Perhaps she suspected a coded message. It was the sort of thing the Censors were always looking for and suspecting.

I became very attracted to her and used to look at her like a love-sick choir boy. When I was in the choir, aged 14, I was practically seduced in my surplice by Clarice—the organist's daughter.

She goosed me when I was trying to get High C! I got it, but it was a bit trembly! Clarice was always feeling her way around, I think she had a crush on each and everyone in turn. Probably got her own organ by now, she was always playing it. But I digress. I used to think about Britta all the time. She told me to say "I love you" in Norwegian —the Finnish words were too difficult for me, and she had Norwegian antecedents so "*Yea Elska Day*" became my password. It also made her fall about because of my pronunciation! Which was good for my ego, making her laugh! She was as nervous as a frantic Finnish faun, she even shied away at a raised eyebrow. When I first offered her a slab of chocolate, from my clothing parcel, she politely refused, saying it was forbidden to accept gifts from prisoners.

"But that only applies to the Jerries" I said "Not to you."

"I am subject to the same rules" she said.

"You're not, are you?"

"They would not shoot me at dawn, if that is what you are thinking."

"No,"I replied.

"What you are saying is— if you were caught in a compromising position, with me, say, you would be put in a military prison, yes?"

"Well, no, but I would be in disgrace and lose my job and be sent back to Helsinki. And that would not be good."

"Do you mean not good because you are collaborating with the Germans?"

"What does that mean—collaborating? Everybody works with the Germans in my country. We prefer them to the Russians."

"But surely, wouldn't you prefer to be working in your own country?"

"Well, yes, but at this time it is very difficult."

Just then, three cups of tea and biscuits arrived, supplied by Smudger, and she was invited to partake.

"The English tea—always at 4 o'clock." We tittered politely and dipped our shortbread biscuits in the tea, as one does!

Just before she left I told her to look out for some "secret" coded messages to Smudger and myself.

"Oh" she said (all mock serious) "You are both spies?"

"Oh—Yes" I replied, looking as if to the horizon, "We belong to M, I.8."

"M.I.8? she queried, mystified.

In unison, we said:

> "EM.I.8?— EM.I.9?"
> 'ow'm I doin'— Mighty fine!
> EMI5?   EMI6?
> EM I doin' it for nix?

Slightly bewildered, and not quite sure about the whole thing, she withdrew, giving a nervous friendly laugh to cover herself. The door closed and opened again almost immediately and she was about to say something when I declaimed:-

> "Oh—Come what may
> *Yea elske day—*
> My love flows like the river Shannon.
>
> Come fly away—
> *Yea elske day*
> *Mein schoen Liebling Britt Luukannen*

Well—you try rhyming something with Luukannen! It's not easy Buchanan.

The Romance never really caught fire. The spark was there and the ignition was turned on but no conflagration. Mind you, it was very pleasant nonetheless. There were many long searching looks and much fluttering of the eyelids on her part and shy frustrated glances and trousers stirrings of my part, but nothing ever happened though when I was near to her I became as jumpy and nervous as she. I wrote her affectionate notes declaring my love and she wrote guarded ones back with lots of crossings out as if on second thoughts she'd censored it!

I held her hand whenever possible when she came into the office but it was such a tense "affair" that I wearied of it and being concerned for her, I too became like a startled rabbit, flinching guiltily at the opening of a door and leaping backwards to the corner of the room as if she had suddenly got Finnish Black Fever which means the end of everything!

A month or two went by and she forced herself to accept some coffee, chocolate and soap, freely and genuinely given. In return, she kept asking me—What could she give me? An uncensored letter of her love I said. But in vain. Looking back, I can't think why I didn't ask her for a session in the photographic room. Maybe I did, and that was why she had the nervous breakdown and was away for a couple of weeks. The thing was, outwardly she was, as they say, very outgoing, but in actual fact, she was terribly nervous. We were now on Christian name terms, and it was quite a thrill to hear a feminine voice saying "Zahm" (If you come from the North it rhymes with "Trahm"). I used to call her Bridget (the equivalent of Britta I presumed).

"Bridget—Don't fidget. Don't fidget Bridget please!
You've censored Sam already—and now he's ill at ease!
It may be a Finnish custom to thwart him at the start.
But thwart him with a gentle hand and don't disturb his heart!"

So my dreams told me but in reality it didn't work out. The nearest we ever got to a passionate embrace or involvement was when one day she asked me to take her to the Education Reference Book Library which was on the third floor.

Attached to it or nearby was a sort of attic or loft room where books and games were stored and stacked. Now in order to enter this room one had to climb some rickety steps.

There was a door but it had been pushed right back against the wall and blocked by a load of stacked books, leaving the attic permanently open. The place was stuffed with reference books, looked after with loving care by a Sergeant from the K.R.R.C., Sergt. Bill Wright. I preceded her up the rickety steps and gave her a helping hand to follow me, and then, on the pretext of looking for some reference in a *Thesaurus* I led her behind a stack of books and pulled her towards me and kissed her. Very gently and very tenderly.

She looked at me half afraid and half not. Her head motioned me not to but her eyes and mouth said "Yes!"

I kissed her again, on each corner of her mouth and then full in the sensuous centre. I held her very close in a tight embrace and she pressed herself against me like the other half of a salami sandwich. I could feel her heart racing but mine was beating hers to it in the "photo-finnish"! I whispered *"Yea elske day, Britta"* in her left ear and as I kissed it and nibbled the lobe she shivered and stiffened (and so did I) and drew her breath in sharply.

I tried to kiss her again but she pushed me away, saying "No,no no Zahm. Not here." I ignored her plea. I pulled her to me roughly and kissed her passionately on the mouth and her lips opened and her tongue met mine. Finnish saliva mixed with British and I found it to my liking. Like pepper with mint. I ran my tongue along her firm strong teeth (they were her own) and she trembled and breathed in longish sighs. As for me I was almost going anyway—my eyeballs were moving upwards towards my forehead—my tongue was exploring the rest of her minty mouth and my hand was searching for a way in through her blouse to fondle her breast. She weakly said "No" and half pushed my hand away, shaking her head from side to side as if to emphasise it, but stopped in a kind of ecstasy when I kissed her fiercely again and almost touched her tonsils with my tongue. In my urgency and desire I pushed her back against the pile of stacked books and they fell to the ground with a great clatter. Like the dropping of several German bricks. After five seconds of holding our breath and waiting, Sergeant Wright's voice called out "Everything all right?"

"Yes—er thank you!" I answered weakly. She was already doing up her blouse. "Just having a bit of trouble finding the *Thesaurus*."

Our beautiful moment was lost forever.

CHAPTER 8
"Prisoner's Pie"

Meanwhile back at the Fort, because of the advancing Summer, we decided to soft pedal on the big three-act plays and concentrate mainly on band shows which were equivalent to variety shows. Nevertheless we set up and started rehearsing a three-act comedy play called "Happy Days" that I've mentioned before, which was intended for performing on the Camp 13A stage. The designing and building of the set and the running of the show were to be the responsibility of the camp 13A Stage Staff and the Producer and Actors were supplied by the Fort.

To keep fit I was playing Soccer fairly regularly on the Camp 13A sandy pitch, which was tough on the calf muscles. In addition a large square on top of Fort 13 had been turned into a Netball or Passball (as we called it) pitch. The rules were more or less the same as the normal ones (3 paces only before bouncing the ball and must pass) but the barging and boring and warding off of shots at the net were a good deal rougher than would normally be allowed.

Eventually a Passball League was instituted and the groups of supporters became very vocal and very partisan.

As daylight took longer to recede, sporting activities became more numerous.

Down at Fort 15 where they had a large Australian population taken mainly in Greece, they had laid a proper wicket and Test Matches between England and Australia were the weekly show piece.

Fort 15, by this time, had become the "non-working" camp for N.C.O.'s from the rank of Corporal upwards who chose not to work for the Reich. This was allowable under the Geneva Convention as also to the Germans in British hands. Not all of the N.C.O.'s took advantage of the ruling, quite a large number preferred to be with the men and were usually in charge of a working party.

Fort 15 was almost split down the middle—with the non-workers from Crete (The Aussies) and the non-workers from the British Army.

King cricket was one way of satisfying their pretended animosity! The Germans were completely bewildered by cricket, and were discouraged to understand it, especially by the Aussies, who took great delight in confusing them. For instance, they informed the *Unter Offizier* that the slang word for cricket ball was "bollock". So you can appreciate what it sounded like to a newcomer, hearing for the first time from German lips the words—"You play Creeket today cobber wiz ze bat and ze bollock…"

Or

"Ven ze bollock is bowled six times at ze wooden schtumps ze mann is Not Out but Inn and ze maiden ovair, she is finished—Cobber!"

Rumours were flying around of "repatriation" of the incapacitated—soldiers with lost limbs—the blind—and for those who for lack of proper treatment wouldn't last the year out.

Mostly the rumours came from Fort 14 Hospital but the false alarms had been so frequent that wolf had been cried too often. The cruellest operation of the lot was when a complete Repatriation Party got as far as France to the actual exchange point, and then had to return because of some extra demands made by the Germans. They insisted that the British should include certain German high-up officers in the exchange and actually named them. The British of course wouldn't hear of it. Consequently, no exchange!

On the other hand, there were many blokes who at the time of the inspection for repatriation were definitely return cases, but by the time the Swiss Commission Board came round to see them they had fully recovered from their illness. I did hear of one p.o.w. who chewed and swallowed a packet of 20 cigarettes on the assumption that his heartbeat would slow down, but all it did was to make him violently sick and give him a nicotine complexion!

Eventually, the first Repatriations took place at the end of 1943. By which time quite a few of them had succumbed to their illnesses and were lying in Thorn Cemetery with a wooden cross to mark the spot. A helluva lot died of despair and hopelessness.

About the second week in September as far as we, the entertainment brigade, were concerned, there occurred in stalag XXA one of the greatest tragedies of our p.o.w. time. It all happened so suddenly that even to this day I'm still confused and bewildered how it occurred.

Danny Faulds, a very close Scottish friend, a much thought of drummer in the band, was taken ill with a sore throat and heavy cold. Within a week he had died. I just couldn't believe it. I had known Danny since the Fort 17 days (1940), and shared with him when we had been sent on the working party to Weischeltal, and later when they had all come back (the Kommando had closed down) I had made great efforts to get him to come to Fort 13.

But because of his prowess and affability, he had been coerced into staying at Camp 13A, along with the rest of the Scottish contingent, Micky Bain, Johnny Wilson, Jock Mcdonald and Bill Thompson. They wanted him desperately for their band anyway.

I was terribly cut-up at his death; it was as if my own brother had died and at the funeral which was unfortunately limited in numbers (otherwise half of the Camp would have been there) I was one of the pall bearers.

The procession through the streets of Thorn to the cemetery was very impressive. All that was lacking was a Scottish piper. In an appreciation written by Bill Thompson and pinned on Camp 13A notice board, he said ….

"Rarely can we say of a man that he was universally beloved, but no one will ever deny to Danny Faulds the right to have claimed the sincere affection and respect of all who were fortunate enough to come into contact with him or privileged to be counted among his intimate friends….

"He will be remembered by everyone for his superb showmanship as a drummer, his unerring and illuminating strokes with brush or pen, and his skill and immaculate sportsmanship on the football field. . . . his quiet charm, his sense of humour, his patience and conscientiousness and the uprightness and strength of character which he showed throughout the good times and bad."

Poor Danny. We missed you, Danny. I and several others wept at the burial during the Last Post. They don't make them like that nowadays. Well, maybe they do, but they're awfully hard to find.

My long association with Knocker Noake (we'd been together off and on for 18 months and it hadn't seemed a day too long!) finally came to an end when he decided to go to work on a farming party where he was to spend the rest of his captivity much to the farmer and his wife's satisfaction. The herd of milk-giving cows cared for him too —it was that delicate touch of his! Once or twice when he came back to Stalag to collect the mail or Red Cross (he was almost the local *fuehrer* by this time) he tried to persuade me to join him in his agricultural pursuits. But—not for me—I preferred the wild and reckless life of Fort 13, being at the hub of things in swinging Thorn! Knocker once brought a British p.ow. back who'd been discovered feeding razor blades to the pigs "To help the War effort" he said. He got 28 days for sabotage which didn't please him. The pigs were a bit cut up about it too! "All our pigs use Gillette blades for their chops!" Or "Hairless pigs for sale, all have had close shaves with Gillette!"

So—I was on my own again, that is, I looked after myself for a time but not for long. James Woolcock or Jimmy to his intimates asked me to join him and we became a two-some. Jimmy was a very clever cartoonist who eventually, with Dave Hawley, took over "Prisoners Pie", our own magazine, written, published and distributed by p.o.w. 's. (The actual printing was done by a firm in Thorn.) Jimmy was a great character. He came from Barry in Cardiff and was a sign writer by trade. As I said he was also an excellent cartoonist and the best reproducer of (Fake) German Documents that I'd ever seen.

The original Editor (Freddie Foster) and Publisher (Dave Scotland) of "Prisoners Pie" decided to bow out (both were Sergeants and entitled to be non-workers if they so chose, but that wasn't the real reason as you'll see if you read on!).

Jimmy Woolcock became the Publisher and Dave Hawley the Editor. The "Prisoners Pie" Office was situated in the Stalag building on the third floor at the rear looking out towards Thorn Military Barracks and the road to Thorn ran alongside.

Unknown to me at that time Freddie Foster's reason for giving up the sinecure job of Editor was to rehearse and concentrate on a spectacular escape across Germany to the Swiss border. He had as his companion or I should say his guide and mentor, one Tony Coulthard, known affectionately as "The Professor" on account of his education (B.A. First Class Honours Modern Languages) and understanding, who was in charge of German lessons at the Fort.

Tony had lived and studied in Germany before the War and spoke German better than most Germans! Certainly more correctly and grammatically perfect.

Freddie of course spoke German like a Deutsch bumpkin. *"Jah!" "Nein!" Nicht cigaretten raucken* or inhalin'. "Mein Herr—needs cutting!"

But don't misunderstand, Freddie was the bloke to have a go, he had guts, application and a sense of humour. Through Tony and otherwise, he learnt to behave as a Siemans-Bau representative or foreign Hungarian worker who had spent nine months in Germany. At the end of the training period (his own personal period in the camp) he would have fooled you and me. And with Tony alongside him, it was a doddle.

Jimmy Woolcock made the passports or *Ausweises* for them (every civilian had one rather like an Identity card) and it entailed getting hold of a special green folder type file, which when left exposed to the sun faded to the identical official pastel-green colour of the *Ausweises*. Then a small photo, like a passport photo, had to be stamped with the German Eagle and Nazi emblem and some official German wording was copied exactly by Jimmy and reproduced so that Himmler himself couldn't have told the difference.

I watched in amazement as Jimmy carved the Nazi emblem of Eagle and Swastika, first out of a potato and then out of soap. He was a genius. If ever anybody deserved recognition in the way of a decoration Jimmy did. But he never got it. Not even a mention. By the end of the war there must have been quite a few of his faked German documents floating around and being accepted officially.

The Freddie Foster—Tony Coulthard escape from Thorn took place on August 23rd 1942.

The attempt was a glorious, successful, heart-breaking failure. They progressed all the way by train with many a tense moment to Lake Constance after stopping off in Berlin, where Tony showed Freddie the sights. Imagine that. The further they got away from Stalag XXA the cheekier they became. They took the train for Munich after being questioned by a woman detective on the station who reported them to a civilian who was of course connected with the *Berlin Kriminal Polizei*— a branch of the Gestapo. They were asked to produce their identity cards, which with acknowledgments to Herr Woolcock they did, were apologised to and allowed to proceed on their way!

Indignantly they Hailed the Fuehrer in a goodbye gesture, took the train and then stopped off at Magdeburg where Tony had studied for some time and actually ate at a restaurant which he had frequented when he stayed there.

Leipzig was next where they again went on a sightseeing tour and then on to Munich. From there it was a short run to Lindau which was the frontier town prior to Lake Constance but unfortunately from here (Lindau) the train turned towards Zurich. And then it was that disaster struck. Apparently there was a normal halt of two hours whilst the train was searched and the two boys decided to go into the Town for some food. Tony had actually gone on ahead and got through the barrier when he noticed that the frontier policeman was questioning Freddie about his pass and for some reason was highly suspicious. Tony sportingly returned to Freddie's assistance only for both of them to be taken to the police station and held as spies! After a long gruelling and exhausting grilling they admitted that they were p.o.w.'s and were consigned to the dungeons of Lindau Fortress. Ironically they could see the Swiss shores of Lake Constance from the cell window!

When they were finally brought back from Lake Constance to Fort 13 under guarded escort of course, a reception committee clapped and cheered their efforts as they entered the Fort gates on their way to the Bunker.

Freddie and Tony Coulthard got 14 days detention each. Freddie Foster applied to go to a *non-arbeiter's* (N.C.O.'s non-working) Camp and towards the end of 1943 Tony Coulthard attempted to escape again, this time via Sweden. He and his companion arrived at Gdynia safely, the port from which they hoped to leave, but they were held up for a week waiting for a particular boat to arrive. They decided to get on to any boat as long as it was Swedish, were observed doing so by an Italian labourer who informed the Gestapo, and it was all up! They got another 14 days detention. For a while Tony was classified as an habitual nuisance and escapee and sent to a camp which had been set up for his kind to discourage escapes. The work was extremely arduous and after his health broke down he was returned eventually to Fort 13. He was on the 800 mile march from Thorn to Hamburg which I refer to later and at Schwerin was admitted to hospital suffering from dysentery and foot trouble. Unfortunately he was not allowed to stay there, his illness not being considered serious enough. He and several others were forced to march on foot and after crossing the Elbe were put into a barn at a place called Domitz. He died there in the early morning of March 24th. Two weeks before his 27th birthday.

In the London Gazette, Nov. 23rd 1945, there appeared this notice. "The King has been graciously pleased to approve the posthumous award of Mention-in-Despatches, in recognition of gallant and distinguished service in the Field to Lce. Cpl. J. A. R. Coulthard (Intelligence Corps)."

The German High Command in charge of prisoners made it a practice to switch around the Commandants of each camp periodically, partly to keep the Jerries on their toes and not to allow them to fraternise too much with their charges and partly to keep the prisoners themselves on their toes. Some Commandants were lenient at letting things through (at the gate at night on the return of local working parties) and there would be no search, but others, usually newly-appointed would be the very devil to get past which made it rather awkward when we had something going like a schnapps party, for instance. But usually some diversion would be devised to enable us to outwit even the most fervent searchers.

There was a classic occasion when a new Commandant who spoke a little English addressed the Camp at Roll Call.

He started off with the usual crap about Victory for the Fatherland against us and the Soviets and he hoped that it would not be long before we were reunited with our loved ones etc... and that if we played fair with him he would play fair with us... but we must remember that he could not stand by and allow us to bring illicit and forbidden articles into the Camp. He went on: "Ze trouble wiz you

Englanders ist zat you zink I know bugger-nozing ven in fact I know bugger-all!"

During the late summer of 1942 there arrived at Fort 13– (arrived! he just walked in under his own steam!) a certain prisoner of war who seemed to have the authority to come and go in and out of camps without guard or supervision. He produced official papers from the *Wehrmacht* (the German War Office or High Command) to prove to both sides that he was genuine. He was certainly English or so it seemed and his aim was to foster good relations between the British and the Germans. We were warned privately to have nothing to do with him but I must say that I was curious about his mission—so called—and encouraged him to talk.

He said he had come from Berlin and had gained the ear of a high up German officer who was sympathetic to his cause and that he had finally been granted this roving commission to sound out the lie of the land. I remember one hairy Corporal of the Durham Light Infantry saying that it was his intention, if he could get him to go to the top of the Fort alone, to throw him into the moat below. He called him a "bloody traitor" to his face.

The newcomer asked me if I was aware that the Germans were contemplating introducing a British Free Corps to fight against Communism and did I think there would be any volunteers? I replied that I had heard a rumour to that effect but to my knowledge nobody from our Camps—13A and Fort 13–had volunteered.

It wasn't until I was in Berlin in 1944, when the Irish question came up again, that I did in fact see three British soldiers in German uniforms with a small Union Jack as a shoulder title flash on each shoulder. Whether they ever fought against the Russians I very much doubt. I would say the nearest they got to making a stand was in bed with some German Fraulein! I know that one or two of them did broadcast to our detriment on Haw-Haw's wavelength, and were apprehended at the end of hostilities, and charged with treason. One with whom I had a casual acquaintance got eight years for his change of heart, or was it his foibles?

But to return to our mysterious freewheeling visitor—he only stayed about a week in Fort 13—which was just as well because things looked like boiling over when he left, with him in the frying pan. About a year later, or maybe less, we heard the news that this self same person (I can't give you his name simply because I can't remember it) had arrived safely back in England via Sweden and had been recommended to be decorated for his audacity and daring. He could have been a double agent, but to this day, as far as I'm concerned the whole thing's still a mystery.

The sunny Polish summer came to a close and I'll say this for Poland, though there were sub-Arctic conditions in the winter that even the celebrated brass monkeys would be hard-put to survive, the summers were ideal. Very hot and sunny and dusty and sandy and thirst provoking, which encouraged a surfeit of beer-swilling, there being no shortage of beer. Not the good old Kentish hops quality, I admit, but usually a lager of Carlsberg Pilsner vintage which wasn't a bad substitute.

What we did produce, in great quantities, was a home brew known as "Snake Juice" or "Two cupfulls and I'm anybody's!" It was made from all the dried fruit you could lay your hands on and there was quite a variety. Prunes, figs, raisins, apricots, pears, apples, etc., plus sugar, yeast and, of course, water. The trouble was it was never given the required amount of time to ferment properly. Patience was not a virtue as far as the prisoners' drinking habits were concerned, so before it was ready they would immediately swill it down and get severely drunk at the drop of a raisin! Well, there alwaysh hash to be a raisin for livin'—in a prison camp especially! I remember seeing some Scotsmen and an Irishman melting down some tins of boot polish— Cherry Blossom vintage—and handing that flaming blue-smoke concoction around as if it was the "hard stuff". As you guessed, it tastes *awful*.

On the war front, the reverses or "strategic withdrawals" that the

Jerries were having in Russia and in the desert towards the end of 1942 somewhat deflated their customary arrogance. The *Sieg Heil* barometer was falling an inch or two and as they had to tighten their belts a little and at the same time tolerate the prisoners letting theirs out (belts, I mean) so the situation could at times get rather tense.

The younger Nazi soldiers were still confident of victory.

At this time we used to have a very friendly German guard— Frederick—we called him "Freda"—who spoke a little English. He would come into our room after lights out, supposedly to check up that everything was all right but in actual fact he would come in and dally for some considerable time giving us his "patter" and the local gossip ... "what the *Unter Ofizier* said". "Freda"… a Berliner, was very amusing, and hated Poland, the War, the Army, the Fuehrer and everything connected with it or them!

For a consideration, chocolate or cigarettes, after having put his rifle against the wall, he would stand in the centre of the room raise his right arm in the well known Hitler salute and say camply "Fawk ze Fuehrer!"

For an encore, to an accompaniment of Cheer up my lads, Bless 'em all and Widdicombe Fair which we'd patiently taught him, he would render:-

"So scheer awp my lads, fawk em all—ze long und ze short und ze tall" (then into the Widdicombe Fair bit)

"Mit Adolf Hitler hairy Himmler—Von Ribbencrap—Septic Dietrich—Ugly Goebbels and old Fatty Goering and all!. .."

(And the whole chorus would join in)

"And Old FATTY GOERING AND ALL!"

If we reminded him that if he were overheard and reported it would be the Eastern Front for him, he would say "I do not care. I give myself up to a handsome Cossack who vill look after me!"

He would say that everything was "*Deutsch* Propaganda" and "*Ersatz!*"

He literally hissed that word Airssatzzzzz! He preferred

everything English (especially matelots). He had an English uniform for when the Russkys came and he said he would pretend to be an Englander and would say "HEIL STALIN! HEIL SCHURCHILL!" and sing—"Old Uncle Winston and all!" and "Old Uncle Winston and all—Old Uncle Winston and all—OLD UNCLE WINSTON AND ALL!"

Sergeant "Smudger" Smith of the Red Cross Parcels Dept., was approached with a proposition by the driver of the Diesel lorry which each month or so came to Stalag from Graudenz to collect their parcels, mail and the like.

This driver, so it was said, was a contact for Partisans and for a consideration involving a large amount of German marks (real German marks not lager geld or camp money) the inevitable Red Cross Coffee, Chocolate, Soap and Cigarettes, would practically guarantee the safe arrival in Sweden of any prisoner involved.

The first or one of the first of the prisoners to get home by this method was Joe Curry who really took the biggest chance. Who was to know that he would not end up in a ditch with his throat cut? Joe bravely risked it and arrived home safely. Robin Doubleday, another military acquaintance of mine, also made it safely, and it became known as the "Cook's Tour" Route!

Most of this carefully guarded information was of course an open secret to the p.o.w.'s at the time. How can you keep a secret in a prisoner of war camp!!

In all, culling from memory, approximately 28 prisoners escaped via Sweden with the help of our Partisan contact friend from Graudenz. We also heard stories of p.o.w.'s who escaped to Warsaw, being heavily involved with and helped by the Partisans there, but to my knowledge very, very few got through to the Russians and the reception when they did wasn't all that hot! Well, you know how suspicious they always are, believing everything the British Tommy tells them and then throwing him in jail to rot for two or three years whilst they look into things! They are *thorough*!

Rifle Brigader Harry Smith who had originally organised the affair was himself given the opportunity to "take off" and everything was arranged. On the night concerned Harry was to be picked up at a certain point and whisked on his way to Freedom, but Fate, in the shape of Captain Bob Moody, came to Harry in a flap and reported that a certain British officer would be arriving at the Fort two days before the escape, on his way to be court-martialled in Danzig for some serious offence. Harry was soft-soaped into giving up his place to the officer and in doing so lost his chance to go. The opportunity never came round again. Needless to say the officer got home safe and sound.

After the first successful escapes by this route and method, an Escape Committee was set up to decide and organise the lucky volunteer.

My own name came up and was proposed and seconded, and then turned down by Captain Bob Moody, because, as he, with typical Kiwi cunning kindly told me afterwards, "You are too valuable for the sake of Morale to let you go."

I had to be content with a badge which the Y.M.C.A. sent me. It was the normal triangular Y.M.C.A. badge but in this instance had gold barbed wire entwined around the capital letters.

"For your unstinting contribution to the enjoyment and entertainment of the British soldiers captive in Stalag XXA."

So said the Citation.

I never heard from the Y.W.C.A.

I could have done with a Y.W.!

Out of the blue I was offered the Editorship of the monthly p.o.w. Magazine "Prisoners Pie". Dave Hawley, the Editor, found that he'd had enough or wanted to do other things like meditate and decided to "jack it in". He was actually in the R.A.M.C. and was on the Repatriation Party the following year, and got home, but whether or not giving up the job had anything to do with it I'll never know. Fate pointed a finger in my direction—well, I did "muck-in" with the

Publisher Jimmy Woolcock for a start, so no one could have had a more helping hand from Fate than that!

Anyway, Dave's swan song or last number (the issue of the magazine I mean!) was the Christmas 1942 edition in which Lieut. Col. McKay, the S.B.O. (Senior British Officer) who lived—lived?—he *existed* at Fort 15, gave his usual Xmas message, ".. this time next year we hope"— etc., etc., (which he repeated the following year! Monotonous, wasn't it!) and I quote "From the Red Cross Society, which has done great work on our behalf, we can expect Xmas fare. From those in different camps who have worked so hard to produce it, we can expect entertainment! (He was right! We were up to our eyebrows!) My best Christmas Wishes to you all. May you continue to preserve the spirit, which has carried you through your captivity, and may the coming year bring us near to that which we all desire."

I was in fact hard at it rehearsing the Pantomime "Mistletoe Bow" written mainly by Stan Hobday and Derek Lunn. It was more or less a pot pourri or in the mould of "Pantomania" previously produced in 1941, but this time the linking theme was "Scrooge". Other panto favourites like Sinbad, King Cole's Fiddlers, Jack & Jill, and Speciality Dance by George Tyler and Johnnie Gaskin "The Toy Soldier and Doll Dance" were included. Also Papa Nicolina. Who was Papa Nicolina? They must have dreamt him up. I don't remember any panto character of that name! I was Simple Simon and played it like Lobby Lud!

"Mistletoe Bow" was a success and was followed by "Rookery Nook", the Aldwych farce made famous by Ralph Lynn and Tom Walls. It was the first of many Ben Travers farces that we were to do, and it went down extremely well. Norman Freebury played the Tom Walls part, Wally Kersey the Robertson Hare part and I played the Ralph Lynn character. Norman and Wally were excellent. They all were. Gonzalas Vargas who had aspirations to become an actor (but didn't) was a sensation as Putz. The whole cast were absolutely first class, and as I said before, the format was entirely suitable to our set up—usually one set with maybe eight to ten characters, all identifiable by the audience, and obviously enjoyed by them, judging by their comments, so it was no hard decision to take to concentrate on Farce or Comedy. Funnily enough the three leading characters, Norman, Wally and myself were all Queen Victoria Rifles blokes, if that is at all significant!

Having left my job in the Books Department, and being transferred upstairs to the P.P. ("Prisoners Pie") office, I found that I had taken over at a rather difficult period. In the first place the Jerries had had to cut down on the amount of paper to be used, so we were unable to print as many copies as before, and we had to reduce the number of pages. There was a very strong rumour that the magazine was going to be closed down altogether and it was only after strong protests to the German officer concerned that we were allowed to carry on, providing we kept strictly to the rationing as promised.

Eventually when the Germans did stop supplying the paper the good old Y.M.C.A. came to our rescue and sent us supplies from Sweden. By this time we were having to make one issue cover three months, and finally in 1944 the magazine folded completely. But in the meantime we survived, albeit precariously.

I think I mentioned before that we had in our midst what the Germans call a *Vertrauensman*—a sort of Ombudsman—or Man of Confidence or "Confidence Man"! He was appointed by the Jerries even though in rank he was inferior to several R.S.M.'s and C.S.M's which was always a bone of contention.

And he incidentally was another Queen Vic. Colour Sergeant Grainger. They certainly got about! He obviously wielded a lot of power, being in a position to do so, both over the British and the Jerries. All the Red Cross information was addressed through him and he, in turn, passed it on to the camps and working parties using the columns of "Prisoners Pie", to do so. This was in addition to the sending of memos and official bumff to the parties concerned for posting on their notice boards.

He had to approve of my being the editor of "Prisoners Pie", and although paying lip service to my capabilities, he delayed somewhat the decision to say O.K. Perhaps he had somebody else in mind—I never thought of that at the time.

He had an important job and gave me the impression that he knew it and would use the power he commanded if he had to.

He was rather reticent, in a way, and didn't socialise much with the P.P. lot.

He said to me once—"There are too many Queen Victoria Rifles employed at Stalag XXA" So what was *he* doing there living the life of Reilly? Oh Really? Yes really!

The introduction to the "Prisoners Pie" Office was quite an occasion. Jimmy Woolcock had rustled up a couple of bottles of Schnapps from somewhere, and at a certain time, 4 p.m. to be exact, a small gathering was invited to "Wish us Luck" and to Bless all who sailed in her!

In this instance the job of editor was more one of sorting out the contributions, the serious, the humorous, the instructive and last but certainly not least, in fact the most important, the Red Cross Parcels information.

Jimmy did the funny cartoons and illustrations and we both checked the proof copy from the German printers when it showed up which was invariably late. I wrote several articles which we never used but were always kept as a stand by.

Obviously everything was Stalag slanted because everything was happening there, but I did try to encourage the working parties to send us contributions and information about their activities. Most of them couldn't be bothered. Sports items from home were greatly appreciated and of great interest, especially Football.

My gentle affair with "Britta" or Bridget the Fidget, in racing parlance "never got out of the starting stalls". The Starters Flag would go up all right but it was the only thing that did; there seemed even less chance of our Love ripening to fruition mainly because we were now on the third floor back—the "Prisoners Pie" office that is, and she was on the ground floor along with the rest of the Censors. So the consummation looked even more remote although as you know "Where there's a Will there's a way" or so I kept hoping.

One or two of the male censors came to visit us, purely to give themselves a break from work and to cadge anything free that would be going, like a cigarette or maybe a cup of genuine coffee. Hans Richter a very friendly Bavarian aware of the set-up brought Britta along with him to visit us but after a cup of tea a fag and a chat (there wasn't actually much to see) she left almost immediately. Hans, the Bavarian fool, didn't think of leaving us alone, although Jimmy Woolcock had given him a broad hint like "Let's go to the Library, Hans, and see what they've got!"

Britta knew what I'd got but she was apprehensive about our slender liaison getting too well known although she had apparently confided in Richter about her feelings for me.

You see there was no justification for her coming into our office, except for a query visit, and she seemed to get more nervous as the months went past.

But it was pleasant to have this affectionate female phase in my p.o.w. existence.

The year meandered on with dwindling fortunes for the Germans —Stalingrad retaken by the Russkys and successes for the British. Fort 13 became rather like a Summer Holiday Camp—with brown bodies strolling around—to the strains of *Chattanooga Choo Choo, I Know Why* and *In the Mood* wafting across the top of the Fort from the portable gramophones (by kind permission of Red Cross and Glenn Miller—and sometimes the luscious harmonies of the Andrews Sisters. Tommy Dorsey too, was a great favourite and some unknown vocalist by the name of F. Sinatra).

Jimmy and I had acquired a new partner, Johnny Murray, a Scot with a great sense of humour and quite a skill in the rhythm section of the dance band. He played the guitar. Well, in fact he doubled with

Nigel Plunket (guitar, I mean) and had aspirations to be an actor. Everybody wants to act! He eventually achieved his ambition by giving a bouncing and cheeky performance as "Flo" the Chambermaid in "Thark."

So the three of us formed a Celtic trio—Johnny from Scotland, Jimmy from Wales, and Kyddy from Ireland! Johnny spoke German and was always in demand somewhere or other as an interpreter. His favourite job was at the *Wascheri* or local Laundry situated not far from the camp and used mainly by the German Military authorities.

Johnny at this particular time had his eye on a Polish girl there who was in charge of the mangling facilities much to Johnny's satisfaction. She looked after the mangle and Johnny encouraged her! He was the world's biggest ram. No woman was safe when he was sniffing around like a sheep dog. A Scottish sheep dog to boot. And they're the most persistent! He would regale us with his tales of how he'd had Krystinya or Katya in the pile of "dirty washing" whilst his shirt, pants and vest were bubbling away in the boiler. He was certainly a clean Casanova!

It was his Celtic charm that did it (not the one he had around his neck!) *that* and his gift of the gab—mainly soap! Soft soap!

Sometimes on hot Sunday afternoons or balmy evenings the Dance Band would play up on the platz on top of the Fort, not the Netball platz because that was inevitably in use at most times of the day, morning, afternoon and evening, but on the equivalent space on the other side of the Fort.

We had one or two Light Orchestral Concerts in the Fort 13 Theatre—playing anything from Bach to Beethoven, and Strauss to Gilbert and Sullivan. Well attended and well appreciated.

And then we started rehearsing "Thark" another of the Aldwych Famous Farces, with Johnnie Gaskin blossoming as the girl-friend Kitty. He was so realistic in fact and pretty (as the girl-friend) that when on the night of the first performance I walked into the dressing room and saw a beautiful slim dark haired girl in panties and bra adjusting the seams of her stockings, I stammered "Sorry" and turned as if to go and suddenly realised we were of the same gender. It was Johnnie Gaskin!

The big feature about this show was the fact that Norman Freebury, who was so good in the Tom Walls part in the previous "Rookery Nook" show and was due to repeat the character in "Thark" was suddenly, at a moment's notice, and in spite of our protestations to the Jerries, sent away to a working party. This happened about ten days before we were due to open, but miraculously, a fellow p.o.w. Alf Gosling, (not unlike Norman facially) volunteered to take over the part and after a hectic night and day rehearsal gave a marvellous performance.

After each major production a self-appointed critic would write about the show and the notice would be pinned up on the Fort notice board for all to see. Whether or not the rest of the p.o.w.'s read them is questionable. The actors and everybody connected with the show certainly did. So, about "Thark" it was said:

"Thark was one of the last of the Ben Travers successes and its plot shows the signs of strain, although the lines have their usual sparkle. It is however, not my duty to criticise the play but the players, so we will turn first to the female players. First of all I would like to say that we have seldom seen in our shows three such attractive looking girls as those portrayed by Johnnie Gaskin, Ernest Seabrook, and John Murray.

"The most satisfactory portrait of a lady was given by Edgar Andrews as the 'Lady Benbow'. He had the 'Lady of the Manor' manner, as it were, even though his accent was rather too 'refaned'.

"Turning to the men—the male characters—pride of place must certainly be given to Sammy Kydd as 'Ronnie Gamble'"(Why do you think I'm quoting this critique!?)—"Sammy acts with such authority that the other players seem to gain in stature and confidence when he is amongst them. He has developed a comedy style and a sureness of touch all his own.

"In spite of the fact that his services were only called upon at the last moment, Alf Gosling was a success in the Tom Walls part of 'Sir Hector Benbow'. Although his timing was not perfect he gave a genuinely fine performance and his rumbustious manner was in excellent contrast to the quieter subtlety of Sam Kydd's.

" 'Death' in the hands of Gonzalos Vargas was an effective portrayal of that humorously macabre figure.

"The other butler Hook is a typical Robertson Hare part in that it would not be a particularly funny part if divorced from the Robertson Hare accent and expression or lack of it. These, Walter Kersey imitated very well. He dithered and teetered, and got every laugh out of his part.

"The costumes and dresses were, as usual, of a very high standard, so once again the Repertory Company add another feather to their already well furnished cap."

(He liked it!).

After "Thark", I dreamt up a show called "Diversions" which was actually a succession of variety acts and song scenas. We did several sketches sent to us by "The Crazy Gang". I had written to Bud Flanagan asking if he could spare any material and he very kindly did so.

After my show we went immediately into rehearsal for the Pantomime, this time, "Sinbad the Sailor". I know that every now and then I came out with the classic line "Somebody's split my mainbrace and it don't half hurt?" and "Hello Sailor". And that Clifford Winterbottom was a riot as "Bella the Bumboat Woman" but apart from that I can't remember much about it.

But first of all an even bigger production—completely unrehearsed—was about to take place.

The FIRST REPATRIATION of British Prisoners of War from this Stalag began on October 16th 1943. The blind and the limbless and the incurables were after all this time, 1940-1941-1942-1943 (and many false alarms), finally going home.

Along with the wounded were a percentage of R.A.M.C. Personnel—and the night before they moved off people were dashing around saying "goodbye" to those who were going—giving addresses to be written to or called on to reassure—phone numbers of wives and mums and girl friends.

Here are some extracts from a couple of letters received later.

It was grand to be home again but I find I am missing a lot of the things I so much enjoyed out there (Ai, Ai!), particularly the shows. I don't know whether I have become over critical but so far I have not seen one film which I have enjoyed . .

. . (how about that for a recommendation?!). *I'm gradually getting accustomed to freedom although I'm not at all sure that I am used to it yet. It was very strange at first talking to a girl without thinking of the consequences! I was in a blue funk the first time I took a girl out, I thought I might have disgraced myself, but I am glad to say that I acted with perfect decorum. . . .* (Blimey!)

And the second one.

I have come back from my four weeks leave and have rejoined my unit. At the moment we are in extremely nice barracks, food is excellent and all is well.

We have to do a little, drill and the rest is mainly P. T. Games, and Cinema shows (consisting mainly of all the films we have missed during our captivity). We also have talks on ABCA (Army Bureau of Current Affairs). This morning's lecture was on Education. School leaving age was discussed. Types of schools, Grammar, Technical, Modern, etc., and we followed that with an Army Trades Lecture for the RAMC. Apparently they are trying to fill up the gap in our lives and if they carry on as they are doing they will undoubtedly succeed...."

And a letter came from the former editor of "Prisoners Pie"—D. W. Hawley—. . . *Having scrounged a lettercard from Vargas, who is seated broodingly beside me, I'm inflicting myself upon you while he sips a cup of Naafi tea.*

The ubiquitous and intriguing Vargas is wrinkling a fastidious nose over his tea and a sheaf of scripts for his forthcoming broadcasts to South America. I have contented myself with a few modest guineas writing articles —the titles of which wouldn't pass the censor at your end! So between us we're keeping the racketeering flag flying vigorously! We've both managed to keep on the right side of the guard-room window so far, though how Vargas manages to keep his crime-sheet clean beats me.

Best Wishes to P.P. and All the Boys. ..

Gonzalos Vargas who was a very active member of the Concert Party and very sorely missed, was later to volunteer for the Parachute Regiment and after being dropped at Nymegen was again taken prisoner for the second time. He missed the shows so much he wanted to rejoin us!

CHAPTER 9
The Cockney Obergerfreiter

I never got around to playing "Malcolm" in "George and Margaret" because with only two days warning the Jerries decided to have another go at coercing the Irishmen into becoming traitors, and the order went out that all of them, no matter what shade of Green — Light, Dark, or even faded—were to assemble together at Fort 17; which was now being used as a Military Food Supply Depot.

We were there for over a week whilst the Celts on outlying working parties from all over Poland were brought in. It was another Irish Sweep, but this time there were no winners. Certainly not the Jerries. From all points East of Prussia they poured in, with their parcels under their arms.

Our Shamrock section or Celtic contingent from Fort 13 banded together in a tight little group. I found myself with Clifford Winterbottom ("Bella the Bum Boat Woman!")—Johnny Gaskin ("Kitty" in "Thark") and Richard Kelly from Derry.

We made up a foursome syndicate and were put with all the others on a goods train travelling to Berlin. I was appointed *Dolmetscher* (Interpreter) so I saw to it that there was no possibility of being packed into the wagons in the way we had arrived at Thorn in the first place, when they tried to break the record by squashing 75 men into one truck. 20 or 25 per wagon was the permitted allowance. We insisted; after all we were V.I.P.'s going to Berlin! Also we refused to move until we had a legitimate issue of Red Cross parcels—to which we were entitled. It duly arrived. Which was lucky for us because nothing had been organised in the camp we were going to— not that we knew that then.

When we arrived at Berlin or just outside, our train was brought to a halt by an air raid warning, which moaned like a mournful banshee. The guards considerately locked us in and then took cover under the trucks. We'd have all gone together if there'd been a direct hit. After two hours, nothing seemed to have happened, nothing had happened, well, at least not near us as far as we could see through our slit holes.

We started to sing, and then the "All-clear" sounded, and the train began to move uneasily and spasmodically towards Luckenwalde —our ultimate destination.

Luckenwalde is about 36 Kilometres from Berlin—it said so on the road sign. (*Nach Berlin. 36 Kms.*), and near to the main *bahnhof* (station) was a huge military hospital with white crosses painted on the roofs.

We unloaded our gear, which was considerable, and marched in a straggling column to the gates of this vast complex of prisoners. It was like a small town with a main road running through the camp intertwined with numerous compounds, containing thousands of emaciated Russians, excitable Italians, and phlegmatic Frenchmen.

(There were two types there, the Vichy French, who were volunteer workers from France and the ordinary French soldiers who'd been captured in France in 1940.)

There was no love lost between them. They just about tolerated each other.

We were met at the gates of Luckenwalde camp by a German Corporal. He wore thick pebble glasses and reminded me of Stan Laurel of Laurel and Hardy fame, the way he ambled up to us. But I couldn't believe my ears when he spoke in a thick Cockney accent and exhorted us "not to muck about" but to "bleedin' well lineup an' be bleedin' well counted." Which we dutifully albeit noisily did.

We couldn't get over this phenomenon and were very keen to hear his explanation. But first we had to be deloused! We were highly indignant—we had been free from lice for over two years now—and complained bitterly, at the same time enjoying the showers forming part of the operation. What was even more degrading was the fact that all our uniforms, after the delousing, had the letters KGF (short for *Kriegsgerfangener*—p.o.w.) about 3 inches high stamped or stencilled in the backs of our blouses and on the map pocket of our trousers. This was the last straw!

We demanded an audience with the *Sonderfuhrer* or the Commandant.

Treating us prisoners, especially Irish prisoners, as though they *were* prisoners, it was unheard of, undignified and certainly didn't tie up with the special treatment that we had been promised!

"Foureyes", (our cockney German), for that's what he was nicknamed, promised to do something about it in the morning. "In the meantime" he said, "let's all get our 'eads down and sort it aht later!" Reluctantly we complied, muttering threats as we did so.

We were shown into a vacant compound that had been previously occupied by the "Eyties" and smelt appalling! The beds were three tiered shelves about the length of the hut and there were very few facilities. The bogs were deplorable and the ablutions were one long trough with five or six trickling taps.

We had been featherbedded too long and had reached a degree of comfort and civilisation in our old camp unknown in this area—we were back to 1941 days! (Later I was to discover that the rumours that filtered back to our old Fort 13 Lager were that we were having a great time—fraternising in Berlin with the local "ladies"—Having everything of the Best, three parcels per man per week—walking about without guards. All untrue, of course, but a certain percentage of the English believed it. "Those bloody Irish," they probably said "You can't trust them an inch." So at least in that respect, the Jerries achieved a division. Perhaps the stories were put about by the Germans as propaganda, if so they succeeded!

"Foureyes" took great pains to tell us that he was really British. He had an English mother and a German father and prior to the War had been a steward on the Nordeutscher Lloyd line playing between Harwich and Hamburg. On the outbreak of the war he had been caught at the wrong end and been called up into the German Army ("Bleedin' shanghaied", he called it!) If questioned he would vehemently reply "It's the bleedin' trooth mate an' I'll tell you annuver fing, they'll never catch me for this bleedin' lark again. Directly this lot's over I'm orf 'ome to Stepney".

His accent was authentic and his manner I thought was likeable but he was not trusted. Quite a few suspected him as having been planted by the Germans and others just didn't like him anyway. Whenever he was around, which was often, I engaged him in conversation. I asked him about the "Eyeties". What were they doing in this camp? "Most of them come from the Eastern Front," he said. "They flung their rifles down and refused to fight." He looked left and right before going on. "Mind you, I don't blame 'em, but don't tell 'em I said so!"

Everybody complained to the *Sonderfuhrer* (the propaganda officer who of course spoke English with an American accent) about everything. He promised to "do my best to put things right, boys, just give me a chance", but he never had a chance. The Irish were impossible. If they weren't quarrelling with the Jerries, they were quarrelling amongst themselves. The newly captured Irish prisoners quarrelled with the older variety, and the Northerners didn't always see eye to eye with the Southerners!

The lunchtime soup had to be collected in a huge container from the French compound, and then "Foureyes" would announce to all and sundry, still lying in their beds, because there was nothing for them to do.

"Soup up" or "Come and get it!"

"Ach, rub it in your fuckin' hair" would be the inevitable reply.

To which Foureyes, all hurt, would reply:

"Now, don't be like that—it's better soup than wot we get you know."

"Well, God help ye! No wonder you're losing the bloody war!"

On June 6th we learnt about the invasion from Foureyes—but practically every member of the Camp knew about it and we wondered how the boys were doing. Most of the Jerries were subdued —they'd been led to believe that their fortifications along the French coast were invincible and there were always photographs appearing in the papers of some distinguished General inspecting their impregnable Atlantic Wall.

One could always smell a rat when the War Communique used the well worn phrase "withdrawing to positions of strength". To us that was always a retreat. Another favourite was the "strategic withdrawl". That was another Red Herring used on both fronts! But the biggest news was yet to come. In July we learnt about the attempt on Hitler's life.

Foureyes imparted the news.

"Looks like Adolf's 'ad it"—he said, out of the corner of his mouth. "Somebody's planted a bomb in his brief case, but the Fuerher's safe! Well, that's what the papers say." He showed us his *Volkischer Beobachter* and spelt it out for us.

"Our beloved Fuehrer safe from dastardly bomb plotters."

I think Dr Goebbels must have written the headline—he was the propaganda Minister.

We, of course, we are all derisive and said that the Fuehrer had had it! Was *kaput*. They had put an impostor in his place. Actually an actor from the Berlin Opera House!

Foureyes, on hearing this, thought for a second and then gave his own opinion.

"Nah," he said. "He's too bleedin' lucky. They'll 'ave to use a land mine to get rid of 'im! Preferably under 'is bed when he's on top of Eva!"

He didn't care what he said when he spoke in English (making sure there was no other German around just in case) but when he spoke in *Deutsch* to his superior officer he was more servile and Heiling Hitler all over the place. I'll say this for him though, if he caught your eye during one of his crawling performances, he always winked both eyes at the same time as if to say "I'm only acting!"

A clear case of running with the hare and hunting with the hounds.

We were addressed daily by the *Sonderfuhrer*. We were not going to be put to work like all the other prisoners but were going to be subject to "Special Treatment". He was always harping on about this "Special Treatment" but the signs of it were a long time coming. He did mention something about "special privileges", nothing concrete, but just generalising. When I tried to ferret out of Foureyes what was happening, he looked at me, pityingly and replied "Nuffink —you don't really believe 'im do you?"

We had no Red Cross Food Parcels for over three weeks, but eventually they did organise them and we caught up with our issues. Foureyes lit up like Eighteyes when he saw the contents! He accepted gratefully a bar of Cadbury's chocolate. "My favourite!" he said. We were awakened midnightly by the Mosquito bombers overhead making for Berlin. It was a fascinating sight from our point of view— 36 Kilometres from the Target! The flares—the searchlights playing around in the sky. The ceaseless Ack-ack. The despairing wail of the siren. Occasionally but not very often the sight and sound of a Focke Wolf Fighter.

At first we used to make for the rear of the compound where air raid trenches (they were just holes in the ground) had been dug out by the Eyeties.

On the first occasion Foureyes had appeared blowing a police whistle.

"C'mon lads, everybody out! Everybody out! Bleedin' Mosquitoes over 'ead!"

After a while, we got bored with the whole proceedings and just slept on.

One day, I approached our Cockney *Gefreiter* friend and asked him if it would be possible to put on a show in the French Theatre, which naturally enough was in the French section, a compound not far from us. Foureyes said he didn't see why not, but he'd have to ask. He came back shortly afterwards, saying the *Sonderfuhrer* was "'ighly delighted" and had detailed him (Foureyes) to give us every assistance.

I had him announce it on parade and say that if anyone were interested, would they contact me. Clifford Winterbottom, Johnny Gaskin and I arranged to do a sketch we had previously done at Fort 13 and I auditioned several of the Celtic Thespians. We had quite a number of accordionists—almost enough for a band, singers ("When Irish Eyes are Smiling") and one Irish jig dancer. Also a very funny "Old Men" cross-talk act. We weeded them out and some sort of

Shamrock Revue was produced. We had magnificent dresses lent to us from the wardrobe of the Berlin Opera House. I went along with a guard to select them and travelled on the Berlin underground to do so.

Nobody seemed to smile much and dour and grim glances were flung in my direction as I sat in my seat with my guard.

I smoked openly and defiantly, and stayed glued to my seat!

A large contingent of French p.o.w.'s (mainly theatrical types) watched the show and invited a party of us into the compound for a glass of wine afterwards. They appeared to have unlimited supplies of wine which they organised through the Vichy French Consulate office in Berlin, and there was certainly no shortage of food. I made a particular friend of a designer called Pierre Chezanoff who hailed from Paris and had several meals with him and his syndicate. They hated "Le Bosche" and were very pleased that the Second Front had become a reality and was being so successful. We drank many glasses to an Anglo-French Victory.

Most of them had been captured at the same time as ourselves but they certainly bore no resentment and never once referred to the *"A bas les Anglais"* days. They showed scant respect for the Jerries and seemed to have "Carte Blanche" about coming and going without guards.

During the first week in August we experienced our first 1,000-plane daylight raid, presented to us by the Yanks! It was a fine, thrilling and yet fearful site to see those glistening monsters flying ponderously as if pregnant with bombs, towards Berlin. You could see the sun reflecting on the fuselage as they turned and wheeled over Luckenwalde—they seemed to be completely unopposed—a covey of German fighters took off from a nearby flying strip, not to attack but for evasion purposes. You could see the ack ack bursts in and around the bombers, but they sailed on majestically with their cargoes of death and destruction.

We stood up in the trenches and waved and somebody shouted "Let 'em have it Yanks!". Everyone cheered in assent and suddenly almost within seconds the whine of descending bombs could be heard. There was a tremendous Crump! Crump! Crump! seemingly in the direction of the station (they missed and hit the hospital) but we didn't wait to have it confirmed. We all dived head-long into the trenches on top of the bodies already there, cowering down trying to evade the bomb blast.

Another bomb fell on the outskirts or perimeter of the Russian compound wiping out a few Soviet soldiers in the process, and everything juddered and shuddered as the explosion rent the air.

The Germans didn't make much comment about the bombing, perhaps they were used to it, but the Irish did. "Bloody Yanks" they said "Trust them to make a balls of it!"

The conditions in the camp and the quarrelsome attitude of the inmates made me think hard about stopping there, and I vowed to myself that somehow I must get away. Preferably back to my original stalag, to Fort 13 where all my friends were, and the days were cushy and comfortable, and one could live the life of O'Reilly!

On my mother's side, there was Scottish blood in the family (her maiden name being Anderson) with a bit of Spanish thrown in. On my father's side was a tattooed shamrock, which proved he was Irish, but in any case he was born in Ireland, and so was I.

I determined to approach Foureyes, my cockney *Gefreiter* acquaintance, and lay my cards on the table.

"Supposin', " I said "Supposin' there was a mistake in registration and somebody who you thought was Irish turned out to be English, would it be in order —I mean—in that case, would the person be returned to his original Stalag?"

"What are you on about?" he said, knowing perfectly well what I was on about, and playing for time.

He looked at me sideways, so that I could see the thickness of the glass on his Army issue spectacles, and said:

"What mistake?... What mistake? You're not 'intin' that *I* should get hold of your record card and alter it—are you?!"

"Well, that was the general idea" I said.

"Christ—it's more than my life's worth. If I was caught doin' somethin' like that, it would be the end of the line for me. The *Russian Front line.* Oh, no, no. Sorry mate. I couldn't possibly do that."

He seemed so final that I didn't broach the subject again until two weeks had gone by.

The conversation ran on roughly the same lines, but this time I came straight out and told him "I'll make it worth your while".

He hesitated, and looked at me, and then said

"They'd shoot me if they caught me. I'd be 'ung for treason. *Kaput*! You know that don't yer!" He waited a couple of seconds, and then said " 'ow much?"

"Name your price" I said magnanimously, now that the fish was nibbling.

"Well, it would be very dodgy, yer know. Very dodgy indeed. On the other 'and"—

"Yes?" said I.

"It *could* be done. Somebody like me could possibly do it"—he nodded to reassure himself. " 'ow much?" He reiterated.

"Coffee? Soup? Chocolate? Cigarettes?" (As if I were in charge of the Red Cross Food depot).

"Yeah—'ow much?" he again said.

"How much? I echoed.

"Yeah—'ow much of *each*?"

We settled on three packets of coffee, six bars of soap, three bars of chocolate, two wedges of butter, 100 cigarettes and a tin of cocoa.

I told the others—Winterbottom, Gaskin and Kelly of the arrangement, but they decided to wait to see what happened to me before joining in the exodus.

I paid him half the butter just to keep him sweet and the rest was to be handed over just before I left—if ever!

One week passed and nothing happened. Each time I looked at Foureyes questioningly, he either winked encouragingly or hurried off as if he'd just remembered a pressing military engagement.

Just when I began to think that I'd backed a loser, it happened.

On the tenth day after the "Agreement" my name was read out at morning roll call ordering me to appear at the German Company Office at 14.00 hours to see the Commandant.

I looked straight ahead, slightly apprehensive that perhaps things had gone wrong, that they had caught Foureyes in the act and I would end up as his accomplice at the court-martial for seducing him into treachery against the Fatherland. A reassuring winking nod from the

Cockney *Gefreiter* left me none the wiser. It could've been "I'm only acting!"

At 2 o'clock I presented myself at the German company office. There was no sign of the Commandant. He never showed up at all, but in the presence of one or two German soldier clerks and an *Unter Offizier,* I was informed by Foureyes in German that there had been a mistake in my registration which had now been discovered and had now been put right. My birthplace as I knew should not have been Belfast but Belper (near Nottingham). He continued in English:—

"Under the circumstances, and on be'alf of the German 'igh Command, I h'am authorised to give you their apologies for any inconvenience caused. Please 'ave yourself in readiness to return to Stalag XXA, Fort 13 Thorn, from whence you came. Heil Hitler!"

That same evening, he came round to collect the rest of his unjust reward. He said he'd altered my record card on the Sunday when so he thought, there was nobody about, but he had nearly got caught. Was it possible for me to throw in a packet of tea for services rendered and old times sake!

I didn't argue (I couldn't). He got his packet of Joe Lyons Tea!

The following day I said my "goodbyes" to the "Sons of Erin" and to Foureyes (Wink—Wink—Heil Hitler!) And was escorted by an obliging guard to Luckenwalde Station where we picked up a local connection for Berlin. There we caught the Cheap Day Non-Return Excursion Special to Thorn. In Poland. And Stalag XXA.

The others followed in about a months time. Foureyes true to form, had upped the payment, but as he had them all by the short 'n' curlies, they had to pay!

They re-joined me—*not* at Fort 13, which had been by this time, evacuated, but at a new camp which was called "*Einheit Drei*". It was only about three or 4 miles from the old Fort and was quite civilised!

We were housed in Nissen-like huts and slept in two-tiered bunk beds—it was all quite nice but some of the magic had gone. I expected to go back to the old Fort and it wasn't the same going to a camp in the open.

I missed the theatre for a start, and I had looked forward to working in it again.

I often wonder what happened to Foureyes. I bet he purloined a British uniform and got himself repatriated as an Englishman cut off from his unit!

Probably runs some flourishing supermarket at Shepherds Bush or somewhere by now. On second thoughts, he undoubtably owns a chain of them!

CHAPTER 10
"Alles ist not Verboten"

The Camp, *Einheit Drei*, as it was called—was quite tolerable. The accommodation was superior, civilised tables to eat off, proper Continental bogs—feet-astride-in-the-footmarks and I hope I hit the hole in the middle type! Plenty of room to walk around. A Concert Hall of sorts although as yet nothing had been attempted there in the way of shows. The cookhouse was run by the admirable Jimmy Hooks who supplied the B.B.C. Bulletins which were read out every other night in the huts. There was also a library and a new innovation was the Saturday Night Dance.

In addition there was horse racing, which encouraged heavy betting in *Lager Gelt* (Camp money). At the throw of a dice, the horses were moved around the floor from start to winning post.

And on Sunday evenings, at sunset, a bugler (usually Jackie Blakey) would blow "Abide with Me" on his trumpet.

It was eerie—odd, and moving.

"Prisoners Pie" was no longer in existence. The office had been closed down by the Germans and Jimmy Woolcock was on a local working party.

For some reason that I can't remember, I decided to be a lone wolf and did not rejoin Jimmy and Johnny Murray as a trio but continued on my own. Frankie Coburn who was a permanent indoor worker orderly for the hut, sometimes cooked some meals for me when I returned from the daily working party.

I worked in the German Barracks about two or 3 miles down the road towards Thorn proper, but the work was not hard and quite enjoyable in a way. We practically roamed about the barracks guard-free. There was only one guard and he was an oldish chap who was quite content to leave us to our own devices as long as we did our designated jobs and re-assembled at knocking off time with the minimum of fuss. There were 50 of us altogether and it was really "fatigue" work we were doing. Unloading coal, sanding the roads when slippery or icy, unloading German rations and assisting in the

213

German Cookhouse. And driving around with a van to help collect swill for the German Piggery. For the pigs I mean.

It was at the "*Offiziere Kantine*" that I met Lucy Ogbolavitch or some such difficult to pronounce Russian name. She along with her father a Professor from Sebastopol University, had been brought back to Poland as prisoners. Her father had been carted off to Berlin (so she said) and she had been assigned to work at the Officers Canteen in the barracks or *"Kaserne"* as it was called. The officers had their meals there and I and a couple of other blokes used to call (as I said before) to collect this swill. She, herself, was a collector's "piece" but was dead scared of anybody handling her!

She spoke German and told us about beautiful Odessa, how it was before the war. She was about twenty years of age and from the moment I met her I became pro-Russian. Much later, not so!

She was a Jewish jewel. She was dark with a sallow complexion, long black hair fell to her waist, and she had dark, burning intense eyes. We never really got the truth out of her, she was probably very lucky to be where she was in the light of what happened to the rest of the Jews. She gave me a photograph with "Love from Lucy" written on the back. Later I found she'd given the others photos with the same inscription on the back. It was an old *Russian* custom, or perhaps she just liked playing the field. But anything of beauty was a joy forever, and a pretty diversion to have around. She profited, of course, having chocolate and whatever she fancied heaped upon her. That's a custom as old as the hills!

At the end of the day we would regroup and march back to camp at about 5.30. 8 till 5.30 were quite decent hours. Almost civilised.

The Jerries by now had seen the Light—it was red—coming up from the East in the shape of the Russian hordes. Warsaw was in the process of falling and being circumnavigated and the icy Winter was the only stumbling block in the path of the Soviets.

The invasion of France continued to be a great success and the German army was rapidly withdrawing from Italy. Wherever you looked on the map, Germany on all fronts was falling back. It could be over quite soon but it could also dwindle on and on and on! As we well knew.

The Commandant of the new *Einheit Drei* Camp had seen service in Africa and Italy before being wounded and then seconded to the p.o.w. camp. He was a bit of a bastard and did everything to the letter of the Military Law—in other words he regularly searched everybody, even though they'd only been working in the German compound a stone's throw from the camp! His strict orders were that anything found on p.o.w.'s contrary to regulations was to be confiscated!

Of course we had to find ways around it, which being British, we did!

To put you in the picture as to the geography of the camp— coming from Thorn you hit the perimeter of the barbed wire about 400 yards before the entrance gates of the camp loomed up, so one had ample time to hurl one's haversack full of loot over the wire into the waiting arms of some confederate or companion. On one occasion I had the misfortune to suffer the loss of two bottles of Schnapps which I had stuffed into my haversack. I had arranged with Coburn to be there at a certain time in order to catch it as it came hurtling over the high wire wall. He was there alright but mistimed the catching bit, consequently my haversack reeked of illicit Schnapps for days afterwards and I was for ever finding bits of broken glass in the lining!

The following week, not to suffer the same loss, but risking the searches, I prepared to bring in one bottle at a time, in the following manner. I tied a thick piece of Red Cross string around my waist, and then around the neck of the bottle, so that the bottle dangled between my legs making it slightly difficult to walk (not unlike a cow with a full udder that keeps hitting the inside of her knee). However, when we arrived at the gates of the camp and came to a halt to be searched, I thrust the bottle towards my rear and clamped my legs together as the

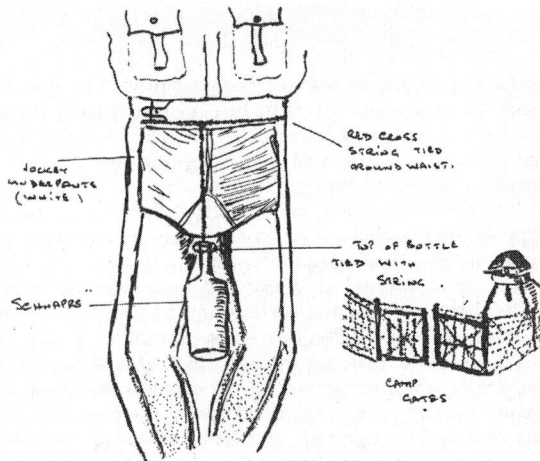

FULL BOTTLE FRONTAL
AS SEEN THRU' THE EYES OF
OUR X RAY ILLUSTRATOR.

searcher's hands went down my trousers in front. And then, when he went round the back and repeated the groping routine. I performed the gymnastic feat of thrusting forward so that the bottle pushed forward as if bursting to get out. It fooled the searchers in the end, but I practically castrated myself marching into camp, and trying to appear nonchalant at the same time!

On another occasion, when we were going to hold a party, the problem of how to get the drink into the camp (in this particular case quite a lot—three bottles of Schnapps, two of Slivovitz, three of unknown vintage brandy, and some other bottles, containing some supposedly wine concoctions never seen before or since!) was solved by my fainting on the job (pretending of course!). The guard was in on it, so it was O.K.from our end. They procured a stretcher from the barracks, putting the bottles under me, down my legs and up in my battledress blouse, so that I looked like Bessie Bunter's mother, with two bottles of Slivovitz where my bosom ought to be; they covered me with a blanket, whitening my face with powder, and darkening my eyes with shadow make-up to heighten the effect, and there I was, almost a "goner"! They watered my hair and left beads of water to indicate sweat or fever as we approached the camp. I uttered fervent moans and pitiful cries for my Mother, Father, and/or Doctor, and because it was just after lunch, and the Commandant had not yet returned from his, the urgency of the fever was impressed on the *Gefreiter* deputy, and we sailed through without loss—not even a leak. And a good time was had by all.

Owing to the move from the Fort to the new camp and the Theatre not being fitted out so professionally as the dear old Fort one, it took some time to organise any show, but eventually we did. A Revue of sorts was put on and I wrote a cross-talk act for Frankie Coburn and myself. We were a couple of deep South plantation workers—he was the flashy dame, and I was the "Steppin Fetchit" boyfriend! We finished off the act with a song and a semi soft shoe shuffle. I enjoyed it, but there wasn't quite the same enthusiasm around as there had been at the Fort. I can't put my finger on why. Perhaps the air of inevitability and depression was seeping into the p.o.w.'s as well as the Jerries—after all it was coming up to the fifth Christmas away from home and still no concrete sign of when the war would be over.

We were aware of course, of the rapidity of the Russian advance, but they had been held up before (especially outside Warsaw) and could be again.

The German Press and radio were full of a new "Secret Weapon" (the Atom Bomb as we now know) which was going to win all their battles and end their reverses, and was supposedly more devastating than the V2 Rockets which were still raining on London.

In the meantime it was no secret that a Dance was being held in the Concert Hall on Saturday night and it was billed as "Come to the Saturday night Hop!" I sorted out my number one shirt, pullover, and trousers and along with my best behaviour which I also put on, I attended my first prison camp ball!

There was a slight smell of cheap sent about the place, (where that came from I'll never know,) and the live quartet of piano, guitar, double bass and drums played all the old (and some of the new) favourites,. Everybody knew everybody else of course, it was just a question of who was going to be "He" or "She" when it came to the Spot Waltz!

The "Excuse Me" dances were a bit of a dilemma—once or twice I found myself being the dame and if you're not used to it—it's not easy going backwards.

At Christmas there was a Gramophone Recital and the machine was electrically connected up with amplifiers situated at each side of the Concert Hall Stage.

To our amazement and great delight we suddenly heard the King of England's Christmas Speech booming out through all the speakers!

I can't remember what he said now but I can tell you that there was not a "dry eye in the House"!

The radio in Jimmy Hooks' charge (in the cookhouse) had been secretly connected up (by previous arrangement of course!) at the crucial moment and when the rest of the camp heard what had happened they cursed their non-attendance at the recital. "Track 29! Boy, you can give me a shine! Chattanooga Choo-Choo won't you choo-choo me Home!!"

After Xmas and into the New Year the rumours came thick and fast.

We knew for a fact that the Russians were getting up "steam." Warsaw had fallen and the Jerries were retreating. But then would come a lull, a temporary hold up, perhaps of two or three weeks duration. Then gradually the Soviet Steamroller inched along another few miles further into Poland.

What would they—the Germans—do with us? That was the great talking point! At first, it seemed a matter of indifference to the guards and officers, who pretended that nothing was happening and carried on with the day-to-day duties. As we did too! But naturally, there was this suppressed atmosphere of anticipation. What if the Jerries just abandoned us to the advancing Russkys! And took off themselves. They were quite a few who thought that this was on the cards, that these were the secret orders.

One day on our way to the barracks as usual we saw what, at a distance, looked like a tattered and battered Company coming towards us carrying picks and shovels like a Labour corps.

The company turned out to be about a hundred Jewish girls who had been ordered to dig "tank traps"—pits of 20 or 30 yards wide and

20 feet deep. It was a helluva job as the ground was frozen solid on top and severer weather was obviously on the way. Needless to say they did it. Each of the girls had her hair shorn and wore a scarf or a bit of cloth to cover her shaven head. The majority of them had no shoes or boots, but their feet were wrapped in old rags and sacking held together with paper string. They were mostly very young, 18 to 22 years of age, and looked as if they could do with a square meal. They were guarded, brutally and fiercely, by black-uniformed S.S. guards, who knocked them about and brandished revolvers at them like gangsters in a film.

We were forbidden to speak to them and were told that they were criminals. But fate, in its peculiar way, made sure that later we would all meet again.

The grapevine or latrine rumour *was* that we were going to march back into Germany proper and be rehoused in new camps.... Just in case, I started collecting stout pieces of wood, mostly from bed boards and began to make myself a decent sized sledge. As it turned out, it was just as well that I did.

The Trek.

It was the 22nd February 1945 when we started the Great Trek. The order had come from Berlin and then on from our Stalag XXA.

"All British Prisoners of War confined in *Gefangen Lagers* in Poland will move back into Germany proper...."

In any case the Russian guns could be heard not too far away and the Red Air Force had flown over on three occasions, endeavouring to bomb the bridge which spanned the River Vistula. A clutch of bombs had fallen near the camp which didn't say much for their marksmanship. On the other hand they could have mistaken us for a German barracks. So said the Soviet sympathisers, forgetting the barbed wire and high look-out posts all around us!

And this was the very early morning of the 22nd., the dawn streaks appeared in a grey and lifeless sky and snow was everywhere. The wind from Siberia was bitter and the below-zero air was heavy with frost making us all look like frozen Father Christmases with an icy fuzz on our hair, our eyebrows and our whiskers. And even the hair in our nostrils froze as solid as fishbones. I wore a balaclava, my Polish Cavalry hat, two pairs of Army issue long johns, two sweaters, battledress, a pair of German Army Jackboots and my overcoat tightly buttoned—well almost tightly buttoned!

My goods and chattels were strapped onto my home-made sledge, and my haversack bulged with tins of Red Cross food and bars of chocolate. I was ready.

We paraded for the last time in *Einheit Drei* Camp and were given a buckshee issue of German black bread and some damaged tins of Red Cross food; some bars of chocolate which were promptly scoffed, and some English cigarettes.

I answered my name—Kydd 13745—for my last roll call in the camp and by the time an inch of snow had fallen we were on our way.

The Great Trek of approximately a thousand prisoners had begun. There were about three companies of German soldiers to guard us, including those originally based at the camp. At first they were their usual officious and frantic shouting selves but as the day wore on and the column became more extended, and the going became more joyless, they inevitably relaxed a little and were finally as weary as the p.o.w.'s they were supposed to be guarding.

On that first day we marched and slithered 36 miles towards Germany heaving and hoeing our sledges behind us. As night fell we were guided into a huge field which was 12 inches deep in virgin snow. Here we were to spend the night, a cold, sleepless night, for on hearing the drone of aircraft engines the order was given that no fires were to be lit. The prisoners showed dissent—vocally—but they complied.

Ready for the 'Trek'.

I opened a tin of corned beef and polished it off, and had some biscuits and jam for afters, and then tried to settle down for the night, but it was too cold to sleep. I tried kipping across the sledge. I tried huddling up with some blokes from my hut, but the night air was so raw, that cold penetrated the clothing (even my well padded extras).

Eventually after spasmodic dozing and waking up and shivering, we saw the first streaks of dawn appearing. This was the signal to start a fire, and soon the field was blazing with small fires everywhere, like an Indian reservation. Everybody brewed up; with melted snow! The German guards collected around the various fires to warm themselves and one with whom I had been on friendly terms, helped himself to a sip of tea. (There was nothing laid on for the Jerries at all.) During the pleasantries, one of the wheels from a cart carrying the German Company stores was whisked off and thrown onto the fire to keep the blaze going, which was understandable, but not to the Germans! They went mad when they discovered it and my German tea-sipping friend, hastily rescued it. I gave him a hand to put it back, and although partly burnt and slightly singed, it continue to revolve dutifully, albeit a little drunkenly!

Whilst doing his rescue act, the guard had inadvertently put his rifle down (trusting fool!). And this too had been cast into the fiery furnace until I rescued it.

We appeased the "good guy" guard by "borrowing" another guard's rifle and substituting the burnt and singed one in its place.

We never found out how *he* got on. Perhaps he too switched and so it went on right down through the company.

I imagined the scene:

Sergeant: "For inspection—Port Arms! 'ello! Vas is dis?"

Herr Soldat: "Mein rifle got singed in that nacht air in Poland."

Sergeant: "Vas?"

Herr Soldat: "Jahvol—I vas rescuing der vheel from the fire und altho it vas singed it still vorked, und then my rifle got singed too, but it fires all right—I zink."

Sergeant: "Put zis man in ze bunker for 14 tags."

At about 6 a.m after the early morning shenanigans we started out on Day 2 of our Trek.

This time we knew more or less what to expect. No grub from the Germans and a gruelling lot of marching.

As we made our way along the road, the small coterie of p.o.w.'s of five years acquaintance (with whom I was intimately associated) hitched their sledges to the back stay of the German Military cart we were behind and thus we travelled for about 5 miles. The German driver with whom we had a nodding friendship accepted the fags we plied him with and said nothing.

It was as well that we did hitch our sledges to the cart because the snow began to flurry down and swirl around as if someone had opened the snow trap door and the going became very uncomfortable and arduous.

By this time our extending column had been joined by a large group of evacuating German civilians—mostly farmers and their families with two or three farm wagon carts piled high with Polish loot and their belongings (Most of them had taken over farms from the Poles who had been dispossessed after the rape of Poland).

It was all reminiscent of the pioneer days of the American covered wagons, with the Russkys as the Redskins and their guns as the war drums.

As we slowly progressed, the column became more and more extended, some falling back as the going got tough and others forging ahead.

The underfoot conditions became very treacherous indeed. A curtain of snow continued to fall, and several horses plunged and fell in an effort to retain their foothold. The prisoners were detailed to get them back on their feet and the hold-ups were frequent and many. If it had not been for a hitch-hiking effort, our group would have fallen far behind. I was mentally congratulating myself for my foresight in hitching my sledge to the cart when the rope broke, and my belongings began to slide down the incline we were mounting!

I hastened to forestall it, but to no avail. The sledge finished up at the bottom of the hill at the side of the road. Out of breath trying to retrieve it I sat on top of the sledge and surveyed the scene. The Retreat from Moscow was never like this but it had similarities. The p.o.w.'s were carefree and retained their sense of humour—it was all a Great German Jape! But the Jerries were all "Doom and Gloom" personified and were beginning to show it!

I lit up a cigarette, and was joined by the guard whose rifle I had retrieved from the fire. I offered him a fag which he took, but did not smoke. He put it carefully in his pocket. "*Naher*" he said sadly, he would smoke it later. He was wearing a small green scarf (German soldiers' issue) over his nose, mouth, and ears, like a yashmak, and he looked very cold and very fed up.

He wasn't a bad chap really. A man of about 50, from Berlin, who had been a prisoner in British hands in the 1914/18 affair.

He leant over me and bent down so that his mouth was close to my ear. "*Sind zie O.K.?*" he asked.

"Yah—just taking a pauser—a break."

"Don't let the *Feldwebel* catch you sitting there."

"You know what he can do" I replied unfeelingly.

"*Jah*, I know" he said, "but he can be a swine to us as well as to you."

"O.K." I said, "Where is he?"

"One mile down the road" he smirked, "His Jeep has broken down!" He gave a guttural laugh. "Ho! Ho! Ho!"

I laughed (in English) "Ha! Ha! Ha!"

"Hans, I say?" I queried "Where are we bound for?"

"Lubeck, *Ich glaube*."

"LUBECK! LUBECK? That's bloody miles away. It'll take us weeks in this weather."

"*Jah*, I know, *Verdamt krieg! Damn Vor*!"

I got up off the sledge and shouted after him as he moved off, cupping my hands for him to hear better.

"Hans?"

He stopped and turned round.

"*Jah?*"

"Hang onto your rifle, you may need it!"

He grinned wryly and said "*Schiser Krieg*!"

I followed him, slowly, dragging my sledge after me.

Round about two o'clock the snow stopped and a watery sun half-heartedly shone. By this time I had caught up with one of my fellow p.o.w.'s I had known for a long time. He had been in the same room as myself at Fort13 and was a professional musician who played the cello sensitively as if he loved it. He had played in the camp orchestra, alto sax, doubling clarinet, and I had been associated with him in innumerable shows. He was a quite likeable bloke—shrewd, with a very dry sense of humour. His name was Richard Davis and he came from Bournemouth. "Proper bloody caper this is" he said as I caught him—still trundling on.

"Yeah—Hans tells me we're making for Lubeck."

He looked at me as if I'd offered to decorate him with the Iron Cross—Second-class!

"Lubeck! We'll never survive. We'll be lucky if we get to Bromberg, never mind Lubeck!"

"Oh—anything can happen" I said "The Jerries might surrender before then."

"Some hopes. You've been saying that for the last two years!"— he retorted cynically.

"Oh well, we'll see. Do you fancy a cuppa tea?"

"Yeah, why not".

Tea was the panacea, the Elixir of Life. When in doubt—brew up!

He possessed one of those home made contraptions called a "Blower" invented as far as I know in prison camp. It worked on the bellows system and could boil a pint of water from a meagre flame in about three minutes flat! We stuffed the dixie (the German type—we found they were better than the British) with snow, and he produced a methylated tablet from somewhere, and before you could say "Lubeck's not the place for me!" the water was boiling. We made the tea and I opened a tin of meatloaf and cut it in half, cut 4 slices of German bread, whipped on the ersatz margarine and there we were with a picnic lunch.

The German military bread tasted slightly sour and sawdusty and we had to accustom ourselves to eating it again. For the last year or so we had managed to acquire from our racketeering sources a white loaf per day and had given the issue-bread away, which tells you what heights we reached in the bartering stakes! We were just mad about white bread!

As we munched and supped, the column continued to file past—singly, spasmodically, and then in bursts of groups.

We estimated roughly and idly that the 1,000-man column must have now swollen to over 2,000 with the civilian additions and that it now stretched over 3 miles or more, all plodding towards the Fatherland, *Deutschland*. No longer *uber* (over) but very much *unter* (under), *alles*!

We gathered up our goods and chattels and "sledged off", towards Bromberg. For that was the next objective. I discussed with Davis the possibility of "taking off" from the column.

"We could" said I with all my great military know-how, "take off and await the arrival of the Russians. After all they are our Allies. They can't be all that far away; in fact unless they are held up, they could overtake us in a week at the pace we're going. On the other hand (I mused) they had sat outside Warsaw for months. Just waiting. They *could* do the same again, and it could be dangerous for two p.o.w.'s marauding on the loose."

"We could take off right now," said Davis, "but the country is far too open."

He was right of course. The country *was* far too open, there was no cover and we were miles from civilisation.

We decided to talk about it later when we'd seen how the land lay. Our thoughts and speech were interrupted by an Armoured Transport Column on the retreat, on its way back to Bromberg or further, to regroup! They scurried past in the snow churning the road up with their steel tracks. There were several troop-carrying vehicles for the battle-weary German soldiers looking very sullen, listless and fed up. Some were wounded and wore bandages, and most of them were unshaven. They were very young chaps.

We silently watched them go past and noted their mental attitude.

In contrast, I remembered how cocky and confident they had been four years earlier when they had first invaded Russia. I was working on the *bahnhof* (railway station) at the time, and I remembered the trainload after trainload of happy, smiling, singing, victorious soldiers. At that time they were going through Russia like a hot knife through ersatz margarine, and when they caught sight of us prisoners, they called out—inevitably—"*England, kaput! Deutschland, Uber Alles!*" And that was invariably the cue for one of their marching songs, which they sang extremely well, in some cases like a specially trained Welsh choir with harmonies and everything. I must say, I was impressed the first time I heard them. Then they would sing another popular ditty called "*Gegen England*" which was all about the invasion of England. They didn't sing that much nowadays —it wasn't in the charts at all!

Mind you, fair's fair. After the fall of France in 1940 you didn't hear *us* singing "We're going to hang out the washing on the Siegfried Line".

When the last of the retreating trucks had gone through on the way to Bromberg (or Bydgosh in Polish) we took up our places in the *strasse* and followed in their wake.

We had travelled about three miles when we came upon the 100 Jewish girls whom we had seen outside *Einheit Drei* camp when they'd been about to dig tank traps. They were resting at the roadside and their appearance was sad and almost indescribable. When we got close to them we could see that their clothes were mainly rags and in places patches of bare skin showed through. Their shovels and pics were piled high on to a farm cart which they were pushing and pulling along by themselves. The black uniformed S.S. guards were continually shouting at them, ordering them not to fraternise with the soldier prisoners.

They hit and pushed some of the girls and sent them sprawling, —but to no avail—the soldiers still fraternised.

Several of the girls spoke English, and I conversed with one from Hungary. She told me that they came from many countries—Rumania, Yugoslavia, Hungary and Poland. She was 20 years of age and had been away from home for two years; she had last seen her parents in a concentration camp at Maidanek in Poland.

I gave her a bar of chocolate and some cigarettes and finally I took my German Jackboots off and handed them to her. I had a pair of British boots in my kitbag which I proceeded to get out and put on.

She was overcome with gratitude and fell on her knees and sought to kiss my hand murmuring "Thank you, oh thank you!" and then tried to help me do up my laces as if I were a little boy, but embarrassed I waved her away.

One of the S.S. guards came up and kicked her away and she fell back into the snow, still clutching her precious boots. He rounded on me shouting "*Verboten! Das ist Verboten! Los! Los*"! and he came towards me, thrusting his enraged face into mine.

I stood my ground. I started quoting the Geneva convention appertaining to the treatment of Prisoners of War, in brief "You touch me, and I'll report you chum!" I might as well have addressed the air.

He screamed as if he would burst and drew his revolver from its holster and discharged several shots into the air. The situation was getting tense and rather ugly. I wasn't going to retreat, and neither was he!

Luckily for me two of our guards arrived on the scene and intervened ushering me on my way, rather like protective fathers or Deutsch Uncles.

As I moved off, I turned to take a last look at the girls and wondered what would happen to them, little knowing that our paths would cross again two months later—in Warsaw.

Around about 8.30 p.m. in the evening, we entered Bromberg, scene of the famous or infamous massacre of Germans that took place on a Sunday at the beginning of the war, which became known to every invading German soldier as "Bloody Sunday." Though subsequently the role of German activists in the killings has muddied the truth.

We blundered our way through the streets. It was very dark and a heavy blackout was being enforced. Nonetheless, it seemed warm and comforting after the open road and the wind and the snow.

Soon we were corralled and directed to a large and disreputable factory, which was to be our home for the night. Davis set to work to produce the magic brew whilst I went in search of some bedding straw and wood shavings, which had been dumped in an adjoining warehouse. There was a helluva scramble going on to collect the choicest pieces because the early birds or first arrivals had snaffled most of it. Some of them were burning the wood shavings to heat their tins of food and to warm the place up. The air was thick with smoke and altercations!

Davis and I had just about sorted ourselves out when the German *Feldwebel* (Sergeant Major) came in and blew his whistle several times like a referee at a football match. The majority of prisoners ignored him completely and continued with the domestic and sleeping arrangements. Some catcalled and told him what to do with his whistle. He ignored their sallies, waited for 20 seconds, and then as if winding himself up for the effort, bellowed, at the top of his voice, "ALLES RAUS!"—ALLES RAUS!!" (everybody out).

The reaction was almost the same as he'd been given for his whistling. There was a momentary pause of five seconds, and then the catcalls continued.

"Get stuffed", "Get knotted" and the well worn "Fuck right off!"

Finally, he could take it no longer. He took his revolver from its holster and discharged three rounds into the rafters! He got what he wanted—silence and complete attention.

He bellowed "We must march through the night to reach the border."

It was no joke. It was obviously an order and he was going to see that it was carried out.

Grumbling and groaning and cursing and moaning and persuaded by the guards who had appeared on the scene to help implement the order, we reluctantly started to gather all things together prior to getting out.

We were marshalled and lined up more in a military fashion than we had been when we straggled in. Unfortunately, or maybe fortunately, some of our stragglers were only just arriving, and they were trying to force their way in, not knowing that we were coming out, and for awhile chaos reigned.

Eventually some semblance of order was restored and after half an hour we were on our way again.

Davis and I were forced to abandon our sledges—well, we'd started to break them up for firewood to cook a worthwhile meal before we'd had to evacuate, consequently we were now forced to carry our bulging haversacks on our backs and our overfull kitbags on top of that! In addition we had transferred our precious tins of Red Cross food to one huge bag which we carried between us—stretcher fashion.

Thus we marched through Bromberg, overloaded, undernourished, tired, fed up, sulky and complaining!

The German guards (not our camp ones) although tired themselves, forced the column to keep closer together. There was much shouting and bellowing as if to impress the natives, and eventually we found ourselves at the bridge which spans the River Vistula. There, in the blackout, we were halted to allow a fleet of German Panzer Tanks and an Armoured Column to cross the bridge, on its way to the shrinking Front for a last ditch defence of occupied Poland.

Unfortunately, the tracks of one of the Tiger Tanks on the bridge came off, and a huge chaotic traffic block ensued.

The prisoners were not allowed to cross the bridge until the debacle was sorted out.

We waited. We stamped our feet to keep warm. And we protested. As one does. They were a very long time sorting things out. Some of the guards looked as fed-up as we did, but they had to put up a front and pretend to be concerned with the situation. You know the sort of thing—peering into the blackness when the *Feldwebel* was about—"Not finished yet? Oh dear. Ah well, accidents will happen. Not long now, I expect."

Hans, our singed-rifle friend, appeared on the scene, surreptitiously smoking an English cigarette. He took one look, said *"Krieg shiser"* and disappeared again!

By this time, p.o.w.'s were milling about, as if outside a football stadium with the ground full up.

" 'Ow much bleedin' longer are we goin' to wait?"

"The Russkys'll be here in a minute!"

"Bloody Hellfire!"

Civilians were filtering among us. One civvy looking very much like Trotsky, in cape and floppy hat, sidled up to me, and engaged me in conversation. I thought first of all he was after some bartering goods, but on the contrary, he asked me if there was anything I wanted?

"To get out of this…" I started to say, but he cut across me.

"That could be arranged if you'd like to make it worth my while."

I was taken aback a bit.

"You mean you'd help me to escape?

"That is the idea" he confirmed.

"Could you take two of us?" I queried.

"*Nein!* Only one."

"Oh, well it's no good then, is it? My friend must go with me."

(Might have ended up in a ditch with my throat cut and all my goods and chattels gone. And you're no good without them, are you?)

With a shrug of the shoulders he disappeared into the crowd. I looked after him, and then went in search of Davis who was sitting on top of his kitbag and mine, smoking a cigarette and ruminating.

I told him of my encounter with the civilian and of how I had said that it would be all right if the two of us could go together, but that I wasn't going alone.

"Well, you're a fool," said Davis unfeelingly, "You should have taken a chance and gone, *I* would have."

I didn't believe him, but I felt a little hurt him having said so.

"All right then, if you feel that this is the time and the place, we can take off when we get over the other side of the bridge. I know this area, I was here with a portable cinema outfit, run by a guy called Kunnemann, helping Freddie Foster recce his escape route."

"So?" said Davis.

"On the other side of the bridge the main road continues for about half a mile or just over and then veers to the right past a V -shaped minor road."

"So?" said Davis, most helpfully.

"Well, we'll arrange for some of the boys to cause a diversion up in front in order to distract the guards, and then we'll with luck, march to the left down the main road."

Davis cogitated for a second.

"Well, what do you think?" I said.

At last he nodded his agreement.

"O.K." He said. "Anything is better than marching through the night, which I'm not cut out for." And then, as an afterthought...

"Yeah, if we're going to make it, better to go in Poland. It'll be no good in Germany."

I really did know the disposition of the roads the other side of the bridge, having visited a camp there with a travelling cinema two years earlier. I had sweated carrying the projector and *knew* that the road forked about three quarters of a mile further on.

And that, *mein freunds,* was the plan of escape, if that is what it could be called!

In due time—well it was well past shivering time, the bridge was cleared with the assistance of a troop carrier towing the stricken de-tracked tank.

In drips and cold drabs we shambled across.

The further we got from the bridge the darker it became, and although there was a strictly enforced blackout, a slight reflection came from the moonlight on the snow. Our breath showed up on the midnight air and it was already freezing.

At a shrill wolf whistle signal from Kydd the "diversionists" struck up their song, which was ironically *Wenn wir Fahren gegen England,* when we got to the fork in the road. The few guards who were near or alongside us moved up the column to quell the choir and the two would-be escapers simply walked to the left—down the minor road. Some of the p.o.w.'s behind—not in the know—shouted.

"Hey, you're taking the wrong bloody road!"

We ignored them and continued until we were swallowed up in the blackness down the minor road, which unfortunately wasn't a yellow brick one!

We quickened our pace, not looking back and slithered on for about a quarter of a mile—not speaking, but then taking the odd furtive look around to see that we hadn't been spotted. So far—so good. Finally we cautiously stopped and spoke only in short whispers.

"What now?" breathed my companion exhaling steam and sweating profusely as he spoke.

"Find a garden and sit it out till the column has passed", I answered perspiringly.

We looked around and over to the left was the very thing—a garden with a tall hedge all the way around it looking like a white wall of snow. A perfect cover. But therein lay a danger too. The houses were spaced out. Detached. And quite presentable. Which could only mean one thing—they were occupied by German or "Gummy Deutsch"—people who would have no hesitation in reporting us to the authorities should we be discovered. We didn't have much alternative. We decided to take a chance and soft-shoed over, entering the garden very quietly. Well, as quietly as we could, because here and there the odd piece of frozen snow would crackle, causing you to halt in your step and hold your breath half expecting a window to be thrown up and a guttural voice to call out "Who's there?"

Luckily, nothing happened. All was quiet. Or comparatively so. There was a slight distant hum from the direction of Bromberg which was probably German troop activity.

We made for the corner of the garden, dumped our gear and sat on it.

And then we got our breath back.

After about 15 minutes of just sitting, and looking, and chancing a cigarette which we took turns to inhale, cupping the fag in our hands, I suggested, whispering, that I should go and find, or try and find a warmer billet. I would have to reconnoitre the neighbourhood and find a poor-looking cottage which would signify a Polish occupant. Davis agreed and was about to say something, when we heard a voice—two voices—arguing. We both stiffened like pointer dogs and, alerted we strained to listen.

A whispered altercation between two men was going on in the middle of the road about 15 to 20 yards away.

I listened intently and heard one say "Ach, shure they didna see us."

I thought to myself—I know that voice.

And then the other replied "We ought to go a wee bit further—just to make sure."

I recognised them. I knew them both. And so did Dickie Davis.

They were two Scotsman by the names of George Clare and Ian McRobbie who had been in the same room as ourselves in the camp we had lately vacated.

I stood up and in a loud theatrical whisper hissed "Psst—Psst. George! McRobbie! Over here."

"Who the hell's that?" came the Glaswegian answer.

"It's me. Sam. Sam Kydd and Dickie Davis. Over here in this garden."

They edged over and I was right. It was George Clare and Ian McRobbie.

They had taken off from the column in exactly the same way as we had done. They told us they had no fixed plan, only "taking off" to avoid the long march through the night, and providing they were not picked up, to await the arrival of the Russians.

It was agreed that because of my pre-knowledge of the area I should endeavour to find a safer and warmer billet for the rest of the freezing night. And so, eventually, after about two hours wait by which time the cold had got into our bones, I decided to go.

I took some coffee, chocolate and cigarettes, also a tin of corned beef and two bars of soap as barter-persuader material!

Stealthily and a bit apprehensively, I made my way down the road. Back along the way we had come.

I hugged the trees which lined the left of the road, the frozen snow crackling under my footsteps, pausing every now and then to see if I were detected, but all seemed well.

I came at last to the fork in the road which I approached very slowly and cautiously and peered into the inky blackness.

There was no sign of troop movements—either British or German.

I waited for some time to make sure and was just about to dash across the major road when I heard a snuffling noise over to the right of me, as if someone were suppressing a sneeze. I dropped to my haunches and looked into the darkness, to the right and then to the left.

Something rushed across the main road and started to lick at my face. It was a dog! A mongrel. He jumped up and put his paws on my shoulder and I overbalanced and fell back into the snow—cursing! I got up and shooed him away by pretending to throw an imaginary stick. He retreated about five or six yards and then stopped and looked at me—quizzically with his head to one side. I picked up a piece of frozen snow and lobbed it at him. It hit him on the rump, and he yelped off. I made a mental note to contribute to the Polish S.P.C.A. in retribution and collected my thoughts.

I had gone even colder and clammier with fright and I could feel my heart pounding as I looked up and down the road and then left and right again, checking that the road was clear.

All was quiet and nobody was to be seen, so taking a deep breath I shot across the main road and hared towards a track which bordered a huge field leading to some small terraced houses, about 250 yards away. I kept going, till I reached them and then decided to approach from the rear. I circled round making a complete U-turn and knocked timidly on the door of the poorest looking house and waited. Nothing happened. I knocked again, harder and more urgently. And then I heard a shuffling movement. The door was unbolted, the catch withdrawn and an old, wrinkled and poorly dressed woman appeared in the opening.

In a Polish accent and poor German she asked me what I wanted. *"Was wollen Sie?"*

I whispered that I was English—*Angelski*—a *Kriegsgefangener.*

I crossed my hands at the wrist as if handcuffed to confirm my words and she gave me a long look not quite sure of me. She then opened the door and beckoned me in.

I found myself in a sort of scullery-cum-kitchen, lit by a very low oil lamp.

She faced me and I told her again that I was a prisoner of war and that I had left the column that was being marched to Germany.

Could I stay in her house for the night? For somewhere to sleep?

She looked at me as if she were studying my face so as not to forget it and then said "It is very dangerous for us—I must ask my husband."

At that moment a very old man of about 80 years of age, with white hair and bushy moustache, appeared at the doorway and came into the room. She went to him and told him who I was and what I wanted and he came towards me.

"It is very dangerous for us" he said in halting German "If we are caught with a prisoner, then (he made the sign of a knife across the throat)—*Kaput!*"

"I know," I said. "but only for three or four hours." I produced a packet of cigarettes, which I handed to him and the tin of coffee and a bar of chocolate to the old woman.

She said "*Drinkuyie*"—Thank you, and so did the old man.

I replied "*Prosser Bardza* (phonetic—It's a pleasure)."

"Sleep here for the night" said the old man.

Then I had to tell him that there were three other comrades in the same boat as myself, hiding in the garden, waiting for me to return. On hearing this, he became very agitated at first, but his fears were overcome when I produced the tin of corned beef, some soap and another small bar of chocolate.

He bade me hurry to fetch the others and warned me to be extra careful when we returned to the house. I said "Yes, of course", and then made my exit cautiously and quietly. I hesitated at the back of the house, and then instead of retracing my steps, I skirted round in front of the terrace of houses and proceeded along another dirt track path which led to the main road.

Still all was quiet and there was no sign of movement as I made my way towards the major road. I had come to it a considerable way down to the left, that is, the fork in the road was quite a few yards to my right.

I edged slowly behind a building on the side of the road and paused before stepping across.

I was just about to cross when a hand was clamped on my shoulder from behind, and I was spun round. A powerful torch was shone into my face, momentarily dazzling me. I could hardly see my captor's face but I could make out that he was a German officer by his elegant boots and overcoat.

"What are you doing here?" he said harshly and deliberately, in German.

"Er—my sister—er is a—is sick" I stammered. "She lives with her mother—er my mother, and I have been to see her over there." I pointed vaguely from whence I'd come and babbled on with lies explaining that my sister was very nervous and that I was the sole support of my relatives.

He waited patiently until I had finished, still shining the torch in my face, and then let me stew for a bit.

Finally, he said "You are a Tommy, *Jah?*"

"*Jah*" I replied, deflated.

"Why did you leave the column?"

"Pardon?"

"Why did you leave the column?"

He obviously knew about the prisoners' movements.

I coughed, for time, and thought quickly.

"I–er–was feeling ill–unwell–*krank*, and-er-as I used to work here in a working camp two years ago and I made a friend of the German *Arbeiter Meister* (Workmaster Foreman) and I knew that he lived here, and I went to visit him to say "Goodbye" before going on my way to Germany." (I nearly said Fatherland.)

"*Nein, nein, mein lieber Freund*" he said "You intended to stay here, and await the arrival of the Russians. *Nicht?*" (Isn't that so?)

"*Jah*" I said.

"There is no *Arbeitmeister* is there?"

"*Nein,* no, *Arbeitmeister.*"

"What were you doing over there?" He pointed the torch in the direction of the houses.

"I had gone to relieve myself and found that the column had passed." (I was a born liar.)

He thought for a moment—no doubt sceptically—and then came to a decision.

"You are foolish to think that the Russians would care for you. They are animals. They would rob you and shoot you. I know them. They are barbarians."

I made no reply. What could I say?

"Follow your comrades to Germany. There you will do better."

He snapped off the torch and pointed in the direction of Schneidermuhl away from Bromberg.

"*Los—Marsch!*"

"*Danke schoen, Herr Kapitan*" I saluted and clicked my heels and started to walk vaguely in the general direction he had indicated, but at a certain half left inclined angle, so that I could rejoin the minor road to the left of the fork.

"Halt!" he shouted. And shone the torch in my direction.

I halted and half turned.

"This way" he shouted. The torch weaved and pointed in the right direction.

"*Jah, Herr Kapitan.*" I did a right turn and marched off. I must have gone about a quarter of a mile before I felt it safe to stop. I bent down, pretending to fix the lace on my boot and at the same time cocked my head to see if I could see him.

There was no sign of the Kapitan. Well, I couldn't see *him*, and if not he certainly couldn't see me. I edged back along the major road till I finally without incident, came to the minor one again, and scuttled down it thankfully. I plodded on till I heard a frantic "Psst–is that you?"

I veered over in their direction. "Blimey–you took your bloody time, didn't you! Eh? Bloody freezing here I can tell you!" "Where the hell have you been?"... ad infinitum.

I told them—feelingly—and we moved off to repeat the process.

Now that we had all our kit with us—carrying it I mean, it seemed to make the going harder. Perhaps we were just getting tired.

We came to the main road and I scouted ahead, but there was no sign of any activity or the officer.

I waved them up and we scooted across the road as if our trousers were on fire. We half walked, half ran till we got to the back of the cottage, me in the lead, of course, and after the old man had met the others we started brewing up and making a meal. The old boy insisted that we have his bed, their only bed, and after the grub in which he and his wife participated, we decided to turn in.

We bedded down, two at each end and although it was a bit of a squash (we didn't undress in case of emergency) it wasn't long before we were all fast asleep, snoring our heads off. It seemed that we had just put our heads on the pillows when we were rudely awakened by the old couple.

They were very agitated and scared and entreated us to leave.

They kept saying "Gestapo! Gestapo!" And you could hear a lot of shouting and the odd shot being fired.

It was either the Gestapo, or perhaps the Polizei, or maybe German soldiers looking for sleeping prisoners! We didn't hang about to find out! We were away out of the back door as quick as a rat up a drain pipe.

Naturally, we didn't want to be retaken but more importantly we didn't want to incriminate the old man and his wife.

Bent low we scurried across the fields, ignoring the path, our steps crackling loudly on the frozen snow, leaving a trail of foot marks like the wake of a ship.

Out of breath but unchallenged we finally came to the main road again, and started to plod slowly down it—towards Schneidermuhl the German border town. There was no point in going back to Bromberg, especially if they were searching for p.o.w.'s.

At first, we were a bit fed up, but as the dawn streaks appeared our sense of humour gradually returned. Not that we'd ever lost it. It had just become subdued a little.

We began to sing and whistle—mostly Scottish airs—led by our two Scots.

In this carefree mood we put our best foot forward and carried on down the road, and after we had travelled for about three miles across flat open country with here and there a shack but no houses as such, we came to a bend in the road. To our right sitting back in a sort of lay-by was a moderately large roadside inn, called a Gastatte. The bottom windows were boarded up as if for protection against looting but the top windows had been left and at each of the four windows we could see several faces peering out. British faces. British p.o.w. faces! There must have been 20 or more ex-p.o.w.'s there—and not a sign of a German, civilian or soldier.

They catcalled out to us derisively shouting "What are you marching for? They went thataway" (pointing) and finally in song "Come and Join us—Come and Join us—Come and Join the Salvation Army!"

We shouted out in similar vein and took steps to join them!

The front door, however, was locked and bolted, so we went round the back.

Here too we were denied entrance by another locked door and despite our entreaties and constant banging on the door, they refused to let us in.

Luckily there was a huge covered henhouse at the bottom of the garden and this we immediately made for, and after shooing the birds away we dumped our gear and rested or should I say "roosted"!

We were more tired than we thought and soon we were all fast asleep.

We slept all through the day and woke in the evening, completely unaware of what was going on outside.

As darkness fell, we had been joined by the hens and chickens who walked amongst and over us, as if we'd been there since the hen -house was built.

I woke the others and made a fire and we had tea and a tinned hot stewed steak meal. We were very tempted to have "Chicken à la Poland"—I mean it was there for the asking or catching, but we thought we would leave it till the morrow, and then we could ring its neck in the morning, pluck the feathers, draw it and have it ready for cooking, either roasting, or boiling in a bucket for the evening meal!

We could hear some motor traffic, all apparently making for Schneidermuhl, and we decided not to venture out in public but to lie low for a couple of days, so we didn't go around the front of the Inn at all. (I gathered afterwards that neither did the others in the house.)

We slept well through the night, apart from the occasional clucking when a hen was disturbed, probably dreaming about the overtime at Easter or the Cockerel from up the road, and I woke up once or twice. It wasn't too bad in the coop. We were huddled together and had a ground sheet and blanket underneath us and two blankets and overcoats over us. We never undressed, of course. Unfortunately we were woken very early by the bloody cockerel, who although chased away, continued with his chronic German crowing long after dawn. We practically earmarked *him* for the chopper for his unseemly behaviour, but Dickie Davis pointed out that being the male he would probably be tough and leathery, so luckily for him he was given a reprieve. Nevertheless, one of his harem had her neck rung the following morning in preparation for the evening "boil-up"!

The day passed tranquilly; nothing much happened. We didn't venture out, except to brew up. We collected 24 freshly laid eggs and had a massive omelette. 6 eggs per person–Total 24. Chicken soup from the boiled chicken to start off with, followed by chicken and meat loaf for the main course, then Ambrosia Rice for afters (topped with raspberry jam!) and the inevitable tea rounded off an excellent evening meal, and as we bedded down for the night, replete, someone remarked that always missing was a drop of Schnapps!

We'd almost forgotten about the war situation, but in the early morning hours, before cock crow, it caught up with us.

The Red Army arrived!

CHAPTER 11
"Tovarich! Angelski!"

Suddenly— just before dawn the yard of the Inn was filled with our first sight of Soviet Front line troops.

They were tough and fierce-looking and like the Germans they shouted at us in Russian expecting us to understand. I don't know which was the worse of the two—the Germans who first captured us and screamed at us or the Russians who liberated us and shouted at us!

We, of course, were quickly out of the coop to welcome them
"Tovarich"(Comrade)*"Angelski"* (English)
"Stalin-Churchill Colleague!!" (Colleagues) *"Dobra"* (Good).
"Germanski ny dobra!"(Germany no good!).

They looked at us as if uncertain about us—whether to believe us or not. And then for the moment they appeared to decide to go along with it, but it was very difficult and very risky without an interpreter. It wasn't advisable to speak to them in German, some of our fellows did and that might have aroused their suspicions. One or two of our chaps had their watches whipped off their wrists before you could say "Maskelyn and Devant" (the two well known magicians) —well it was hopeless to try and argue with them. They seemed to be obsessed with watches and clocks of every conceivable shape and size. Even Grandfather clocks! Later on I saw two Grandfather clocks being wheeled away in a cart, by two Mongolian Russkys. They, we found, were the worst types and no one ever got close to them, not even their relations! I once offered a cigarette to a Mongolian Russian and he knocked the packet out of my hand and then kicked the packet away (obviously a non-smoker!).

I don't think the Anglo-Soviet public relations Board would have approved. The Anglos who were with me at the time certainly didn't. It did give us the warning to be wary of them—which we subsequently always were!

Being trigger-happy was another of their little failings—if anything moves, fire at it. If anything doesn't move, fire at it and after two or three bottles of Vodka keep firing at it. Fire at everything and anything! Anywhere and everywhere! We were, eventually, through a Polish interpreter, told to line up with our gear and march towards Schneidermuhl where, they said, we would be able to pick up transport that had gone through with stores and would be going back to base—probably Warsaw.

Again in the snow and at an unaccustomed fast pace, guarded by Soviet guards, we marched towards the German border. En route we were passed, and spat on, by several Russian tanks—big black monsters with a Soviet star on the side. Some of the p.o.w.'s, well -versed in these things, said they were British tanks supplied by us as part of our "Aid to Russia" Fund and christened "Churchill" tanks. But the Russians would have none of it. *"Niet English"* (Not English) *"Russky"!* They were adamant about that. But they were wrong.

Strategically and militarily the Russian Armoured columns had by-passed Bromberg and then returned in a huge pincer movement sweeping all before them. The tanks were miles ahead of the infantry who were consolidating at their leisure and at their own pace. That first day of marching under our Russian Allies we must have marched 38 kilometres and towards evening we came to a small town called

"Nertzhal". By this time we were an International column consisting of British p.o.w.'s, French dittos, Germans, Eyeties, and a sprinkling of Lithuanians who had mostly been picked up in and around Bromberg retreating from the Russians, but not fast enough!

As we entered the outskirts of Nertzhal some spasmodic firing broke out ahead of the column obviously directed at the Soviet guards who returned the fire.

The firing was coming from strategic points mainly the roofs of houses manned by the *Volksturm*, the equivalent of our Home Guard. They had no uniforms, wore civilian clothes with white armbands, upon which was written *"Volksturm"* under a Swastika and German Eagle. They were either very old men or very young boys of 14 and 15 years of age.

We marched on, ignoring the shooting (a British Sergeant Major shouted "Anybody who breaks ranks will be court martialled!") when suddenly a very large explosion, seemingly mortar fire, was heard not far from our position. The column immediately scattered—ignoring the C.S.M.—and Davis and I belted up a side turning and kept going. It was a cul-de-sex, I mean sac, but a "sac" with a difference. At the end of the street stood some huge wooden gates topped with barbed wire, and at the gates, waiting to receive us, stood a crowd of about 70 or 80 women, all dressed alike in, as it turned out later, prison garb.

The place was a women's communal prison run on self supporting and collective farming lines and the women incarcerated there were serving time for mainly minor offences. Most of them were Polish but several came from Germany and had been convicted of "looting" during or after air raids.

All the officials, including the Burgomeister, who had a house adjoining the prison and was responsible for the administration, had long since gone, leaving the girls to fend for themselves, and as far as I could see they seemed to be fending very well. They varied in age, height and beauty and none of them seemed undernourished. There was a link in sympathy and understanding in the fact that we were all ex-prisoners and they made us very welcome. Especially Davis. He looked very thin and in need of mothering—which is one way of putting it—and he lost no time in getting involved with a blonde

German dame from Hamburg, by the name of Lisa or Elsa who said she was pro-British and hoped the British won the war (he'd just given her a bar of chocolate, mind you).

She had been sentenced to two years corrective training (imprisonment) for "looting". Davis sympathised with her and carried on with corrective training not specified in the sentence. In other words he didn't sleep alone! She was about twenty-four, had served a year of her sentence, was very good looking with grey-blue eyes and liked chocolate, coffee, soap and Davis. In that order! Maybe I'm maligning her or perhaps I was influenced by my "pièce de résistance" Krystina Obelinsky from Bromberg, who was Polish and hated all Jerries, male or female. Her father had been killed in the war and she didn't know where her mother was and her brother had been taken prisoner and he too had disappeared.

At first we were the only representatives of the British Army, but as the evening wore on the place became littered with them—all staking their claims!

Some dozens of Frenchmen somehow drifted in (trust them!) as well, till in the end they outnumbered the British, and it became a case of "*Ne poussez pas les Anglais*" (Don't push the English) —well not too far!

Jimmy Hooks, our erstwhile cook and purveyor of B.B.C. News, turned up and immediately started taking an inventory of the place! He did a tour of the piggery, the cow's byre, the bakery and last but not least the cook-house. He could assure us, he said, that Roast Pork would be on the menu on the morrow, especially if I would assist him by knocking one off for him to carve up. Secure in this knowledge and after sharing my Red Cross meal with Krystina—corned beef hash and beans followed by Ambrosia Rice and (a bar of chocolate for her) a cup of decent coffee, which she and the blonde dame went into raptures about, we settled down for the night.

She snuggled into my arms and told me that she was serving a three year sentence for insolence, disobedience and for cohabiting with a Scottish p.o.w.! That wasn't so bad except she kept calling me "Jock" every time I got near her which wasn't conducive to good love making, but I ignored it and soldiered on!

After the Act of Love which wasn't the greatest, she asked me to tell her about England which I'd had to promise I would take her to, in order to seduce her (I suppose "Jock" had told her about Scotland! "Och aye I'll take ye hame to the wife all right!") and as I started to extol the virtues of Merry England I realised that she had fallen asleep. I pulled the blanket over her up to her chin and then looked around the barn littered with bodies and straw, and saw that most of the ex-p.o.w.'s were also asleep except for those in the act of intertwining and those that were just lying there too tired even to "twine". For the next two days we lived and slept like "fighting cocks".

Everything was there for the taking—and that included eggs, hens, potatoes, pork, milk, cheese and flour—and crumpet. We'd have been there still if what I'm about to relate hadn't happened.

I had taken the tea bucket early on the third morning to get the water for the tea from the pump in the exercising yard when I saw what looked like a German soldier, wearing his white sheet camouflage outfit, padding across the track.

"Hey—Hallo." I shouted *"Was machen zie hier?"* (What are you doing here?)

He turned and saw me holding the bucket and looking surprised at seeing him. "Was machen *zie* hier?" (What are *You* doing here?) He said.

"If you must know" I said, advancing on him, "The Russians brought us here. They have captured all this territory including Bromberg and you'd better watch out or it'll be Siberia for you!!"

"Nein-Nein" he said, shaking his head from side to side pityingly.

"Our company withdrew when the Russian tanks came through but now we have come back and retaken the town of Nertzhal."

"Nein!" I said *"Nicht verklich?"* (S'not true).

"Jah-jah ist verklich" (It's true) said the white clad clot.

"The War is not yet over, mein freund! We shall attack the Russkys. *"Sind zie allein?"* (Are you alone?)

"No, there are English and French ex-prisoners here recovering from the March." (I conveniently forgot to mention the women.)

"Good!" he said "I speak with my officer."

He turned and plodded off in the snow to speak with his beloved officer.

Forgetting about the water I rushed quickly to the barn and told them the News!

They too couldn't believe it, but sure enough within the hour, the officer, a German Major accompanied by a section of soldiers, turned up and ordered us all out on parade. The girl prisoners on one side and the men p.o.w.'s on the other. He strutted about, very much playing the part of the officer in charge.

"We have retaken this Town," he said deliberately. (It must have been a silent takeover, for we heard nothing!) "and the Russians will not defeat us." (Well everybody's entitled to their own opinion.)

"You," he said, pointing to the ex-p.o.w.'s, *"You* will be required to dig trenches to assist us to defend the town. And, anyone found committing an act of sabotage will be shot!"

I, foolish fellow that I am, stepped forward.

"Entschuldigen zie mir, Herr Major!" (Excuse me Major.) I ventured.

"Jah?" he replied from his great height *"Was ist los?"* (What is it?)

"According to the Geneva Convention relating to all prisoners of war in enemy hands we are not allowed to assist the enemy, in this case, *Deutschland*, in any act of war such as digging trenches, working on war machines in factories etcetera...."

He looked at me coldly and started to unbutton his holster, preparing to take out his pistol ...

"Except of course," I hurriedly went on "We should consider that it would be in our own interests to accede to your request. Where do we find the picks and shovels?"

I wasn't going to be a martyr for anyone at this late stage, least of all for the Geneva Convention!

The unbelievable thing was to find ourselves in German hands once again, we thought we'd left all that behind ages ago! We duly marched away and dug slit trenches at either side of the road which wasn't easy because of the frozen state of the ground. But like the

Chinese have found, nothing's impossible if you put your mind to it, and digging slit trenches out of frozen concrete slabs is child's play—to the Chinese! It wasn't the way I would have chosen to spend my third day of Freedom but you've got to be prepared to accept anything that comes along. And at the end of the day I was exhausted and very glad that we had been marched back to our prison billets and gathered up in "dem lovin' arms!"

The Jerries put a board across the gates to make sure we wouldn't get out and then repeated the homily about shooting on sight anyone caught in an act of sabotage and departed to their slit trenches, saying they would be back on the morrow.

The girls or each syndicate, prepared a meal with the usual char (tea) and then we bedded down for the night. We were slightly apprehensive about our future. We were all right if we stayed where we were, we argued, but if the Jerries decided to evacuate and came to take us with them—well, that would be a bloody awful kettle of fish.

We needn't have bothered discussing it because Fate in the shape of the Russians had it all laid on.

We were all fast asleep when there was an ear-splitting crash and something exploded and ripped through the roof, tearing a gaping hole so that the night sky could be seen. Nobody was hurt as far as I could see but everyone was certainly wide awake, eyes staring and looking up.

This was immediately followed by another crash and the windows on one side of the barn all shattered like broken ice, showering the glass everywhere. Then came some shouts—a short silence—and then a burst of machine gun fire. In the barn, panic set in, and a frantic general exodus took place. Everybody, including myself, bolted outside to a corridor which separated our building from another barn, but once there nobody seemed to know what to do. Where to go? What to do? Some began to scream hysterically and others sobbed. The women weren't all that bright either. I told Krystina to wait for me while I went back to rescue my haversack and overcoat. I went back inside and scrabbled around, found my jacket and put it on, also my overcoat, grabbed at my haversack and managed to put one strap on, and dragging my kitbag along the floor I returned to the corridor.

There was nobody there. Absolutely nobody. It was as if a magic wand had been waved. I shouted Krystina's name. Then "Dickie Davis", and waited. All I heard was another crash on what sounded like the roof again. Then, again, nearer this time, and casting care to the winds I bolted along the corridor to a door at the end of it. As I opened it, I was greeted by a hail of bullets, country of origin unknown. Just my luck, I thought, to be mown down by "British Aid to Russia Fund" ammunition! I waited, for two or three minutes or maybe five, and then with my kitbag under my arm I flung open the door and ran like a Chinese hare—sideways—pursued by whining bullets thudding into the wall.

I made for the wooden gates which were now wide open and dashed down the street zig-zagging and trying to get away from the fusillade of fire which followed me. At the end of the road I was brought swiftly and suddenly to a halt. A slant eyed, evil-looking Mongolian with a machine gun at the ready (B.S.A. Aid to Russia) was pointing the serrated barrel at me. I dropped my kitbag, put my hands up and said "ANGELSKI!—*Angel—Anglichan—Niet Germanski* —TOVARICH! ANGELSKI!"

He looked at me coldly, I could see his Asiatic breath on the night air, and motioned me to pick up my kitbag, which I did and then came behind me and prodded me in the back to move along in front of him. At machine gun length I lurched down the road till we came to a house that had been taken over as an Emergency First Aid Post. There he handed me over to the Russian doctor or Medical Officer who luckily for me spoke pidgin English and like most of them was anxious to show it off! Mind you any English at all was music to my ears and from the mouth of a Russian it was even sweeter—and a relief!

He had a leathery face but kindly eyes and he told me he came from Moscow.

To my surprise he offered me a Will's Gold Flake cigarette which I took. "I smoke only English" he said, showing me a packet which had the inevitable "Aid to Russia" written on it!) He made his excuses and then left me to attend to some of the wounded. I noticed that he and his orderlies were using paper bandages to bind the wounds, the paper being not unlike thick crepe toilet paper. Several severely wounded lay on the floor but the less so, comprising the majority, were suffering from minor injuries such as flesh wounds. The Germans apparently were putting up a stiff resistance (from our slit trenches no doubt!) but their cause was hopeless, they were outnumbered by four to one!

So said the Doctor.

He went on "Ambulance come you go Moscow—much Vodka drinking! Plenty women—Russian women BEEG—Strong! They fight! But they give in! Ho—Ho Ho!"

He laughed heartily as if it were a big joke, and not wishing to offend I joined in.

At the end of the laugh session he said "You—London?" *"Jah*—er—*Da Da"* I said, hurriedly switching languages and trotting out the usual. "Me not speak Russian" (That was very obvious "Me know only—(Wait for it) *Dobra* (Good)—*Angelski*—(English)—*Ny dobra* (Not or no good) *Niet* (No)—*Da-Da* (Yes—yes my Russian baby sez yes-yes!).—*Germanski* (German) and finally *TOVARICH"* (Comrade).

"TOVARICH" He roared "Zat is good! *Tovarich! Russky— Angelski."*

He slapped me on the shoulder almost dislocating my blade and then seized my hand and pumped it as if he were jacking up a car! He handed me a packet of German cigarettes as a parting present and said "Come".

I wasn't quite sure what was happening but when we got outside, the ambulance turned out to be an old farm cart! The badly wounded were put on to the cart and covered with blankets and the walking wounded, which included me, followed on behind.

I smiled at the Russian driver in a friendly way and offered him one of my German cigarettes which he put in his mouth and then realising it was German spat it out in disgust saying—"Germanski!" as if I were trying to poison him. He was very distant after that and I gave up my attempts to be a good "ally".

As far as I could gather we were making for the Russian Army Base that had been set up not far away. The badly wounded moaned and groaned when the cart bumped over some uneven frozen snow and when the horse fell on its knees, slipping in the icy road, the driver wouldn't allow any help but lashed it till it scrambled to its feet.

There were several dead soldiers lying around on the sides of the road, both Russian and German, and most of them were frozen into grotesque positions like some macabre "Statues" game. We were fired on twice by some solitary sniper but we all marched stoically on and the fire wasn't returned. No one was hit. Our small silent convoy plodded on through the night, or what was left of it and after a while the dawn started to come up and about half an hour later we arrived at a huge encampment which was obviously the base.

I was handed over to a Russian officer who in turn passed me on to a political *"Kommissar"* who cross-questioned me in German for five minutes and then detailed a Russian guard to take me away. I was escorted to a small building like a Martello Tower and pushed through the doorway almost to fall into the arms of —guess who?—my friend and compatriot Richard Davis!

He and all the others had been marched there from outside the barn and had gone in a different direction from mine. The girls had come too and had been put in another adjacent building. I told him of my meeting with the doctor and he informed me that they had been warned to get ready for interrogation; in fact they thought when I was bundled in that the interrogators had arrived!

There was still this slight atmosphere of distrust about the Russian attitude—slight suspicion of our stories—were we telling the truth?

I may be maligning them but only when they were drunk did they become friendly—too friendly sometimes! It may have been this fatalistic outlook on being taken prisoner which they certainly didn't seem to approve of. Some of them, like the doctor, were more civilised in their approach, but in general a dog in the manger attitude was levied on the p.ow.'s. Especially the British.

The interrogation followed the usual pattern. Name—Rank—Number. Regiment. Where captured? Why hadn't we escaped before?—"NEXT."

This rather dim view of us was most noticeable during the whole interrogation, unmindful of the fact that there were also thousands of

Russian p.o.w.'s. Not that the poor devils ever got any parcels from home (there was no mail!) or through the Red Cross. Russia was not a member of the Geneva Convention and did not bother about prisoners. Literally thousands of them died of malnutrition. At our last camp, the new one, we were about a mile away from a camp for Russian p.o.w.'s established up the road, and daily a cart piled high with their dead— emaciated skeletons —would be wheeled past our camp to some communal grave.

Once we collected a large amount of food to be sent to the Russian camp but the Jerries would not allow it. The Germans hated them, feared them, and murdered them.

After our interrogation we were segregated into sheep pens. One for the British, a large one for the Germans, one for the French, and one for the Italians and Lithuanians.

After a wait of nearly two hours (no grub issued) we were ordered out of our pens and marched down the road and halted.

There we were joined by the girls. I looked in vain for Krystina and one of the women told me that she had "taken off" for Bromberg.

Lisa or Elsa (or whatever her name was), Davis's girl, was there, wearing a pair of British Army trousers and a khaki ground sheet thrown over her shoulders like a shawl. They had obviously been given to her by Davis. Later he gave her a balaclava, and after she had put it on she could easily have been mistaken for a British soldier— apart from the feminine walk! This, of course was Davis's intention!

I told him he was "off his rocker" dragging her along with us. She was bound to be found out sooner or later, but ignoring me he told her to pretend that she was French (she spoke a smattering apparently— like *Oui* and *Non*!) and to answer only *"Je suis Francaise"*.
"Je suis *Francaise*. O.K. Lisa?"
"Jer swee Francesay-zar" this in an obvious German accent.

She sounded about as French as my foot. She had no chance.
I told Davis so, but he had a mad light in his eyes that spelled "sex".
I'd seen it once before when he had the cello clasped firmly between his knees, fiddling away, so I didn't pursue the matter.

We were marched across fields to a large farmhouse which we understood was Marshal Zhukov's H.Q. As we came into the farmyard we had our first sight of a Russian woman soldier. She was in uniform and was wearing the highest award that the Soviet Army dishes out—the U.S.S.R. Gold Star, received for bravery in the Siege of Stalingrad. She was very buxom and very handsome in a Soviet-Tucker kind of way. Draped round her neck was a strap to which was attached a machine gun. This in turn lay against her ample bosom. She stood with one foot—her right foot—planted on the neck of a frozen dead horse.

To our surprise all the German prisoners were ordered to fall out from the column and told to undress to their long johns, in the bitter cold. This they reluctantly and slowly did, so much so that the Russian sergeant in charge shouted *"Los, los"* at them, to hurry them up. Then these pathetic creatures were made to form a huge circle round the Russian woman. There was a long pause. Davis looked at me, apprehensively. I looked away. This was no time for conversation. Suddenly in German the Russian woman screamed "RUN" *"Los; los; los!"*

As they slipped and slithered and attempted to run around her she followed their feet with intermittent bursts of gun fire and one or two fell to the ground wounded in the legs. Others were wounded more seriously—-a sort of Russian roulette really. Not a charming sight. But when you think about it perhaps she had a personal score to settle for Stalingrad.

After this macabre exhibition we were ordered to get moving again and within minutes we were on our way to Posen (in Polish, Poznan). As we filed past the end of the farmhouse the door opened and the Marshal himself came out to look at us.

I nodded and said *"Tovarich"* and he half-smiled and saluted! We arrived in Posen very late that evening after a frenetic march from Zhukov's Headquarters, it had snowed the whole way and the Russian guards of whom there were six did not believe in rest periods or taking a break. But in the end we stood up to it—just!

In Posen we were housed in a German prisoner of war camp for the Americans which really opened our eyes.

We thought that we did well but they, the Yanks, *they* had a surfeit of *everything!* They discarded things that we prized, like Red Cross Food parcels!

The camp, in places, was like a club, with all home comforts, armchairs, carpets, deck chairs, cigars and "Hershey" (Chocolate) bars —the only things missing were Scotch and "wimmen"!

Davis had *his* woman, his home comfort, "Lisa the Looter".

But soon would come the testing time.

Interrogating time! And then we would see what happened to the ersatz Frenchie from Hamburg.

The camp was commanded (apart from the Senior American Officer) by a Russian Colonel, who spoke English like a genuine American! Well, he would, he'd been educated at Harvard.

"Now see here, you Britishers." he said.

"We're aimin' to get you fellas 'Home' to your folks as fast as humanly possible, but first of all there are one or two formalities that we have to go through. I want each and everyone of you to come to my 'awfice' and give me your particulars. O.K? Tomorrow that is. You just take it easy tonight, boys, and if there's anything you want just you ask for it! I'll see ya all tomorrow at my awfice!"

It was during the interrogating interview that Lisa did her "*Jer swee Francesay-zar*" bit. (I don't know why she went in in the first place, perhaps she counted on winning the Russian American Colonel over?) But unfortunately for her the Colonel spoke perfect French too —and German!

So we never saw Lisa again. She didn't even return Davis's spare trousers and he needed them badly. He had a bad attack of diarrhoea and messed up the other pair.

About two or three days later, when even I had got fed up smoking cigars and had acquired carton after carton of American cigarettes, (also about 50 "Hershey" Chocolate bars) we were told that we would be going that day to Warsaw and that transport would be provided in the form of several trucks—some British 15 cwts and other questionable Russian mechanical wonders!

So the same evening we started to trek back—across Poland to Warsaw. I don't know if the petrol was British but at a certain unpronounceable place in Poland, where we had stopped to have a meal, we returned to the trucks to find that the drivers had drunk the petrol! It was not unusual, apparently it was a well known Russky habit!

"Dobra Healthovitch! Down the hatch with Shellski!
The petrol to suit all tastes!"

We arrived at Warsaw after several nightmare rides. As you can imagine, there's a wealth of understatement in those eight words. Suffice to say that it took about four or five days and that the driver whose name was Ivan (we called him among other things Iva—nackeroff!), was never sober! He actually drove best when he was high on Vodka like a Learner who would never pass his Test—Driving or Breath—but he enjoyed it.

He really *did* enjoy it. Every bump or thump was greeted with a Russian war whoop from the driver's cabin! We nearly went through the roof of the truck each time we bumped and we cursed and held on grimly, as Ivan would try to emulate the Dodgems at an Amusement Arcade and skid and slither and slide and then accelerate, so that we got dizzy with the permutation of things that were happening to us.

But we arrived—we finally arrived—and were directed to a *Kaserne* or Cavalry Barracks just outside Warsaw called Rembertova. It was none too clean but it was somewhere to lay one's head and we were glad to get there in one piece, and it was encouraging to learn from the American speaking Russian Colonel that we would only be there a couple of days before moving on to Moscow—probably by plane. The liar! For dinner we were given a bowl of "Kasha", the staple food of the Russian peasant. It looks like a cross between semolina and frogs' spawn and after you've had it seven days a week —it tastes like it!

The third day after our arrival, the Jewish girls who had dug the tank traps and whom we had met on the way to Bromberg turned up. They had been surrounded and their black uniformed guards had been shot before their eyes. Not that that would have bothered them. They'd had a life time of experience in their tender years already. The girl to whom I had given the German boots was still wearing them, and she asked me if I would like them back. I was indignant that she should think of such a thing! Of course I said cornily "No, my dear, all I ask is that each time you put them on you think of me." Which she promised to do!

Each day at the *Kaserne* would bring new arrivals, some from our old camp and some from working parties whom we knew, and all of them with hair-raising tales to tell.

The worst story was about our boys who had rushed out to greet the Russian tanks, waving their arms in welcome, and the Russians thinking they were Germans had mown them down with machine gun fire and then ran over them with their tanks.

Some American p.o.w.'s also arrived and a truck with American Red Cross food parcels, only just in time, as our larder needed replenishing and I was sick of the sight of Kasha. I made friends with a young American from Pittsburgh, Elmer Gall, later to become a teacher, and he still continues to send Xmas cards to me. The *Kaserne* was having to house more people than it could cater for and Davis and I got fed up with the conditions which became daily more intolerable, so we asked the Senior British Officer (a padre) if we could go into the town to look for better billets. Surprisingly, he refused.

He told us we were forbidden to leave the building without special permission. And if it were essential, we had to obtain a special permit from the Senior British Officer.

Davis and I said "to Hell with it" and we left. It was quite easy. We bribed the Russian Guard at the entrance to the *Kaserne* by giving him a packet of American cigarettes and a bar of chocolate and took off for Rembertova itself. We found a block of flats that looked reasonably habitable, not damaged by shellfire as most of them were, and mounted the stairs. At a likely looking door, I knocked. And waited.

After a hesitant wait, a lovely looking Polish girl aged about 19 or 20, opened the door and asked me in German what I wanted.

I said I was a British ex-p.o.w. and this was my friend and would it be possible for us to prevail upon her to supply us with some boiling water for *"tea-machen"*—I also added *herbata*, which is Polish for tea, I think. Whatever it was it worked wonders.

Her eyes lit up and she said "Oh, you speak Polish."

"No, no we just know a smattering, like *chleb* (bread) *Gindobri* (Good Morning) *Yachega* (phonetic- How are You?) *Dobra* (Good)." Her eyes shone even brighter and she ushered us in. It was the easiest thing in the world, she was very trusting and so welcoming. It was very moving in fact.

We made the tea—*herbata* and she had a cup too, and we told her about our travels, and then we waited for her mother to arrive. She had gone shopping. We gave Krystina (yes, another Krystina) a bar of American chocolate to sweeten the situation, not that it needed it. She was bowled over as it was. In due time Mum arrived and she too enjoyed our presence and after a cup of *herbata* for her and another bar of Yankee milk chocolate, she insisted that we stay and have an evening meal with the whole family. Dad would be back shortly from his employment. (She didn't mention what it was and we didn't pursue it.) The flat was very comfortable and obviously they had seen better days but their hospitality was unbeatable. When father arrived and found out who we were he greeted us very warmly. We learned he had been a Professor of Mathematics at the University in Warsaw and was now doing a labouring job! He told us very quietly that they had a Russian officer billeted on them which entitled them to extra rations for his board, bed and breakfast so we need not worry about robbing them of their food. (Actually we hadn't given it a thought!)

We had a good tasty meal of meat, potatoes and greens, and biscuits and cheese and we supplied the genuine coffee. The professor was hoping that he would get his beloved job back once things had returned to normal. He was most apprehensive about the Russians, thinking that Poland would be dominated by them for a long time to come. He obviously preferred the old regime now sitting in London and wished that they could fly in and take over. He had no time for the Lublin Government and said so. After coffee he produced a bottle of Schnapps in our honour and we were all in the middle of toasting Poland and England when the Russian officer arrived.

He seemed quite civilised not unlike the Medical Officer from Moscow. He offered his cigarettes all round. We all took one and then downed half a tumbler full of Schnapps at one go. He said "Good

Night" in German very politely and said "See you in the morning" to us, again in German. He wasn't the ogre they'd made him out to be.

The officer had their only spare room but they said that if we wouldn't mind sleeping on the sofa they would be glad and pleased to have us stay. We accepted eagerly of course and asked if we could help with the washing up? But Krystina and her Mum wouldn't hear of it. Davis slept at one end of the sofa and I at the other and although I would have preferred Krystina, it was infinitely superior to the *Kaserne*! I was lying smoking a last cigarette when Krystina came tip-toeing out of her room to go to the bathroom. She was wearing a sort of white shift and looked very fetching. As she came back Davis was snoring like a pig. I gave him a kick and he sat up saying "Wassa matter? Wassa matter? Oh—hello Krystina." (He thought she'd come out to see him—he never gave up, did he?!)

In English she said—"Good Night Dickie! Good Night Zahm!" (Rhymes with trahm—remember?)

It was rather sweet, wasn't it.

In the morning we had a bath which was a luxury in itself. We looked through Krystina's photograph album of happier times before the war and then after lunch the three of us went for a short walk together. Krystina, Dickie and myself.

In the evening after the meal we ventured out and thus got caught up in the following hair-raising incident.

We were recognised by some tipsy Russian soldiers as being British (by our uniforms, I suppose). Anyway, these very mellow fellows insisted on us having a drink with them which as a friendly gesture we naturally did. But we could not get away. Every time we made a move to go it would be the cue for another round—another Vodka to be poured into our glasses. We dared not refuse. And then we had to emulate them by drinking it down in one go. Next they commandeered some furniture from somewhere, set alight to it in the middle of the pavement and when the bonfire was blazing merrily away sat cross-legged round it, still imbibing, and asking us to do the same. After maudlin time they started to sing songs about Russia, each doing his party piece and being wildly applauded when he'd finished. Then it was our turn—yes, *our* turn, and when we demurred, saying

"Niet" (no), holding throat, "Voice *kaput. Ny dobra*!" one of the soldiers pulled out his gun and fired it into the air—just to prove that it was loaded—saying in Russian something that menacingly sounded like "Sing" and levelling the wavering gun at us. We stood up, Davis and I, and sang "Rule Britannia, Britannia rules the waves, Britons never, never, never shall be slaves!" We repeated it, and when we came to "never, never, never shall be slaves" where the music normally goes down on "shall be slaves" we went up, finishing on a top note for "slaves" which we held for as long as our breath lasted. It was greeted rapturously as if we had just performed an aria at the Moscow State Opera House. Naturally they made us re-fuel with another vodka! In the end we got away when a drunken brawl broke out between them.

The next day at the flat we were told that the local Bureau de Change was changing German marks for zlotys (Polish currency) and roubles (Russian). All German marks were being withdrawn or called in and would not be considered as legal tender after a certain date. I had amassed a considerable amount of marks, legally and illegally, altogether about £50 worth and thought it would be a good idea to change them, especially as we were hoping to go into Russia—roubles for Russia was what we wanted. When we got to the Square where the Bureau de Change was situated it reminded me of a milling crowd outside Wembley Stadium trying to get through one turnstile! Luckily as we were English the Poles fell back as if we were Royalty or the great General Sikorsky himself. We bowed left and right and before long were in the Inner Sanctum, taking out our money and counting it, hoping for a beneficial transaction! The underling who had greeted us motioned us to sit down and then left us for a moment but almost immediately returned. He took our money and started to sift through the notes when his obvious Superior appeared at the inner door to the office. The clerk stood up and put his finger to his lips, giving us the signal not to speak. We were slightly bewildered by this seeming play-acting and looked at each other and then behind us to see if anything was there, but of course there wasn't. The Boss then got in on the act. He stealthily walked in, stopped, turned and closed the door, looking left and right to make sure the walls didn't have ears, and then came over to us and said in a stage whisper "Have you heard the news?"

Davis looked at me and then together on cue we said "What news?"

B.de C. Superior: "The War news!"

D. & K: "War news?"

B.de C. Superior: "England and American troops have entered Berlin and declared war on Russia."

Davis and I were silent. We had had no access to news for several weeks and now in the interim anything could have happened. On the other hand it could have been wishful thinking on the part of the Poles which had developed into a rumour and to them had become a fact. The Poles wished with all their hearts that the English troops would liberate them, led if possible by Churchill himself! Some of them expected English parachutists to drop out of the sky and straighten out the predicament they were now in. The majority of them, at that time, did not recognise the Polish Red Government formerly resident in Russia and now filtering through to Lublin. Many Poles did not wish for their leadership but were faithful and anxious for the Free Poles in London to return.

The Bureau de Change Superior went on "I am glad and yet I am sorry. You will no doubt go to Russia to Siberia!"

I looked suitably apprehensive as did Davis but at the same time we asked for our money, just in case it wasn't true. Mournfully the Superior nodded to the underling to do his duty. We left, with the money mostly in Polish zlotys but also a few roubles.

We hurried back to the flat and asked Krystina if she had heard anything on the Communal radio about England and America declaring war on Russia. She said "No. But is it likely to happen?" Later we asked the Russian officer, tactfully, how far the Red Army were from Berlin or if it had already fallen. He replied that the British, American and Russian Armies were doing well but Berlin had not fallen yet, and was not expected to for some time. Russian troops would obviously get there first, he said, because of the approach— they were in direct line. He was tied up with the administration for Russian troops in the Polish area and obviously knew what was going on, so we took it as being true. Why should he lie? Later Krystina's father turned up to tell us that he had heard that the British and American ex-prisoners were leaving the *Kaserne* for Russia very soon. We gathered up our gear, made our fervent goodbyes—we had already exchanged addresses, promising to write "après la Guerre" (after the war. French! Blimey I was multi-lingual!)—and shot back to the barracks.

Believe it or not, we were refused admission by the Padre officer! "You," he said "chose to leave us when times were bad, like rats deserting a sinking ship. And now that we are on the move for home you wish to take advantage of it. Well. You will have to make your own way home. Not with us!"

We couldn't believe our ears, it could have been a death sentence. The Senior British Officer—-a Padre—refusing to take us? What did he gain by being so bloody spiteful? It was up to us to show the so-called Man of God that we would get there before him if we could.

We walked away from the *Kaserne* straight to the centre of Rembertova, and we asked the natives which road lead to Lublin. They pointed it out so we stood on the corner like two hitch-hikers and waited. Before long a military lorry driven as we found out by a Pole in the Russian Army, took us on board, as far as Lublin. He was actually going further and offered to take us but we said that Lublin would do for now. We rewarded him suitably with chocolate and cigarettes and I gave him half the zlotys I had collected from the Bureau de Change in the morning!

So here we were in Lublin. We were one step ahead of the Padre's lot already! The first thing to do was to find a billet so we employed the usual tactics. We sorted out a comfortable looking house, knocked on the door and asked for water for "Tea-machen—*Herbata.*" It worked—it never failed. Soon we were lying back in the hottest bath we'd ever had—singly of course! There were three daughters in the house but they were babies—eleven, twelve and thirteen year olds—but they were very sweet, adopting us as their favourite ex-p.o.w.'s! We gave them each a bar of chocolate and left our soap in the bathroom. They were ardent Catholics and because I told them I was born in Ireland they assumed that I was too and before I left they gave me a little Virgin Mary Medallion for luck. I've still got it but up to now it has never put me on to a winner! Seconds and Thirds, yes—but a Twenty to One Winner, no! (I think it works in other ways though.) They gave us food and looked after us and let us sleep in proper beds.

It was all very civilised. On the second day in Lublin we took a stroll through the market place and were approached by a member of the Red Polish Government who asked us if we were British and how we got there. Had we been liberated by the Soviets? He asked us to accompany him to the Polish Red Cross Broadcasting Unit where, he said, we could broadcast to the world that we were safe, which we did. And perhaps our parents or some friends would hear the broadcast? (Which naturally they never did.)

I decided to buy some little trinkets for the girls and returned to the market place which was littered with stalls selling everything under the sun but at inflated prices. Unfortunately I found that my pocket had either been picked or I had lost the money that I had changed at the Bureau de Change (well, the rest of it, for I had given the Polish lorry driver half).

So in order to recoup, I had to sell my only respectable pair of brown brogues that I had carted all over Poland with me. I got 750 zlotys for them. We bought the trinkets for the girls and in the afternoon we visited the Concentration Camp at Maidanek where thousands of Jews had been exterminated. We saw the ovens, the gas chambers, the bleached bones and the dentures, but even with all this evidence, I don't think the enormity of it hit us until some time afterwards.

We had become conditioned to a degree and didn't feel much about death, I suppose, because we half expected it ourselves sometime. It was always on the cards.

When we got back to our Catholic family we learnt that a goods train was leaving for Odessa from Lublin very shortly carrying ex-prisoners of war.

We made our hurried "good-byes" and within minutes, only just in time, we were on the goods train and it was chugging its way out of Lublin station. The Russians had issued each man with a loaf of rusk bread which was as hard as the wooden floor we stood on, and a tobacco leaf each. You ripped a piece off the leaf, rubbed it between the palms of your hands and then found some cigarette papers (if you were lucky) or the daily paper or the Common Prayer Book paper (the Best) and smoked it. Apart from the top of your head blowing off, you were left gulping, afraid to breathe out, because you'd never stop coughing. I swear it loosened the teeth as well. It certainly stained them—a browney-black.

Luckily for us we still had a few remnants of Red Cross Food left and some chocolate and Yankee cigarettes.

In each cattle truck we had a small stove with a funnel going up through the roof. The idea was to get the stove red-hot and keep it thus for as long as you could. We had about 25 ex-p.o.w.'s in our truck, 12 of them Yanks. *They* burnt *everything* even their haversacks to keep the fire going. When we got back from bartering one day at a Russian village we'd stopped at, we found that some Yanks had wrested our wagon door off somehow and it was now being fed into the flames of the stove. It was all right whilst it was alight but it had all gone up in smoke after about 4 or 5 hours and from then on it was a case of trying to get away from the freezing blast of air which swept into the truck unimpeded. The next time we stopped we went looking for a good supply of wood to see us through the day. We came upon this privy standing deserted and alone at the back of some shack and we rocked it back and forth till we'd loosened it from its freezing foundations. Lifted it bodily upwards leaving the dry bog behind looking naked and unashamed! I hope nobody had to use it in the middle of the night! If they did, no doubt they blamed the Germanski!

The engine was something out of Stephenson's era but for all that it was a game one! We would come to a small incline and the engine would huff and puff and chug to try to get to the top and sometimes it wouldn't make it and we would roll all the way back again. The trouble was we had no coal and the poor thing had to be stoked up on wood all the time, consequently there was never sufficient steam to get it (and us) over the brow of the hill. But we did it eventually. Sometimes we had to get out and push! It was certainly a Fred Karno journey. We made our tea from the dribbling hot water that came from the engine and when we stopped for any length of time to allow the engine to recuperate and cool down we would wander off in search of a Russian village to see if we could barter anything. In this way we got meat, milk, bread and eggs, usually for chocolate or cigarettes. There was never any animosity shown to us, if anything quite the reverse. I don't know if they would have been so keen on us if we hadn't had something to barter with, or whether they would have given us something for nothing. Maybe . . . We'll never know.

After what seemed a lifetime, actually five or six days, we arrived at Odessa which lies on the Black Sea. Which rhymes with "Taxi" as all old songsters will remember. "We joined the Navy to see the World. Instead of a girl or two in a taxi, we were compelled to look at the 'Black Sea'."

We arrived in the late evening and Puffing Villiamovitch staggered into Odessa station letting off steam and a long gasping whistle to herald our arrival. He didn't do too badly really, a bit short of steam at times but he'd made it and so had we!

200 of us rolled around in dilatory fashion till we were rounded up by two good humoured Russky guards and marched through the Odessa streets to what had originally been a school before it had been bombed. Parts of it were still habitable and the kitchens were intact and it wasn't long before we got our usual portion of "Kasha". It didn't taste too bad this time. I think they'd jazzed it up with some Sebastopol sauces which made it fairly edible. Odessa had been battered mercilessly and there were very few buildings left undamaged. We had been warned not to go near one part of the school where the walls were a bit shaky but of course the p.o.w.'s knew best. Within the week, the wall collapsed, killing and burying two British and four Yanks. Where we slept, obviously one of the classrooms, there was a huge stove in the middle of the floor which glowed red hot all through the night—it was stoked up with coal, but even with that it was still freezing in the mornings!

We were marched to the Communal Baths in Odessa and there the showers, unlike ours, come out of the pipe in the tiled floor and hit you about navel height, depending on what size you are. If you're a small guy you get it in the mouth and if you're inclined to be tallish, it hits you where the monkey keeps his nuts. The attendants at the baths were all ladies, buxom Russian ladies, who for a few roubles would give you a quick massage. These ladies couldn't get over the sight of Darkie Smith a coal black Scotsman from Glasgow whose below-the-navel accoutrements caused quite a stir. (It's all that porridge!) They would point and gape and then burst into uncontrollable Russian laughter. I must say I thought he was a big boy for his size!

He, poor sod, was embarrassed by the whole performance and when one of the ladies offered to massage him running her hands down his legs, he told her to "fuck off" in no uncertain Scottish manner "Ach, stop yer tickling Babouchka!"

As part of our brain washing we were taken to Classical Concerts, Ballet performances, Russian Film sessions and Vodka drinking reception parties to further Anglo-Soviet Relations. The drinking was always with decorum unlike the common Ivans, but the result or effect was the same! After one or two speeches we would toast and drink the health of Joseph Stalin—Marshal Zhukov—Rokossovsky—Churchill —Rooshvelt—the Ruskian sholgiers the Brisssh soljershhs and anybody elshe you can shink of if you're still schtanding up zhat is! One day a British Military Mission arrived from Moscow:—

"Now listen carefully, you chaps, you've got to put on a good show for these damned Russkys, so heads up, chests out, and stomachs in. And let's all be on our Best Behaviour, what?"

And from the ranks of the suffering emaciated lot who had probably seen more action in a week than this "chap" had seen in a lifetime, a fruity cockney voice enquired "who's this big prick?"

Finally after a few days when all our names, ranks and numbers had been duplicated innumerable times and we had said our "Good byes" to the Russian Commandant and the Russian "Kasha" Cooks and the Lady Attendants at the Odessa Communal Baths, we lined up to be on our way. A speech of thanks from the Russian Commandant and a gift for each man—those Russian hand-painted soup bowls and wooden spoons and also a Russian Military Hat each with the Hammer and Sickle and Soviet Star on the front. Wearing the hats, we marched proudly to the harbour as near in step as those Russian Steppes would allow, led by a Soviet Military Band and watched with awe and envy by the Germanski prisoners working on the roads poor devils. We'd done our stint. Now it was their turn to pay. We climbed up the gangway of the "Highland Monarch" which had arrived that morning with Russian prisoners liberated in France, who, now clad in battle dress, lined up on the Odessa quayside. Davis and I went up to the bridge and shook hands with the Captain. He said we were just waiting for some more of our chaps to arrive and then we were off. Almost as he spoke we could see a column marching in the general direction of the harbour and the ship. As they got closer, we saw that the Senior British Officer was none other than our Padre friend from Rembertova. As they came alongside we blew a raspberry and as he looked up we waved "Hello Padre—glad you could make it!" The Bastard!

Steaming out through the Dardanelles, we anchored in the Straits whilst a barge laden with fresh fruit such as bananas, melons, pineapples, grapes and Turkish Delights (Jelly not Belly!) chugged its way to our ship. A present from the British Residents in Turkey. The temperature went up and so did our spirits. Off Crete we had an Emergency alarm, everybody had to don his lifebelt, a German sub had been sighted, but sheered off in the direction of Crete.

There were three or four members of the Fort 13 Concert party with us, namely, Winterbottom, Gaskin, Stan Hobday, Frank Coburn and myself and we were asked by the Entertainments officer if we would put on a show. Naturally we said yes and we got together and remembered some of the sketches we had done in various variety shows in the camp. Unfortunately the Intelligence Officer—a chap called Michael Dennison (yes, him!) rudely refused to allow us to use his office as a dressing room, although it was adjacent to the stage and would have been ideal. However we got over it by borrowing some screens and hanging a curtain over the top. It went off quite well, but it was a little haphazard and we were very limited as to what we could do. The Yanks who came didn't know what it was all about, but they laughed dutifully and clapped politely!

Before we arrived at Port Said we were briefed NOT to give any interviews to the Press, and at all costs there was to be no mention of Russian treatment which in some cases had been very questionable indeed. But Frank Coburn, who'd been engaged in a long conversation with a handsome hairy matelot when the briefing was going on and wasn't aware of any order, told all to the *Daily Mirror* representative. He was reprimanded but it didn't worry Frank. As he said, "I told the truth, what have they got to worry about?" That of course was the trouble—they didn't want the truth told!

The arrival at Port Said was a very emotional one. As the ship nosed its way slowly into the harbour, the Scottish Pipers Band could be seen swinging along proudly in their kilts and regalia and there was a stunned silence aboard as the pipes and drums could be heard reverberating across the water playing "The Cock of the North". A great cheer filled the quayside and many a face was tear-stained. We were given four days leave and went around like dazed tourists. Some tried to emulate the Russkys, drinking in every bar, and some tried to break the record by copulating every night in the Kasbah! And some of the Yanks never returned to the ship. From Port Said we journeyed to Naples, where the rest of the Americans were put ashore. Then through the Bay of Biscay where it was quite rough, a good thing the captain said, it kept the subs quiet. Subs? What subs? Finally we made it ...LIVERPOOL!!!

We arrived late in the evening and everybody was forbidden to leave the ship until the Medical Authorities had checked each and everyone of us. But to the fellows whose homes were in Liverpool, you might as well have addressed the wall. Almost before the Tannoy announcement, forbidding people to go ashore, was finished, they were shinning down the anchor chain, diving over the side to swim ashore—damp but happy!

The following morning some Lieut. Colonel deputising for the Military Governor came aboard and addressed the troops over the Tannoy.

"Welcome Home to England, chaps, after your long and suffering years in captivity.

We are proud to know that even though many of you have lived under trying and wearisome conditions, you have surmounted the difficulties and overcome the worst aspects of such a life and have upheld the noble traditions of the British Soldier on Active Service.

And as the European War draws to a close we hope that after your long and well deserved leave you will come back fully refreshed once again to serve the Colours in that other Theatre of War, the Far East! Much as I would like to say it I'm afraid the War is not over for you yet...."

Didn't somebody tell me "For *You* the War is Over?"

EPILOGUE

Queen Victoria Rifles (K.R.R.C.) Battalion Orders Part 2.
Rifleman Samuel J. Kydd, Army Number 6896304, was discharged 27th September, 1945 from H.M. Forces for ceasing to fulfil Army Physical requirements.
Suffering from *Psycho-Neurosis*.
He was awarded a Pension of 10 shillings per week, subject to review, and lived happily ever after...